THE GERMAN INFLUENCE IN DANISH LITERATURE

IN THE EIGHTEENTH CENTURY

THE GERMAN INFLUENCE IN DANISH LITERATURE

IN THE EIGHTEENTH CENTURY

The German Circle in Copenhagen

1750–1770

BY

J. W. EATON

Professor of German Language and Literature
in the University of Saskatchewan
Saskatoon, Canada

CAMBRIDGE

AT THE

UNIVERSITY PRESS

1929

CAMBRIDGE
UNIVERSITY PRESS

University Printing House, Cambridge CB2 8BS, United Kingdom

Cambridge University Press is part of the University of Cambridge.

It furthers the University's mission by disseminating knowledge in the pursuit of education, learning and research at the highest international levels of excellence.

www.cambridge.org
Information on this title: www.cambridge.org/9781107487505

First published 1929
First paperback edition 2015

A catalogue record for this publication is available from the British Library

ISBN 978-1-107-48750-5 Paperback

PREFACE

THE object of the present work is to indicate somewhat more clearly than has hitherto been done, the very real debt which Danish literature and thought owed to the German writers who were in Copenhagen between the years 1740 and 1770. The idea of the book was suggested to me by Professor J. G. Robertson of the University of London. To me, as to so many other students at home and abroad, Professor Robertson has shown an unfailing courtesy and kindness. Without his generous help and stimulating encouragement, this work would hardly have reached a conclusion. I am also indebted to him and to Mr J. H. Helweg, Lecturer in Danish at University College, London, for assistance in reading the proofs. To the British Museum and to the Royal Library in Copenhagen, I am indebted for a service which was always efficient and willing.

J. W. EATON

SASKATOON
November, 1928

CONTENTS

THE GERMAN INFLUENCE IN DANISH LITERATURE

INTRODUCTION

THE active resentment against the Germans in Denmark after 1750 and the fear that the Danish language and nationality might succumb to the powerful German influence have somewhat obscured the real services, material and intellectual, which the Germans in Denmark in the eighteenth century rendered to the country of their adoption. These reasons, together with the opposition between the two countries during the nineteenth century, explain the fact that, while full justice has been done to the influence of France and England on Danish literature, no adequate recognition has been given to the German influence. The French and English influences were purely literary and did not arouse the ill-will, which the German element incurred by its attempt in the eighteenth century to interfere in Danish politics. Yet it should not be forgotten that it was the Danes themselves who, during and before the eighteenth century, sought German masters in thought and literature and material help in the development of their country. The establishment of an absolute monarchy in Denmark in 1660 had discouraged the development of any native initiative in material or intellectual matters and had served to accentuate the tendency to inertia and apathy among the Danish people.[1] It was natural that the Danes, Germanic in origin as they were and the nearest relations of Germany in the European family, should turn to their southern neighbours.

The relations between Denmark and Germany did not begin with the German circle at the middle of the eighteenth century, nor were they before that time confined to literary channels.

[1] H. L. Møller, *Kong Christian den Sjette*, Copenhagen, 1889, p. 112.

In politics, trade and religion, as well as in literature and art, the connection between the two countries after the Middle Ages had been a close and, for Denmark, an important one. Many of the Danish kings were of German descent and their queens came frequently from German houses. The House of Oldenburg had been on the throne of Denmark since 1448 and had possessed since 1460 the duchies of Schleswig and Holstein. These two duchies formed for a long period the natural connecting link between Germany and Denmark. The Holsteiners were generally regarded as Germans. Hamburg's semi-dependence on the Danish throne under Christian IV and Frederick III was an important link of mediation for German literary influence. Hamburg enjoyed a reputation, which went beyond the German borders, and its connection with Denmark was closer than that of any other north German town. The epigrammatist, Chr. Wernicke of Hamburg, was for some time in the Danish service under Count Ditlev Rantzau and was on friendly terms with the Danish resident in Hamburg, Hans Hagedorn, father of the poet, Hagedorn, who too was for a time in the employment of the Danish government. Wernicke dedicated poems to Frederick IV of Denmark and to several men prominent in Danish life, but he had no direct influence on Danish literature. Barthold Feind, the Hamburg poet, had a political connection with Denmark. C. H. Amthor, the Holstein poet, was a professor of law at Kiel. He played the part of Danish court poet, defended Danish policy in the duchies and celebrated the victories of Frederick IV of Denmark in 1709. He entered the Danish service in 1713, celebrated the king's birthday with a genealogical-historical poem in German alexandrines, entitled *Der königliche oldenburgische Stammbaum*, became royal historiographer and died in Copenhagen in 1721. The connection between Copenhagen and Hamburg was continued by Klopstock's marriage to a Hamburg lady and by his frequent stays there.[1]

For a long time the language at court, except under Christian IV,

[1] For Hamburg's connection with Denmark see J. Paludan, *Fransk-engelsk Indflydelse paa Danmarks Litteratur i Holbergs Tidsalder*, Copenhagen, 1913, pp. 215 ff.

was German. Many Germans entered the Danish government service. In the army the words of command were given in German up to the end of the eighteenth century. In the Slotskirke in Copenhagen the service was in the German language and one of the court preachers was always a German.

The Hanseatic towns maintained active trade relations with the Scandinavian countries and in the wake of the Hanseatic merchants many German settlers came to Denmark. From 1660 until the fall of Struensee in 1772 there was a large and steady German immigration. The declaration of absolutism in 1660 had resulted in hostility between the Danish crown and the nobility, and many foreign noble families, chiefly German, were invited to Denmark by the Danish king. Such Mecklenburg families as the Berckentins, the Plessens and the Moltkes served the Danish crown for generations, and German students followed these noble families as tutors.[1] The great fire in Copenhagen in 1728 had a crushing effect on the Danes and the government brought in many skilled German workmen, who built up Copenhagen under Christian VI and Frederick V. The Germans were similar to the Danes in religion and manners and these settlers brought many valuable qualities, industry, frugality, a sense of order, technical skill and initiative.

During the seventeenth century there were many wandering troupes of German actors in Denmark,[2] and among them were many students. There was at that time in German schools and universities a wide-spread interest in the art of acting and the unhappy conditions in Germany during the Thirty Years' War had had an unsettling effect on the German students.[3] It was a German, Andreas Wulff, who in 1662 obtained the first

[1] L. Magon, *Ein Jahrhundert geistiger und literarischer Beziehungen zwischen Deutschland und Skandinavien* 1750–1850, I, Dortmund, 1926, p. 9.

[2] For an account of these wandering troupes see J. Paludan, "Deutsche Wandertruppen in Dänemark" in *Zeitschrift für deutsche Philologie*, XXV, pp. 313 ff. and Th. Overskou, *Den danske Skueplads*, Copenhagen, 1854–76, I, pp. 80 ff.

[3] The plays, which these German players produced in Denmark, had but little refinement or subtlety. They were for the most part a mixture of folk-scenes, juggling, singing and ballet.

charter to open a theatre in Copenhagen. In 1664 a German troupe was playing as far afield as Bergen in Norway. The Veltheim troupe, well-known as "the Saxon Company", visited Copenhagen in 1707. In 1716 von Quoten was given a charter to perform in the Danish capital,[1] and during the winter of 1718–19, Spiegelberg's company performed there.

It was from Germany that Denmark had received Christianity and the Lutheran Reformation. The Reformation knitted the Scandinavian countries closer to Germany and the religious connection, which it inaugurated, lasted for some considerable time. The protestant character of the University of Copenhagen, founded by Christian I in 1479, was emphasized by the appointment of German professors from Bonn and Wittenberg.[2] To Wittenberg went many students from the noble and burgher classes in Denmark and this University long remained a kind of court of appeal for all academic disputes and the arsenal of learning for Copenhagen University and for the scientific education of Denmark.[3] It was from Germany and the Netherlands that Christian IV recruited the staff for the Ridderakademi of Sorø, founded by him in 1623 for the education of the sons of Danish nobles. Jakob Meursius came there from the Netherlands and the Low German poet and mathematician, Johannes Lauremberg, from Rostock. The well-known Lutheran divine, Johann Gerhard of Jena, however, refused a similar invitation. At Sorø the Danish kings' sons studied and for many years German was the language of intercourse and instruction.

During the seventeenth century and, except for Holberg's works, during the first half of the eighteenth century, there was but little originality among Danish writers. In one of his epistles, Holberg writes: "De forrige anvendte deres meste Tid

[1] That von Quoten was a man of considerable versatility is indicated by the words in this charter: "...som Oculist, Steen- og Brucksnider, samt Tandbrækker at maatte bruge og exercere sin Kunst her i Staden" (Th. Overskou, *op. cit.* I, pp. 110 ff.).

[2] Rudolf Kayser, "Deutsches Leben in Dänemark" in *Preuszische Jahrbücher*, CXXXII, pp. 230 ff.

[3] R. E. Prutz, *Ludwig Holberg*, Stuttgart, 1857, p. 274.

og utroligt Arbejde paa at forklare Autores og et rense dem fra Kopiistfeil, men bekymrede sig lidet om at hæve deres egen Geist højere".[1] There was no drama or epic; the lyric, both religious and profane, was purely didactic. All echo of the old Volkspoesie had died away except in Kingo's psalms.[2] During the years immediately before the time of the German circle Holberg's works had but little influence, and Danish literature was for the most part sunk in a pietistic lethargy.[3] Poor as the German literature between Hans Sachs and Opitz was, it made a considerable contribution to Danish literature. Most of the post-Renaissance ideas Denmark got to know in German form and often through the German language. Opitz was imitated by such Danish poets as Arrebo, Hans Ravn, and Søren Gullænder.[4] Hofmannswaldau, Lohenstein and their disciples were acknowledged models. After the Reformation, Latin and German were much used by the learned classes in Denmark, and the strong and heavy qualities of German were impressed on the Danish language, not always, however, with happy results. The "Fruchtbringende Gesellschaft" gave an impulse to the linguistic endeavours of Pontoppidan and Peder Syv, and Christiern Pedersen's translation of Luther's Bible into Danish did much for the development of the Danish language.

During the first half of the eighteenth century, however, the French literary influence was stronger in Denmark than that of Germany. The movement inaugurated at the beginning of the eighteenth century by such writers as Haller, J. C. Günther, Brockes and Hagedorn had but little influence on Danish literature. Nor did the struggle between Opitz's successor,

[1] Holberg, *Epistler*, No. 306.

[2] In the *Epistola ad virum perillustrem*, I, p. 119, Holberg complains of the prevalence of religious poetry.

[3] "Tørre og aandløse Tanker i en forloren højtidelig Stil og mechanisk klaprende Vers, efter Omstændighederne pyntede op med pedantisk Lærdom eller med smagløse Billeder og Lignelser, Ordspil og Ordkunster" (J. Paludan, *Fransk-engelsk Indflydelse paa Danmarks Litteratur i Holbergs Tidsalder*, Copenhagen, 1913, p. 219).

[4] J. Paludan, "Holbergs Forhold til det ældre tyske Drama" in *Historisk Tidsskrift*, VI, 2, p. 1.

Gottsched, and the opponents of the French influence, Bodmer and Breitinger, mean much to Denmark until the coming of Klopstock at the middle of the century. The connection between Denmark and France dated back to the Middle Ages, when there were French monks in Denmark and Danish students in Paris. In the seventeenth century there were many Danish students of medicine, law, philosophy and theology in France, while in the Danish noble houses there were many French tutors. After 1740 French adventurers, teachers and publicists competed with the Germans in Denmark. In 1750 La Beaumelle was appointed to Charlottenborg as professor of French, in which chair he was succeeded by Mallet, the author of the *Histoire de Danemarc* (1758). At Sorø too the French language and literature were popular subjects of study. The easy transition from the Latin to the French language helped to popularize French with the educated classes. That the French language was threatening the sovereignty of the Latin is indicated by a remark of Godiche, the printer, in the introduction to a translation of du Peplier's *French Grammar*:

> Ligesom vor Nation udi vor Tid har faaet saa stor Smag for de galante Videnskaber,...saa er og det galante franske Sprog kommet udi besynderlig Estime og Credit. Det elskes, det læses, det øves...enhver ønsker sig at forstaae det saasom et Middel, der kan besynderlig recommandere en eller i det mindste distinguere en fra den gemeene Hob.[1]

Although in his earlier historical and philosophical works Holberg took many ideas from such German writers as Grotius, Pufendorf and Thomasius, yet it was to the French influence in Danish literature during the first half of the eighteenth century that he lent all the weight of his authority. The power of the Hanseatic League had been particularly strong in Bergen, Holberg's birthplace, and had aroused his patriotic resentment. Holberg only visited Germany once and then not of his own choice, but as travelling escort to a young nobleman. With the

[1] C. Nyrop, *Den danske Boghandels Historie*, Copenhagen, 1870, I, p. 311 (quoted by Paludan, *op. cit.* p. 447).

German language he seems to have had but slight acquaintance. He found it difficult and unattractive:

> Det tyske Sprog er i sig selv haardt og vanskeligt...thi ved det, at de skille de Ord ad, som Naturen har sammenføjet, og tage det forreste og sætte bagest, kan man ikke forstaa noget deraf, førend man kommer til Enden af Meningen...denne Pinebænk kalde de Sprogets Zir og Gravitet.[1]

J. E. Schlegel tells of having given Holberg his *Hermann* and *Der geschäftige Müsziggänger* and of Holberg having said that he liked his comedy but, as concerned the tragedy, he had no understanding for German verse.[2] Germany seemed to Holberg to possess the same faults in its literature and learning as Denmark. He admits the learning of the Germans, but declares that they have little taste or grace in its presentation.[3]

Holberg's attitude towards German literature threatened for a time to diminish greatly German influence in Denmark. The introduction of pietistic and rationalistic ideas from Germany, however, and the formation of a circle of German writers in Copenhagen joined to make up a stream of German influence, which Holberg's waning authority was powerless to stem. The pietistic movement, inaugurated in Germany by Spener, came to Denmark with the accession to the throne of Christian VI in 1730. Christian was of a puritanical temperament and a strong pietist. He both spoke and wrote German[4] and during his reign[5] many German pietists were called to Denmark to positions at the court as well as in the church and civil service. His wife was

[1] Quoted in *Historisk Tidsskrift*, VI, 2, p. 5.

[2] Letter to Hagedorn, dated October 26, 1743; cp. Fr. von Hagedorn, *Poetische Werke*, ed. Eschenburg, Hamburg, 1800, V, pp. 290 f.

[3] "Thi skrive andre Nationer zirlig, da skrive de Tysker grundig...". But Holberg goes on to say that the German writings "synes snarere at være Samlinger end vel indrettede Værker" (*Historisk Tidsskrift*, *ibid.*).

[4] On one occasion, when Christian VI used the Danish language in court society, one of the Germans present exclaimed: "Es ist doch sonderbar, dasz Eure Majestät der einzige Ausländer in ihrem eignen Hause sind" (M. Koch, *H. P. Sturz*, Munich, 1879, p. 58). In Christian VI's reign a monastery at Clitau was actually consecrated in German. See Rahbek and Nyerup, *Den danske Digtekunst under Frederik V*, Copenhagen, 1819, Introduction, p. lxvii.

[5] 1730–46.

a Brandenburg princess, unable to speak Danish and reputed to dislike all things in the country of her adoption. She is said to have inspired many of the harsh pietistic measures passed in Christian's reign, such as the closing of the theatres and dancing-places and the banishment of actors from Denmark. The pietistic movement in Denmark did not develop through literary channels so much as through personal contact: the Danes who had studied in Germany, and German priests and German students who took positions as tutors in Danish families. Pietism had many devoted and influential adherents in the aristocratic Danish families, more especially in those of German descent,[1] who had come to Denmark in the seventeenth and eighteenth centuries and who maintained their connection with Germany by their close and frequent contact with relations in that country. With the death of Christian VI in 1746 and the accession to the throne of Frederick V the force of pietism spent itself in Denmark, but the German influence still continued through the introduction of Wolff's rationalistic philosophy. Of this philosophy Eilschov had been since 1740 an eloquent disciple, while from 1741 to 1753 Stampe expounded its ideas in the University of Copenhagen. It quickly became the fashionable philosophy in Denmark and continued to be so until the 'sixties, when it was succeeded by that of the French and English schools. With Klopstock's arrival in Denmark in 1751 the literary supremacy also passed back to Germany.[2] Klopstock's coming to Denmark is the boundary stone between the quiet and sober clarity of Holberg's thought and expression and the sentimental turbidity of the new poetry of feeling.

To the strong position to which the German influence at-

[1] The members of these families played an important part in the life of the literary societies in Denmark at the end of the eighteenth century. See F. Rønning, *Rationalismens Tidsalder*, Copenhagen, 1886, I, p. 60.

[2] The way for the author of the *Messias* had already been prepared by Hagedorn, J. E. Schlegel and Gellert. Gellert's *Fabeln* were extremely popular in Denmark. Under the anti-German Guldberg régime during the 'seventies they were even prescribed in the Danish schools. See Rahbek and Nyerup, *op. cit.* p. 237. Even Holberg finds words of warm praise for Gellert's *Fabeln*. See Holberg's *Fabler*, 1751, Preface.

tained in Denmark during the years 1730 to 1770 the German universities contributed. From the two re-modelled German universities of Göttingen and Leipzig many Danish students brought back German ideas. In the eighteenth century, Göttingen was regarded as a place where the science of statesmanship and government should be studied, and many young Danish nobles sought their education there.[1] Bernstorff, the patron of the German circle, had studied in Göttingen and his influence rendered still closer that university's connection with Denmark. It was there that Tyge Rothe, who later did so much for the development of a patriotic spirit in Danish literature, was educated. Johann David Michaelis of Göttingen was the first to conceive the idea of the famous Danish scientific expedition to Arabia in 1761 under Carsten Niebuhr. The "Deutsche Gesellschaft" in Göttingen had many members in Denmark, among whom were Detharding, the translator of Holberg, and Hauber, who was called as German preacher to Copenhagen in 1746. In Leipzig University too there were many young Danes of noble birth.[2]

The accession of Frederick V to the Danish throne in 1746 meant a new freedom in social life and a revived interest in the arts and sciences. The cruel restrictions introduced into Denmark under the pietistic Christian VI were abolished and under the new reign men of learning could hope for some encouragement.[3] It was well for Klopstock and the German writers associated with him that Frederick V and his ministers did not imitate the attitude of Frederick the Great towards German literature. At a time when the Germans had to give way to the French element at the court of Frederick the Great, Holberg

[1] J. S. Pütter, *Versuch einer akad. Gelehrten-Geschichte*, 1765, I, pp. 15–17; quoted by L. Magon, *op. cit.* p. 202.

[2] Gellert on one occasion was accused of taking more pains with the education of Danish students at Leipzig than with that of the German students. Gellert denies the charge, but assures Bernstorff that the Danish students reflect much credit on the University of Leipzig. See L. Magon, *op. cit.* pp. 202 f.

[3] Letter from J. E. Schlegel to Bodmer, dated October 8, 1746; see G. F. Stäudlin, *Briefe an Bodmer*, Stuttgart, 1794, No. 42.

and the Danes had to give way in Copenhagen to the all-powerful German circle. Some of the most famous names in German literature of the eighteenth century were those of writers who were enabled to write their principal works through Danish hospitality. The unrest caused by the Seven Years' War made Germany a distressful country for all classes, not least for literary men. The German reading public was not yet so large that an author could live by his pen alone, and the interest in literature and writers evinced by Germany's rulers did not develop to any great extent until towards the end of the century. There is ample evidence that contemporary writers in Germany regarded Denmark as a Mecca for German writers and scientists, and its king as the most enlightened of European monarchs. J. D. Michaelis of Göttingen declared that the sciences were in a parlous condition in Germany and that they seemed to be taking refuge in the north, seeking there the financial aid which, in time of war, the German states were unable to offer them.[1] Elsewhere the same writer speaks of Frederick V as attracting men of real learning from all nations and playing the part of benevolent patron.[2] Michaelis declares to Bernstorff that the expression "absolute Monarchy", as it is understood in Denmark, agrees with his ideas of liberty and tolerant government.[3] Gerstenberg and the members of the German circle saw in this "Danish corner of Germany" the possibility of creating a new spirit in German literature. Herder, who himself had thought of the possibility of settling in Copenhagen in order to enjoy the company of Klopstock, regarded Denmark as a country which, under a generous and excellent government, was working for the good of humanity[4]; and

[1] Letter to Count J. H. E. Bernstorff from Göttingen, dated April 11, 1757. See J. D. Michaelis, *Literarischer Briefwechsel*, Leipzig, 1794–6, I, p. 352.

[2] "Ja, ich vermuthe, dasz in Dänemark die Bedingung einer künftigen Beförderung auf unterthänigste Bitte leicht zu erhalten stünde, weil der König die wahre Gelehrsamkeit aus allen Nationen zusammen sucht, und in der That der gemeinschaftliche Landes-Vater aller Gelehrter ist" (J. D. Michaelis, *op. cit.* p. 377, letter to J. H. E. Bernstorff, Göttingen, January 1, 1759).

[3] Letter to J. H. E. Bernstorff, dated May 31, 1759, *ibid.*

[4] R. Haym, *Herder*, Berlin, 1877–85, I, p. 313.

Frederick V fulfilled his ideas with regard to the co-operation of the state in the encouragement of the arts and sciences.[1] The Danish king well deserved the reputation of a generous patron of learning and the fine arts. During his reign the Danish expedition to Arabia was undertaken, Sorø Academy was re-opened, the Danish Society of Fine Arts came into being, the study of Natural History and Economics underwent a particularly important development, and German literary men were invited to make their home in Copenhagen. It is not at all certain that the popular Danish king's attainments in literature and the arts were particularly brilliant, but he was wise enough to take council in these matters with such men as Count J. H. E. Bernstorff and Erik Pontoppidan, at that time vice-chancellor of Copenhagen University. Frederick V was as popular with the German writers as he was with the Danish nation, and Klopstock's elegy, *Rothschilds Gräber*,[2] written on the occasion of the king's death, expressed the grief of the German writers in Denmark as well as that of a whole people.

In Count Bernstorff, Frederick V found a minister as enthusiastic and ambitious in his ideas for Denmark's material and intellectual development as he was himself.[3] In 1746 the reputation of Louis XIV of France was still undiminished, and Bernstorff and Moltke wished their sovereign to emulate on a smaller scale the brilliant example of his French predecessor. Bernstorff was among the noblest and most cultured continental ministers of his time. A man of great powers of work, moral earnestness and deep piety, he was the typical representative of the more enlightened conservative ministers of the eighteenth century, careful for the people's welfare, and, differing in this respect from the ministers of the seventeenth century, setting it before the splendour of courts and the glory of princes. His ideas of statesmanship he had formed largely in France and he

[1] Herder, *Werke*, ed. B. Suphan, IV, p. 212; IX, p. 313; XVII, p. 107.

[2] Copenhagen, 1766.

[3] "Vor elskværdige Friderick skulde havt en Ministre, hvis kolde Overlæg kunde svække hans sværmende Heede" (*Interiører fra Kong Frederik den Femtes Hof*; cp. *Charlotte Dorothea Biehls Breve*, ed. Louis Bobé, Copenhagen, 1909, p. 142).

aspired to play in Denmark the rôle of a Colbert.[1] Most of his ideas were too ambitious and proved to be impossible of realization in Denmark. The greatest contributions, which he made to Denmark, were probably the encouragement which he gave to the liberation of the peasants, the organization of the expedition to Arabia, and the help which he vouchsafed to Klopstock and German men of letters.

Like so many of the men in high political positions about the middle of the eighteenth century, Bernstorff was a north German.[2] During his twenty years' residence in Denmark he took no trouble to learn Danish.[3] His official correspondence with Copenhagen from Paris was conducted in German or French.[4] In Danish art and literature he took but little interest. The only evidence of Bernstorff's interest in Danish literature is that he obtained for the "Selskab for det danske Sprog og de skjønne Videnskaber" (founded 1759) an annual subsidy of two thousand daler to be used for prizes, and the help which he gave to the "Kongelige Landhusholdningsselskab" (founded 1769). It must be admitted, however, that Bernstorff assisted Sneedorff at a time when that Danish writer despaired of obtaining any encouragement from his fellow-countrymen.[5] In his letters Bernstorff never mentions Holberg. The desire for progress and for development in art and literature, which, after 1750, was becoming evident in Denmark, he proposes to satisfy by foreign importations.[6] For many years

[1] For a criticism of Bernstorff's administration see B. G. Niebuhr, "Carsten Niebuhrs Leben" in *Kieler Blätter*, III, pp. 9 ff.

[2] J. L. Holstein, A. G. Moltke and C. A. Berckentin were all from Mecklenburg.

[3] C. F. Bricka, *Dansk biografisk Lexikon*, Copenhagen, 1888, II, p. 168.

[4] C. F. von Gramm thought it necessary to translate a Danish letter into German before sending it to Bernstorff; cp. Aage Friis, *Die Bernstorffs*, Leipzig, 1905, I, p. 269.

[5] H. P. Sturz, *Leben und Charakter des Grafen Bernstorff*, Leipzig, 1777, p. 79. Bernstorff did not consider that Danish architects were able to plan a country house. He advised friends to employ a French architect and to buy French furniture (A. Friis, *ibid.*).

[6] "Berkentin og Bernstorff føle sig som tyske; at de er knyttede til Danmark, spiller ikke den fjærneste Rolle for deres litterære Interesser" (Aage Friis, *Bernstorfferne og Danmark*, Copenhagen, 1913–19, I, p. 239).

before his accession to power in 1751 the immigration from Germany to Denmark had been steady and considerable. The immigrants had been for the most part skilled artisans and merchants, and, under Christian VI, priests and clergymen. With Bernstorff immigration from Germany increased in volume and changed in character. For the next twenty years it was composed chiefly of scientists, literary men and men of learning, doctors, soldiers, secretaries and tutors; and this type of immigration contained a much more serious threat against Danish nationality than had the earlier movement from Germany. It was the realization of this fact by the patriotic Danes and the unashamed manner in which Struensee fostered the German influence, which later forced the Danish nation to defend itself and to assert its national spirit.

Most of the members of the German circle came to Denmark on Bernstorff's invitation. For the rôle of patron to literary men the Danish minister was well fitted. With German and English literature he had a more than superficial acquaintance; and his intimate knowledge of French literature and his perfect mastery of the French language and its subtleties were unusual in a foreigner.[1] Despite the very considerable burden of his official duties Bernstorff found time to keep in touch with the best of European literature, and he maintained a correspondence with several foreign writers of distinction.[2] During the time which Bernstorff had spent in Paris[3] Voltaire was at the height of his fame and influence, and although the French writer's anti-religious ideas had no effect on Bernstorff, yet he had learnt from him that literature was becoming a world power and he had seen in the *salons* of Paris the great honour, which princes and nobles paid to men of letters. It was in friendly and stimulating intercourse with the German circle that Bern-

[1] Büsching, who was in Denmark during Bernstorff's term of office, was of the opinion that Bernstorff took too great an interest in French literature and not enough in German. See A. F. Büsching, *Beyträge zur Lebensgeschichte merkwürdiger Personen*, Hamburg, 1783–89, III, p. 197.

[2] With the French writer, Montesquieu, for example.

[3] 1744–50.

storff found his chief pleasure and relaxation. In winter in his town house in the Bredgade, and in summer at his country place, "Bernstorff", the German writers gathered round the Danish minister and his wife. Towards them Bernstorff's kindness and encouragement were never lacking. It is a proof of his tolerance and generosity that, although he did not agree with Basedow's religious views, yet he appreciated his intellectual honesty and power and, as Basedow himself acknowledges,[1] protected him throughout his difficulties at Sorø. Of Bernstorff's circle Klopstock was the chief member. The minister's deeply religious nature was a strong link between Bernstorff and the author of the *Messias* and laid the foundations of an intimate friendship, the harmony of which was never disturbed. Of the deep and painful impression, which Bernstorff's departure from Denmark made on the Germans there, H. P. Sturz, himself a member of their circle and Bernstorff's biographer, has given a vivid account.[2]

The centre for the social life of the German circle was in the Petristræde, where lived Balthasar Münter, minister at the German church there, J. A. Cramer, Cramer's tutor, G. B. Funk, and Resewitz, second minister at the German church. Between these families and other German families in Copenhagen there was much social intercourse. J. H. Schlegel, Gerstenberg, Klopstock, Resewitz, Münter and Niebuhr met frequently in Cramer's and Münter's houses. From their close and constant association with one another these men received a stimulus which was invaluable for their intellectual and artistic development, and the fashion, which they inaugurated, of forming a literary coterie, was continued at a later date by Danish writers. For these German writers there was already a German foundation in Denmark. Johann Elias Schlegel[3] was one of the first Germans of literary importance to settle in Denmark in the eighteenth century, and his *Der Fremde*[4] helped to prepare the

[1] J. B. Basedow, *Philanthropinum*, p. xxii.

[2] H. P. Sturz, *Erinnerungen aus dem Leben des Grafen J. H. E. Bernstorff*, pp. 109 and 113.

[3] Died 1749.

[4] 1745–6.

way in Denmark by creating a literary public. It was his German prose which taught in some measure the Danish people to understand Klopstock's poetry. The wide circulation and the assured popularity of J. A. Cramer's *Der nordische Aufseher*,[1] the mouthpiece of these pioneers of a foreign culture, showed that the members of the German circle could count on the steady support both of Germans and Danes. Cramer and his collaborators enjoyed the protection of the government and of many members of the aristocracy, some of whom, such as the Stolbergs, had estates in both Germany and Denmark. The clergy in Denmark formed a very considerable part of the educated public and among them were many Germans and Danes, who had studied at German universities. To these Klopstock's poetry made a strong appeal.

For this group of German writers in Denmark English literature possessed a great interest. Young was regarded by them as a saint. Countess Stolberg asked permission to call her son after him,[2] and Fritz Stolberg, always a devoted admirer of this English writer, quoted frequently from the *Night Thoughts*.[3] For Richardson Klopstock and his circle had a strong admiration. It was indeed partly in the hope of meeting Richardson that Klopstock wished at one time to become secretary to the Danish legation in London. Of Thomson, the author of *The Seasons*, the Germans in Copenhagen were enthusiastic admirers.

By her separation from the Kalmar Union in 1523 Denmark had achieved her political independence. By means of the Reformation she gained religious and mental freedom. The path to her free development lay open, but it was some time before she advanced along it. Literature was still far from the masses, the jealously guarded preserve of a narrow circle of learned people. Holberg saw clearly that the greatest obstacle to the develop-

[1] 1758–61.

[2] L. Bobé, *Frederikke Brun og hendes Kreds hjemme og ude*, Copenhagen, 1910.

[3] Translated into German by Ebert in 1751–2. To Young, Klopstock's wife, Meta, wrote enthusiastic letters.

ment of a Danish literature was the absence of a wide and educated audience, and his moral epistles and his comedies were written largely for the purpose of creating such an audience. The periodicals published in Denmark during the period 1750 to 1770 continued Holberg's work in this respect. These were for the most part German. With J. E. Schlegel's *Der Fremde*, Büsching's *Nachrichten*, J. A. Cramer's *Der nordische Aufseher* and Gerstenberg's *Briefe über Merkwürdigkeiten der Litteratur*, only one Danish periodical, Sneedorff's *Den patriotiske Tilskuer*, may be compared in importance. These German periodicals helped to emphasize the difference between intelligence and learning and to stress the fact that to be able to speak and read Latin and Greek did not necessarily mean that one could think.[1] Through his wide knowledge of literature and his lack of condescension in imparting it Schlegel was able to give to the Danish reading public something which it had lacked hitherto. His learning and easy man-of-the-world attitude formed a happy combination, and *Der Fremde* begins in Denmark the movement which brought classical and modern literature before a wider and more popular audience. To *Der Fremde* and its successors in Denmark is largely due the fact that Danish women began to take an interest in literature. Up to the middle of the eighteenth century Danish men and women did not meet together very frequently in social intercourse, and women were not generally regarded as being capable of sustaining a serious interest in intellectual and literary matters. With the German circle a change begins. Klopstock's wife, Meta, became in Denmark the model of the intellectual woman, and Frederikke Brun and Ch. D. Biehl continue the change which she had inaugurated.

[1] F. Rønning, *op. cit.* I, p. 60. Up to the middle of the eighteenth century the standard of classical education in Denmark had been low. Of Suhm's translations from the classics Holberg writes in 1750: "Hr. Kammerjunker Suhm bliver ved sit priselige Forsæt, at fordanske gamle Autores, for at bøde paa den Mangel, som vi tilforn her udi Landet, have havt, saaledes, at ingen uden de, som forstaae fremmede Sprog, have kunnet gjøre sig nogen Idee om de Gamles Skrifter og Lærdom" (P. F. Suhm, *Samlede Skrifter*, Copenhagen, 1798, XV, p. 24). In *Epistola* No. 306, Holberg says: "Udi vore Tider er Prisen meget falden paa de Græske og Latinske Helde".

In the theatre J. E. Schlegel carried on Holberg's efforts to create a wider audience. When Frederick V wished to found a Danish national theatre it was not to Holberg, then growing old, that he turned, but to Schlegel, at that time a lecturer in Sorø; and, although Schlegel's tragedies and comedies gave little to Denmark, yet, in his theoretical works Schlegel indicated the course which Danish comedy was later to take from the Holbergian to a higher type of comedy. Schlegel's two critical works[1] and his comedy, *Die Langeweile*,[2] which was produced at the opening performance of the Copenhagen Theatre, seemed to point to the possibility of the wider German experience of the theatre being of some service to Denmark. The opportunity was not lacking; for it was some considerable time before a Danish dramatist appeared, worthy of succeeding Holberg. The promise contained in Schlegel's works, however, was not fulfilled. Twenty years later, in 1767, Sturz in a letter written as a preface to his drama *Julie*, entitled "Über das deutsche Theater an die Freunde und Beschützer desselben in Hamburg", makes little mention of the Danish theatre, despite the fact that during the intervening period the Danish stage had developed, and that Sturz was as familiar with the Danish language as Schlegel had been. Klopstock's influence had strengthened the patriotic pride of his German friends, and when Sturz wrote, the Hamburg experiment of a German National Theatre was being tried.

Before the introduction of pietism, the Lutheran creed had been predominant in Denmark for many years. Its learned theology was immense and tyrannous, and it gave but little chance to secular philosophy to develop its ideas. The movement in England and Germany which aimed at taking philosophy from a purely academic to a popular audience did not begin until a later date in Denmark. In this change the German circle played an important part through the introduction of new theological ideas

[1] *Zur Errichtung eines dänischen Theaters* (1746) and *Gedanken zur Aufnahme des dänischen Theaters* (1747).

[2] 1747.

from Germany. In Basedow rationalism in Denmark found an able exponent, and his lectures at Sorø roused great interest in religion and church history. The free-thinking ideas, which he boldly voiced, were then prevalent in educated circles in Denmark. J. A. Cramer, while introducing the new historical-critical treatment of theology, was keenly alive to the dangers which threatened Christianity from the attacks of the free-thinkers, and, by stressing the imaginative element in the scriptures, he tried to create an audience for the poetry of Klopstock. Under Frederick V the church was not in as strong a position as it had been under the pietistic Christian VI, and Klopstock's *Messias* brought back the glamour to the Christian faith and, as a Danish contemporary of Klopstock remarked, did more for religion than many sermons of orthodox theologians.[1] The members of the German circle did not favour a narrow adherence to Christian dogma. Resewitz is expressing the opinion of the majority of them when, in a letter to the German rationalistic philosopher, Bahrdt, he says that he approves of all free investigation of religion, provided that it is undertaken honestly.[2]

The period of German predominance marks the beginning of the science of pedagogy in Denmark. Up till that time there had been no consideration of education in the light of general principles, although Holberg, possibly under the influence of Locke's ideas, had attacked learning which was dead and unproductive. In *Der Fremde* Schlegel speaks of the necessity of reform in educational methods.[3] Both Gerstenberg and J. A. Cramer showed a keen interest in psychology and the education of children, but in literature in Denmark between 1750 and 1760 there is little of pedagogic importance save a few articles on education in *Der nordische Aufseher*. In the 'sixties the decisive influences were Rousseau and Basedow,[4] and in *Den patriotiske*

[1] P. K. Stenersen, *Critiske Tanker over de rimfrie Vers*, pp. 5 f.

[2] Letter dated September 1, 1770 in *Briefe angesehener Gelehrten an K. F. Bahrdt*, I, p. 60; quoted by F. Rønning, *op. cit.* I, p. 295.

[3] Articles Nos. 10 and 47.

[4] Basedow was teaching at Sorø Academy from 1753 to 1761.

Tilskuer Sneedorff treats of many of the ideas of these writers. Resewitz, whose educational theories made a deep impression in Denmark, expresses new ideas of school reform, which were in the air at that time. In the development of musical taste and education in Denmark J. A. Scheibe, a fervent disciple of Gottsched, played a prominent part, while Gerstenberg did much to keep the Danes in touch with musical developments outside their own country.

In the eighteenth century intellectual interests and literary intercourse began to break down the old social barriers; it was then that the different ranks and professions began to mingle, and a new social rank, that of the privileged literary class, began to make its appearance. In Denmark, up to a later date than in other countries, it was held that a man should have a more serious interest than that of literature. To be a poet alone, like Ewald, was astonishing.[1] His predecessors in Danish literature, such writers as Sorterup, Wadskiær and Friis, were generally priests or professors. The Norwegian Tullin, the greatest poet at the middle of the century, was a manufacturer of starch and powder, and, since he was successful as such, was honoured at least as much for that reason as for the excellence of his poetry. Klopstock was the first writer in Denmark to live simply and solely as a poet, and to proclaim a high conception of his calling. His honoured position at the Danish court and that of other members of the German circle began the change in Denmark after which writers were no longer regarded merely as the obedient and grateful creatures of rich patrons.

During the period from 1740 to 1770 such Danish journals as there were contained but little real literary or aesthetic criticism. J. E. Schlegel's series of articles in *Der Fremde* on the Danish writers from Arrebo to Holberg is one of the earliest critical accounts of Danish literature. Schlegel was, too, the first writer in Denmark to express any reasonable ideas on aesthetic questions, and, although he denied that he was a

[1] F. Rønning, *op. cit.* I, p. 88.

disciple of Gottsched, yet he expressed such of the ideas of Gottsched and Batteux as could be adapted to Danish conditions. *Der nordische Aufseher* gives a valuable picture of the intellectual and aesthetic movements in Denmark at that time and, by bringing the Danish people into touch with the ideas of countries intellectually further developed than their own, Cramer tried to create a Danish literary audience. Cramer was the first to make the merits of Tullin's *Maidagen* known abroad, and in his relations with Sneedorff he exercised a definite influence on the education of the Danish public. It was from *Der nordische Aufseher* that Sneedorff took the idea of *Den patriotiske Tilskuer*. The *Schleswiger Briefe* of Gerstenberg was the first purely critical periodical of any importance in Denmark; it did much towards keeping Denmark in touch with literary ideas in other countries. The articles on Danish literature[1] gave an insight into literary conditions in Denmark at that time and afforded a much-needed encouragement to young Danish writers. In his *Sorøske Samlinger* Gerstenberg showed a real interest in Danish literature and an appreciation of its real needs; he supported Sneedorff in a demand for a free, fearless and unprejudiced criticism and impressed on the Danes the help which sound criticism could give to the building up of a national literature. Klopstock was essentially German and rather narrowly national. He had not the wide knowledge of foreign languages and literatures and the cosmopolitan viewpoint of Elias Schlegel and Gerstenberg. Yet Klopstock's influence on Johannes Ewald meant much to Danish literature,[2] and it was from the controversy over the *Messias* that a more intelligent criticism and a greater clearness in literary ideas were developed in Denmark. It was Klopstock's work which dealt the first blow at the Boileau-Batteux conception of poetry in the North. His *Messias* illustrated the ideas of Young's

[1] *Schleswiger Briefe* (*Briefe über Merkwürdigkeiten der Litteratur*), ed. A. von Weilen, Stuttgart, 1890, Nos. 19, 25 and 26.

[2] The subject of Klopstock's influence on Ewald has been fully treated of in L. Magon, *op. cit.*, *passim*.

Conjectures on Original Composition, a work which had roused much attention in Danish literary circles.[1]

To the growing interest in the Danish language and literature and in Scandinavian antiquity the members of the German circle made an important contribution; through their writings they helped very materially to develop a national consciousness among the Danes and to strengthen the feeling of opposition to foreign influences to which, later in the century, the German influence itself had to yield. The national ideas of Sneedorff, Tyge Rothe, Tullin and Ewald owed much to J. E. Schlegel, Basedow, Gerstenberg and Cramer. Sneedorff was broad-minded enough to realize that Danish literature and thought could draw profit from the ideas of these foreigners, and he gained from his German friends an encouragement and a stimulus which he sought in vain among his fellow-countrymen. Gerstenberg was always keenly interested in matters concerning language, and his Danish essays contained the most valuable contribution to the theory of language in Denmark during the 'sixties. In *Der Fremde* and his *Coniectura* J. E. Schlegel gives the fruit of his study of Scandinavian mythology and history. He strongly advocates the use of national material in tragedy and comedy,[2] and he recommends Holberg's plays to the Danish public chiefly because they were an expression of the Danish national spirit. The members of the German circle realized the importance of the older Scandinavian literatures. The Danes themselves did not until later perceive so clearly the importance of finding material for a national literature in the earlier history of their own country. To this Holberg was no exception, and the foreign influences, which he himself had been able to use and control, threatened for a time to swamp a literature which possessed no background. Bredal's musical piece, *Gram og Signe* (1756), was a mere caricature, and Ewald's *Balders Død* (1773) was the first native work to catch the real bardic spirit.

[1] In *Schleswiger Briefe*, No. 20, Gerstenberg examines what genius is and stresses the difference between genius and talent. Cramer speaks of Young's work in *Der nordische Aufseher*, Article 159, June 26, 1760.

[2] *Gedanken zur Aufnahme des dänischen Theaters*, 1747.

It was not only in literature that the members of the German circle exercised a definite influence on the development of a spirit of nationality among the Danes. To the unpatriotic worship of Italian music Scheibe offered strong opposition at a time when there was no Dane of sufficient musical prestige to speak with authority. Scheibe's cantatas and oratorios were the first attempt to exploit the Danish language in the field of music. His theory that the origin of harmony was to be sought among the northern peoples was at that time a novel idea, and his admiration for the musical qualities of the Danish language was not without its influence on Ewald.

For twenty-two years Danish literature developed in the hands of foreigners and of such Danish writers as they encouraged. Had this foreign influence continued unopposed it would have made Denmark a German province and her literature essentially German.[1] Only when the Danish language was employed in literature and when Scandinavian antiquity was exploited, did the Danes come into their own. For the apathetic attitude of the majority of educated Danes during these years towards the development of a national spirit and its expression in literature there are various reasons. The pietistic sirocco, which, during the reign of Christian VI, had dried up almost all poetic impulse, still had its effect after that monarch's death and explains in some measure the fact that there were few literary productions in Denmark of any significance during the first few years of the reign of Frederick V.[2] The Danes realized how far behind the rest of Europe they were intellectually. Then, too, the growth of foreign influence in Danish literature was favoured by the Danish national character, by its simplicity, its docility, its tendency to belittle Danish efforts and to admire foreign productions, its lack of independence and of initiative—tendencies which were intensified by the system of absolute monarchy introduced into Denmark on the French model in

[1] N. M. Petersen, *Bidrag til den danske Literaturs Historie*, 2nd ed., Copenhagen, 1867–71, v, 1, pp. 4 f.

[2] Rahbek and Nyerup, *Den danske Digtekunst under Frederik V*, Copenhagen, 1819, p. 4.

1660 by Frederick III. A contemporary and independent observer writes in 1694 that in Denmark the natives are considered less than foreigners.[1] A French traveller remarks in 1706: "Le nom de Danois est à présent regardé comme un terme de mépris".[2] The Danish writer Eilschov says: "Mange Danske holde sig det for en Skam, at de ere fødte i Danmark, og derfor sige: Wir sind aus Flensburg".[3] Although Holberg, Sneedorff, Tyge Rothe and other patriotic Danes were familiar with Montesquieu's *L'Esprit des Lois*, its influence spread even more slowly in Denmark than in the rest of Europe, and the Danish people showed a whole-hearted belief in the omniscience of the crown. J. E. Schlegel said that it was difficult for a republican to believe that a people could submit so willingly to an absolute monarchy as did the Danes.[4] In this period there were few rebellious thoughts, and such as there were were lost in the general love for Frederick V. But this unbounded love for their sovereign was not founded on any strong love of, or pride in their country. There was about the middle of the eighteenth century no real sense of patriotism in Denmark. The Danish writer, Suhm, relates a conversation with a Danish woman at a time when war with Russia threatened: "Hvor mange Börn har I, Mor?" "Jeg har haft syv Drenge, men de ere, gud ske lov, alle døde". "Hvorfor gud ske lov?" "Fordi de skulde være Soldater". War was the king's concern.[5]

The unpatriotic ideas of the educated classes in Denmark were reflected in their attitude to the Danish language. Under Christian VI the upper classes could neither read nor write in Danish[6]; for the learned people there was Latin, for the ladies French, for the gentlemen German and for the people Danish.[7] Several of the foremost Danish authors after Holberg wrote in German and French rather than in Danish. So patriotic a Danish

[1] R. Molesworth, *Account of Denmark*, 1694, p. 83.

[2] De La Vrigny, *Relation en forme de Journal fait en Dannemark*, Rotterdam, 1706.

[3] F. C. Eilschov, *Poesiens Misbrug*, Fortale.

[4] J. E. Schlegel, *Werke*, v, p. 244.

[5] P. F. Suhm, *Samlede Skrifter*, Copenhagen, 1798, x, p. 144.

[6] M. Koch, *op. cit.* p. 8.

[7] N. M. Petersen, *op. cit.* v, 1, p. 94.

writer as Erik Pontoppidan[1] wrote a history of the Danish language in German. Tullin complains bitterly of the low regard in which it is held; he says that it is like a child, which has been chased away to the nursery and the servants, where it can learn only vulgar expressions. He declares that the Danish language has been driven from the court, denied access to the schools and academies, excluded from learned correspondence and not spoken in polite society, and this, despite the fact that when cultivated, Danish is capable of revealing as fine qualities as any other modern language.[2] Before Tullin Holberg had realized the importance of making the Danish language a literary medium and an instrument of culture. Although Norwegian by birth he made a strong plea for a national development in Denmark, and he saw in the revival of the Danish theatre at the accession of Frederick V the possible advantages to the development of the language; he expresses the hope that the native tongue might soon be tolerated in the houses of the great and spoken at court.[3] That at the middle of the eighteenth century Denmark had developed a fairly good prose is due in large measure to Holberg. Had Holberg had a worthy successor, the use of the Danish language would have been encouraged and the Danish national element might have been kept intact amid the foreign influences which surrounded it after his death.[4] Many of the writers, who later secured a victory for Denmark against the German influence, were, like Holberg, Norwegians who wrote in Danish and lived or published in Copenhagen. But the beginnings of Holbergian imitation by Eilschov, Horn and Suhm hardly lasted beyond Holberg's lifetime, and it was not until Sneedorff that Holberg's work of encouraging the use of the Danish language in literature was vigorously continued. In the intervening period Langebek and Højsgaard did something for the cultivation of the Danish language. Langebek had founded the "Selskab for Fædrelandets Historie og

[1] 1698–1764.
[2] C. B. Tullin, *Samlede Skrifter*, Copenhagen, 1770–3, II, p. 35.
[3] Holberg, *Epistler*, No. 179.
[4] Holberg died in 1754.

Sprog" in 1745 and he edited the first six volumes of the *Danske Magazin*. Langebek's style is free from foreign influences. Jens Højsgaard (1698–1773) wrote a manual of the Danish language. He is the first exact and practical observer in Danish linguistic matters.

Sneedorff realized what Herder so often declared, that on the cultivation of a nation's language depends the preservation of its national character, and in *Den patriotiske Tilskuer*[1] he presses for a purer Danish language and the expulsion of the too great number of French and Latin words. He emphasizes the important effect of the national language on modes of thought, manners, education, laws and sciences and declares that the matter deserves the attention of the government.[2] It is rather surprising that Frederick V did not do more towards the realization of Sneedorff's ideas. Although Frederick had been brought up in a pietistic and German atmosphere, yet he had a liking for the Danish language. On the occasion of the king's coronation Langebek speaks of Frederick V's interest in the Danish language and of his desire to see Danish eloquence developed at Sorø Academy as well as the cultivation of other modern languages.[3] Frederick's first wife, Louise, daughter of George II of England, quickly acquired the Danish language, and Pontoppidan preached in Danish in the Slotskirke.[4] That Frederick's loyalty to the language of his country was sincere is evidenced by a remark of Dass in a letter to Suhm concerning the education of the young Crown Prince:

> Den nye Instruction, som er givet Vedkommende til Kronprindsens Information, skal indeholde en curieux Artikel, som er, at al Information maa skee paa Dansk, og saaledes blive flere end een nødsagede til at tale Dansk.[5]

In the fostering of the Danish language and national spirit Sorø Academy played an honourable part.[6] At the University

[1] 1761. [2] *Den patriotiske Tilskuer*, No. 7, February 9, 1761.
[3] Rahbek and Nyerup, *op. cit.* p. 84.
[4] Rudolf Kayser, *op. cit.* pp. 230 ff.
[5] P. F. Suhm, *Samlede Skrifter*, Copenhagen, 1798, xv, p. 204.
[6] See C. Molbech, *Om Sorø Academie*, Copenhagen, 1847, pp. 15 ff.

of Copenhagen, in close touch, as it was with the court and nobility, the German and French influences were particularly strong; but in Sorø there were many learned Danes, who had travelled much, men such as J. Kraft, J. S. Sneedorff, O. Guldberg, Schytte, Schøning, Erichsen and Kongslev. At Sorø was begun the serious study of the Danish literature and language. It was there that the solid foundations were laid for the creation of a new Danish prose. From Sorø was issued *Den patriotiske Tilskuer*, the best Danish literary production since the appearance of Holberg's works, and from there Sneedorff, Kraft and others awakened in the Danes a critical literary sense.

The movement towards a rejuvenation and improvement of the Danish language was part of the more general movement to resist foreign influences. The victory in the 'seventies of the Danes over the Germans was due in large measure to Holberg, Sneedorff and Ewald, and the two latter of these men owed much to German writers. The complete break between the Danish and the foreign elements in Denmark is one of the most important literary events in the second half of the eighteenth century. It was, however, slow in developing. Before the accession of Christian VI there was no real dislike of the Germans by the Danes[1]; that began when, through the influence of the German pietists at the court of Christian VI, rigorous and unfair laws were imposed on the Danish population. Life at the Danish court continued to be most luxurious, and the Danes bitterly resented lavishing money on foreigners, who were taking from them all joy in life. The German immigrants, who came to Denmark during the reign of Christian VI and Frederick V, were not all of the best type. There were among them many of little education or breeding, knights of fortune, pretentious and arrogant, and they were not slow to express their contempt for all things Danish. Nor was this arrogance

[1] It was in 1730 that Christian VI came to the Danish throne. There was at that time a pronounced hostility towards the Swedes. Lysholm, professor of Eloquence and History at Sorø Academy, said that he would rather be a pig than a Swede. A. F. Büsching, *Beyträge*, Hamburg, 1783–9, VI, p. 204; quoted by F. Rønning, *op. cit.* I, p. 159, note.

invariably confined to the uneducated Germans in Denmark. In many of the German writers of the eighteenth century there was a strong racial consciousness, a keen pride in their German nationality. These feelings were shared and expressed by many of the members of the German circle in Copenhagen, particularly by Klopstock. Although Klopstock did not openly express scorn for the Danes, yet his attitude towards them was one of condescension, and his gratitude and that of other German writers was shown to Frederick V and to Bernstorff, and not to the land which had given them hospitality.[1]

For some considerable time, however, there was no frank protest against the German influence in Denmark. It was only with the development of a stronger national consciousness that this muttered dissatisfaction and ill-will became open and decided. The opposition to the Germans in Denmark at first found expression in unfavourable opinions of Klopstock's poetry. Holberg said that he did not understand the *Messias*, and Dass declares that Klopstock's poetry and poetic theory were not suited to his dull understanding, but were rather for "delicate, seraphic spirits".[2] Suhm speaks of Klopstock's *Drei Gebete* as merely "unintelligible and affected nonsense".[3] In 1741 the historian, Klevenfeld, then in Göttingen, wrote to Langebek and said that he had given a letter of introduction to Langebek to a German, who was travelling the usual road for a German, seeking bread in Denmark. Klevenfeld declares that it was a rare thing for a German to come to Denmark and not find employment.[4] On the stage of the time fun was made of the Germans, who, though despising all things Danish, still came to Denmark to make a living. There are passages in Holberg's, Sneedorff's[5] and Ewald's[6] works, which express a

[1] Baggesen reproached Klopstock with the fact that he made no return to the Danish people for the generous hospitality which they had extended to him for so many years. J. Baggesen, *Labyrinthen*, Copenhagen, 1909, p. 63.

[2] P. F. Suhm, *Samlede Skrifter*, XV, p. 233.

[3] P. F. Suhm, *Tronhjemske Samlinger*, I, p. 261.

[4] *Langebekiana*, p. 6.

[5] *Skrifter*, 1775–7, VIII, p. 378.

[6] *Samlede Skrifter*, Copenhagen, 1914–24, I, p. 77.

decided hostility towards the Germans. Ewald cries out bitterly: "Tysk er en Gift for Landet, al vor Fortred er Tysk".[1] A Dane, writing from Copenhagen on July 28, 1769, to Luxdorph, after speaking of the rumours of Herder's going to Copenhagen, says:

> Man ønsker os til Lykke med denne Erobring, og jeg er uforsigtig nok til at svare; at vi hos os selv ogsaa forstaa at kritisere, og at ikke alle tyske skønne Aander kan vænte sig at have den Lykke hos os som en Klopstock.[2]

In 1772 Suhm wrote a letter calling for the abolition of the use of a foreign language at the Danish court. He protests against the immigration of a hungry crowd of Germans and French to the detriment of the native-born Danes and compliments Count Danneskjold on having protested against this condition of affairs.[3] Tullin says that when he hears of a foreigner dedicating a book to the king of Denmark he can take his oath that the author desires to settle in Denmark, where he can find a good livelihood.

In 1770 Count J. H. E. Bernstorff, the patron and protector of the German circle, was forced to resign. Count Struensee succeeded Bernstorff as prime minister under Christian VII. Struensee's arrogant attitude towards the Danes, his failure to appreciate their growing spirit of nationality and patriotism and the strength of the ill-feeling against the Germans, brought the anti-German movement in Denmark to a head. The new minister declared that he had no time to learn Danish; he had all his official decrees published in German instead of in Danish, and he even went so far in 1772 as to propose a law for the abolition of the Danish language.[4] Struensee fell in 1772. The succeeding period under the Guldberg régime was characterized by the fight against the German influence. In 1776 the "Indfødsretslov" was passed, by which only Danes were to get civil service appointments. This law marked the victory of the national

[1] *Harlekin Patriot*, II, p. 8.
[2] *Luxdorphiana*, p. 475.
[3] P. F. Suhm, *Samlede Skrifter*, Copenhagen, 1798, XV, p. 64.
[4] *Ibid.* p. 67.

party in Denmark and the final quenching of the hopes for a continuance of a dominant German influence in that country. German writers could no longer expect to find among their northern neighbours the hospitality and protection, which, during the reign of Frederick V, had been extended to the members of the German circle in such generous measure.

CHAPTER ONE

The FORERUNNER of THE GERMAN CIRCLE, J. E. SCHLEGEL

JOHANN ELIAS SCHLEGEL,[1] the founder of the German circle in Copenhagen, was the first German writer of importance to settle in Denmark, where he spent his most mature years, the last six years of his life.[2] His significance for Danish literature lies not so much in any definite influence on individual Danish writers, as in the contribution which he made to the creation of a Danish literary public, and in the stimulus and encouragement which he gave at a time when Danish literature had little of positive achievement to show except the works of Holberg. He continues the movement which Holberg had begun, that of bringing Denmark into touch with European ideas. For this task he was perhaps better fitted than any of the Danish writers of his time. More clearly than most of his contemporaries, German or Danish, he reflects the movement, the stir and stress of his own time, while his knowledge of the classics, unusually profound in a German of his age and period, was still more conspicuous in Denmark, where, before the middle of the eighteenth century, the standard of classical education was low. His knowledge of the languages and literatures of France, Italy and England gave him a breadth of outlook which no other Danish writer of his time, with the exception of Holberg, possessed. No heaven-storming genius, Schlegel possessed a talent, delicate and penetrating, independent and significant. His intellectual curiosity was insatiable and he possessed an infinite capacity for hard work. His was a conciliatory spirit, supple and receptive to the ideas of others. At a time when

[1] Born at Meiszen, January 17, 1719; educated at Schulpforta (1733–9) and at Leipzig University (1739–42); in 1743 he went to Copenhagen; in 1748 to Sorø Academy as professor; he died on August 3, 1749.

[2] 1743–49.

everywhere thought was hard and narrow, this was almost a form of genius.[1] It was fortunate for the nascent Danish literature that Schlegel did not come to Copenhagen a confirmed apostle of Gottsched's ideas. Although he had been a member of Gottsched's circle in Leipzig he took no active part in the Leipzig-Zürich battle, but quietly followed the path of his own development, undisturbed either by the taunts of the members of the Swiss party, who regarded him as a Gottschedianer, or by the somewhat patronizing benevolence of Gottsched. Before his arrival in Copenhagen Schlegel had moved forward, in theory if not in practice, beyond the narrow bounds of Gottsched's poetics, and his intelligent appreciation of the importance of Holberg's works, and his association with the Danish dramatist, went far towards completing his emancipation.

It was in 1743 that Schlegel went to Copenhagen as secretary to Geheimkriegsrat von Spener of the Saxon legation in that city. There he found an atmosphere which was not altogether foreign to a German. At that time, and for some time to come, the German influence was strong in the capital of Denmark. The consort of King Christian VI had come from Brandenburg and spoke no Danish, and the higher nobility, the official classes and the well-to-do citizens of Copenhagen contained many German elements:

> Bei Hofe und in den vornehmsten Häusern wird gar kein Dänisch, sondern lauter Deutsch gesprochen: alle Bürger nehmen auch deutsche Mägde in ihre Dienste, damit die Kinder von Jugend auf diese Sprache lernen mögen, dasz also die dänische Sprache blosz den Bauren übrig bleibt: welche jedoch das deutsche auch ziemlich verstehen, ob sie es schon nicht sprechen können.[2]

But in spite of this widespread knowledge of the German language, there was but little acquaintance with German literature, such as it was at that period, and, in letters to Hagedorn and Bodmer, Schlegel emphasizes the isolation in which at times he

[1] G. Belouin, *De Gottsched à Lessing*, Paris, 1909, p. 187, note 1.

[2] *Kurtze Reise-Beschreibung von Hamburg bis Coppenhagen im Jahre* 1742, quoted by E. Wolff, *Gottscheds Stellung im deutschen Bildungsleben*, Kiel and Leipzig, 1895–7, II, p. 56.

felt himself to be. The biggest handicap, he said, lay in the fact that he had no friends in Copenhagen who were competent to give an opinion on his works.[1] He had little opportunity of seeing new German books. Although he had the use of a library which contained many Greek, Latin and French works, there were none by German authors. Such German books as Schlegel did see he borrowed from his friend, Kapellmeister J. A. Scheibe.[2] He complains of the distance from the learned world and of the fact that he seldom hears of what is happening before it is already old.[3] He envies Hagedorn his good fortune to be living in a city of learning; and shortly before his death, Schlegel writes from Sorø that, for a man occupying a professorial chair, he has all too little connection with the learned world outside Denmark.[4]

It is true that, in leaving Leipzig, Schlegel was leaving a focus of intellectual life, but he was leaving too the fettering restraints which lay on his free development. In Copenhagen he was no longer under the shadow cast by Gottsched, and in his new milieu he soon occupied a position to which his talents entitled him.[5] To Schlegel Denmark offered a generous welcome. His personal charm, his surprisingly thorough knowledge of the Danish language and the zeal with which he studied Danish history and literature, and, finally, his personal friendship with Holberg, aroused in the Danes a favourable opinion of German writers; and this impression still existed when, one and a- half

[1] J. E. Schlegel, *Werke*, herausg. von J. H. Schlegel, 1764–70, v, 1770, Einleitung, p. xxxviii, letter to Bodmer, 1745.

[2] Letter from Schlegel to Hagedorn, October 26, 1743. See Hagedorn, *Werke*, herausg. von Eschenburg, v, p. 288. Schlegel speaks of writing something on the art of expression in literature and eloquence, but says that he cannot find German illustrations of the rules which he lays down, since he has none of Gottsched's works on these subjects and must draw his illustrations from Cicero, Pliny, Virgil and Boileau. *Ibid.* p. xxxviii (Letter from Schlegel to Bodmer).

[3] Letter from Schlegel to Hagedorn, August 10, 1743. See E. Wolff, *Johann Elias Schlegel*, Berlin, 1889, p. 93.

[4] Letter from Schlegel to Hagedorn, April 2, 1749 (Hagedorn, *Poetische Werke*, Hamburg, 1800, v, 3, p. 299).

[5] The missing manuscript in Schlegel's own hand might have told us much of Schlegel's Danish period. Cp. E. Wolff, *op. cit.*, Introduction.

years after Schlegel's death, Klopstock came to Copenhagen. In von Spener's house there was much social intercourse and Schlegel gained a wider experience in this respect than had been possible for him in Leipzig. His later comedies and his periodical *Der Fremde* show the beneficial effect of these new opportunities. To the libraries in Copenhagen Schlegel found ready access. C. A. Berckentin,[1] whose library was especially rich in historical works, allowed him the use of it, and when Schlegel later went to Sorø, Berckentin on several occasions sent him boxes of books.[2] Von Korff, the Russian legate, who was then beginning to collect his great library, which later went to Russia, gave Schlegel permission to use his books and asked him to prepare a new catalogue for him.[3] Material on the Danish language and literature in which Schlegel was particularly interested he found in the library of Professor H. P. Anchersen, while his historical studies brought him into contact with Professor Hans Gram, the royal librarian and historiographer.

Schlegel's learning and his modesty soon procured him highly placed patrons who were interested in literature and art. He was particularly fortunate in finding in C. A. Berckentin, J. L. Holstein[4] and J. S. Schulin[5] sympathetic supporters. All these men were born in Germany. They were ministers of state and possessed considerable influence at the court of Christian VI. It was Berckentin who, with J. L. Holstein, induced the Danish government to support the arts and sciences.[6] Holstein was much more Danish in his sympathies than Berckentin, who, like his close friend, Bernstorff, saw the chief hope of creating a

[1] C. A. Berckentin (1694–1758) was born in Mecklenburg, and studied at Kiel; in 1740 he went to Copenhagen where he became a minister and a member of the Council.

[2] *Genealogisk og biografisk Archiv*, I (1840), p. 259.

[3] *Ibid.*

[4] Johann Ludwig Holstein (1694–1763) was also a native of Mecklenburg; he was educated in Hamburg and Kiel. As a patron of the University of Copenhagen, he left it a library of 20,000 volumes and many manuscripts.

[5] J. S. Schulin was born in Anspach and educated in Germany and Holland.

[6] The Danish Academy of Science was founded in Copenhagen on November 13, 1742.

Danish literature in the transplantation and encouragement of German writers; the idea does not seem to have occurred to him that Danish literature could be developed from within by native talent. With Bernstorff, then in Paris, Berckentin was in communication and, possibly, absorbed some of his literary ideas. Bernstorff knew of Schlegel and of the members of Gottsched's school. He had followed the literary movement in Leipzig with interest, particularly the drama; for the theatre, so Bernstorff thought, was particularly well fitted to raise the spirit and heart of a nation. French drama he followed closely, and he was always careful to inform Berckentin of the new plays which he saw in Paris. He wishes that the German theatre might be raised to a level with the French theatre; and he deplores the lack of encouragement of German dramatic literature, the eternal imitations of the French drama on the German stage, and that unpatriotic humility, which declared the German language to be unfitted for the expression of a great dramatic literature. It is quite probable that Berckentin passed on these ideas to his young protégé, Schlegel; it may well be that from Berckentin, and indirectly from Bernstorff, Schlegel's impulse to write plays for the Danish theatre gained strength. Schlegel's *Canut* was rated highly by Bernstorff, who thought it the best German drama that he had read. Schlegel's ideas for the development of Danish literature were, as we shall see later, more patriotically Danish than those of either Berckentin or Bernstorff, Danish statesmen though they were.

Schlegel was not the kind of man to stand idly by and take no interest in Denmark and the Danes.[1] He had begun to study Danish immediately on his arrival in Copenhagen, and within two months he had mastered it sufficiently well to be able to understand a translation of a work of Gottsched and to read Holberg's *Den Stundesløse* in the original. He could make himself understood in the language, although the pronunciation seems to have presented some difficulty to him:

[1] "Hele hans Virksomhed i Danmark er præget af Viljen at være dansk; Sproget havde han, som Holberg siger, i Grund udstuderet." C. F. Bricka, *Dansk biografisk Lexikon*, Copenhagen, 1887 ff., xv, p. 172.

Ich habe in den ersten Monaten meines Aufenthalts allhier mit groszem Eifer ein dänisches Buch verstehen lernen, und ich habe es seit der Zeit noch nicht so weit gebracht, dasz ich mich rühmen könnte, einen lebendigen dänischen Mund nur mittelmäszig zu begreifen.[1]

Der Fremde shows how familiar he had become with the social and literary conditions in Denmark; and those pages which deal with ancient and modern Danish writers prove how wide his reading was.[2] Schlegel's last work, *Coniectura*, a historical treatise in Latin, is a tribute to his interest in Danish history, and a kind of introduction to the historical works of his brother, J. H. Schlegel. The attitude which Schlegel adopted towards the literary taste of the Danish public was a fair one, neither flattering nor unduly censorious:

Ich habe niemals den Willen gehabt, weder ein Bewunderer noch ein Tadler, noch ein Vertheidiger des dänischen Volkes zu seyn. Und diejenigen, die mich hin und wieder als das letztere betrachten wollen, können versichert seyn, dasz ich es vielleicht seyn würde, wenn ich erst überzeuget wäre, dasz diese Nation einen Vertheidiger nöthig hätte.[3]

He declares that, although the Danish people had no great literary or aesthetic training, yet their taste was unspoilt. In this connection he quotes Holberg, who had complained of the poor taste of the higher classes and had said that the Danish middle classes had the best taste, and, indeed, a taste which he preferred to that of the French or English.[4] Schlegel adds that he could see the love which the Danes had for "witty and pleasant pieces", not merely from the deserved applause which they had given to Holberg's comedies, but also from the attention bestowed on translations of German pieces.[5]

[1] *Der Fremde*, Letter 1, April 6, 1745; *Werke*, v, p. 16.

[2] See *Der Fremde*, Letter 30, where Schlegel quotes from Arrebo's description of the reindeer in his *Hexæmeron rhythmico-Danicum*.

[3] *Werke*, v, Vorrede.

[4] Letter from Schlegel to Bodmer, September 18, 1747. See *Archiv für Litteraturgeschichte*, xiv, p. 50.

[5] *Äesthetische Schriften*, herausg. von J. Antoniewicz, Stuttgart, 1887, p. 198.

As to the taste of Danish authors, Schlegel declares it to be bad, and says that, since his arrival in Copenhagen, he had not seen a single good line of poetry, while the literary taste in court circles was not so much bad, as lethargic and indifferent.[1] French literature is more popular than German,[2] in spite of the fact that in court circles everyone talks German as well as his mother tongue. Several of the foremost Danish ministers of the Crown are well versed in literature. They do occasionally praise native productions, but more in order to encourage their authors than from any real conviction of their excellence; of such encouragement, however, there has not been enough. Schlegel adds that many of the young Danes of fortune and position do take a keen interest in the history and language of their own country.

From the *Abhandlung von der Nachahmung* (1742), of his Leipzig student years, to 1747, Schlegel had written nothing concerned with the drama except the Preface to his translation of Destouches' *Der Ruhmredige* (1745). During that time Schlegel had changed. In von Spener's house he had met the best society that Copenhagen had to offer; his taste had become more refined, and this was now reflected in his style, in its greater carefulness and elegance; and, just as social intercourse had affected his style, Schlegel now sought to elevate social conditions by his writings. This he attempted to do by publishing in Copenhagen a "moralische Wochenschrift" on the English model. Germany had already had a vogue of such periodicals,[3] a vogue which was declining when Schlegel came to Copenhagen. Schlegel was well aware of the influence of these periodicals; he knew how much they had done to improve the literary taste

[1] Letter from Schlegel to Bodmer, October 8, 1746, in G. F. Stäudlin, *Briefe an Bodmer*, Stuttgart, 1794, pp. 39 ff.

[2] This may be partly explained by the fact that before Schlegel's arrival in Denmark, all that was known of German literature there consisted of the productions of such wandering theatrical companies as those of Spiegelberg and Von Quoten.

[3] "Man hørte foruden tale om poetiske, juridiske, theologiske Spectators, og andre, som vare i Arbejde, saa Folk omsider begyndte at frygte, at der vilde opreise sig Sandemænd udi ethvert Quarteer, ja at der vilde blive ligesaa mange Spectatores om Dagen, som Vægtere om Natten" (Rahbek and Nyerup, *op. cit.*, Introduction, p. lix).

and moral standard of the average man. Their popular style and form had attracted a large circle of readers and had given them an interest in questions which they would otherwise have considered outside their sphere. Before Schlegel arrived in Denmark there had been Danish periodicals, but they were, for the most part, translations or imitations of English, Swedish, and German periodicals. The *Dänische Bibliothec* (1737–9) was edited by Langebek and Harboe and was written in German so that it might circulate outside Denmark. J. Riis' *Den danske Spectator* (1744) was in Danish and was the oldest original periodical on the English model. Its tone was, however, somewhat peevish and sharply critical. Schlegel's journal *Der Fremde*[1] is suaver and less censorious. Its irony is never bitter, always gentle and delicate. In its lightness and urbane elegance of style it strikes a new note in literary periodicals in Denmark. Here is no display of learning, no classical allusions.[2] Schlegel regards himself as a guest, staying with a good friend and desirous of fulfilling a guest's duty by entertaining his host pleasantly, avoiding the extremes of praise and blame. He has chosen German as his medium of expression since almost all educated Danes speak as good German as one hears in Germany.[3] Although he advocates good social manners and taste there is no deeply moral or didactic intention, no wish to castigate vice or extol virtue. In an easy and pleasant manner Schlegel discusses the small failings and weaknesses which he observes in the everyday life around him, the different types and characters he meets. There is grace in his style, variety in his subjects and a psychological delicacy of treatment, which betrays the keen judge of people. Throughout *Der Fremde* we find lively pictures and entertaining descriptions. It does not flatter the Danes; it criticizes their short-comings but praises their good qualities, and its great success, written as it was almost wholly on Danish

[1] Fifty-two weekly numbers were issued between April 6, 1745 and April 6, 1746.

[2] Such allusions as we do meet are rather to the great French writers, as well as to Swift and Chesterfield, and particularly to Holberg.

[3] P. M. Stolpe, *Dagspressen i Danmark*, Copenhagen, 1878–82, IV, p. 241.

subjects, was a triumph of tact. It was written under difficulties, for Schlegel was then only twenty-five years of age, and he wrote it single-handed for a foreign population. Furthermore, it was written for a pietistic audience although Schlegel himself and his friends, Hans Gram, Anchersen and Holberg, were rationalists and opposed to pietism.

Schlegel's periodical is written in letter form. It contains dialogues, short stories and allegories. There are many allusions to Copenhagen,[1] to the beauty of its surroundings and the good manners of its inhabitants. Schlegel gives us an indispensable picture of the Danish capital of the period, a picture which may well be compared to the exact portrayals of the prejudices, weaknesses and habits of the different classes of the population in Holberg's comedies. In *Der Fremde* we find the results of Schlegel's studies in Danish and Scandinavian mythology and history. He calls history by dates a dead thing, and challenges the Danes to write a Danish history in their own language. Sagas and stories of old heroes he takes from Saxo Grammaticus, the *Edda* and other old nordic sources. His knowledge of Danish literature and history is surprising and his celebrated series of articles on Danish writers from Arrebo to Holberg is one of the earliest criticisms of Danish literature.[2]

Schlegel speaks, too, of the necessary reforms in educational methods. He condemns the harsh school discipline and the exorbitant amount of time spent on the study of dead languages to the neglect of the Danish language.[3] He fights against pietism's solemnity, its forbidding of all pleasures, its pedantic learning. He is opposed to all religious fanaticism and upholds the beauty of nature and joy in life against the pietistic conception of the earth as a vale of human woe.[4] Towards the end of the existence of *Der Fremde* Schlegel interferes in so domesti-

[1] *Der Fremde*, Letters 1, 2, 11, 13, 18 and 47.

[2] "Hans Bemærkninger over de danske Digtere endnu idelig efterses og citeres af alle, der lægge sig efter vor Poesis Historie" (N. M. Petersen, *op. cit.* v, 1, p. 14).

[3] *Der Fremde*, Letters 10 and 47.

[4] E. Wolff, *J. E. Schlegel*, Berlin, 1889, p. 122.

cally Danish an affair as the Langebek-Pontoppidan quarrel. Langebek had been forced by command of the king to apologize to Pontoppidan for having ventured to correct some mistakes which Pontoppidan had made in an article on church history in the *Danske Magazin*. Several of the professors of the University of Copenhagen were incensed at the indignity put upon Langebek, and Holberg and Anchersen asked Schlegel to oppose Pontoppidan in *Der Fremde*. This he did in the form of a parable.[1] So thoroughly did Schlegel carry out their request that both Holberg and Anchersen were much perturbed as to the possible consequences for them all. Pontoppidan complained to the minister, von Spener, who called Schlegel before him. Schlegel declared that he had not aimed at Pontoppidan in his article and the matter ended there.[2] Schlegel's happy combination of learning and an easy man-of-the-world attitude came as something new to the Danes. He continues the movement begun by Gram, Langebek and Holberg, of popularizing knowledge, of interesting the middle class in literature,[3] of creating a public to whom a more serious literature than the "moralische Wochenschriften" might later make an appeal. Danish critics have expressed astonishment that a foreigner should have been able to acquire so accurate a knowledge of the Danish national character, history and literature,[4] and that a journal, written by a foreigner on Danish subjects and intended for the entertainment of a popular audience, should have been so successful in the Danish capital.[5] It was the first weekly paper in Denmark of any independent real value, and it did not suffer

[1] *Der Fremde*, Letter 48.

[2] See P. M. Stolpe, *op. cit.* p. 243; N. M. Petersen, *op. cit.* IV, pp. 244–6; P. Engelstoft, *Universitets og Skole-Annaler*, 1806, II, pp. 288 ff.; P. F. Suhm, *Samlede Skrifter*, Copenhagen, 1798, XIV, pp. 243 ff.; W. Söderhjelm, *Om J. E. Schlegel som Lustspeldiktare*, Helsingfors, 1884, p. 129; Söderhjelm states that Schlegel had to stop publication of *Der Fremde* by the order of the king, but this does not appear certain.

[3] In his writings on the Danish theatre two years later, it was with the middle classes that Schlegel thought the best hope for the development of a National Theatre lay.

[4] P. M. Stolpe, *op. cit.* p. 241.

[5] N. M. Petersen, *op. cit.* V, I, p. 14. S. Müller, *Dansk Litteraturhistorie*, 1893, p. 104.

greatly by comparison with the best of the English periodicals. It made Copenhagen a literary centre. Holberg had already made Copenhagen a centre for the theatre, but the educated upper classes rather looked down upon his plays, and *Der Fremde* made this class feel that they now had a periodical which expressed Copenhagen's opinion on matters which were not always narrowly Danish.

Der Fremde was not the only periodical to be edited in Copenhagen by a German writer. J. A. Cramer edited *Der nordische Aufseher*[1] there during the years 1758–61. Cramer's position in Copenhagen was very different from Schlegel's and his periodical reflects the difference. He represented governmental circles; through Klopstock and Moltke he had the royal ear; and he enjoyed great prestige. His periodical was the organ of the German circle in Copenhagen. Schlegel, on the other hand, stood alone. He had made an effort to ingratiate himself with the Danes by learning their language, literature and history; but the party to which he belonged, that of which Holberg and Langebek were the leaders, was opposed to the pietism which, with Christian VI on the throne, was then in favour. The style of *Der nordische Aufseher* is unctuous and heavy, that of *Der Fremde* is delicate and playful.

Schlegel's interest in Holberg's plays, shown by the frequent allusions to them in *Der Fremde*, probably did not begin with his arrival in Denmark. Holberg's *Barselstuen* had been performed in the Hamburg opera house as early as March 29, 1742; it was the first of Holberg's plays to be produced in Germany; and it was followed by *Jean de France*, *Jacob von Tyboe*, *Den politiske Kandestøber*, and several others. When Schlegel came to Copenhagen in 1743 he brought with him a letter bearing the greetings of Gottsched to Holberg. And in a letter to Gottsched of September 18, 1743,[2] he tells him that he has met Holberg

[1] Cp. B. Kahle, Holberg, *Neue Heidelberger Jahrbücher*, XIII, pp. 144–72.

[2] "Mit dem Herrn Prof. Holberg habe ich übrigens Bekanntschaft gemacht und ihm bei dieser Gelegenheit das Compliment abgestattet, welches mir Ew. Hoch Edelgeb. aufgetragen haben. Ich weisz nicht, ob er mir erlauben wird, diese Bekanntschaft fortzusetzen, weil er gar keine Gesellschaft

and delivered the letter, but adds that he is not sure that he will be able to follow up this introduction since Holberg does not like society; in order to see him he had to use a little strategy. In a letter to Hagedorn[1] Schlegel writes in more detail of the same interview, and later describes to him another[2] at which Holberg said that he did not understand much German, but had read Hagedorn's poetry. There is no direct evidence of further meetings between Schlegel and Holberg, but Schlegel subsequently alludes in a letter to Bodmer[3] to Holberg's opinion of literary taste in Denmark, and it seems fairly certain that their intercourse did continue. Holberg was interested in *Der Fremde* and later made strenuous efforts to get Schlegel appointed to Sorø. In the biography by his brother, J. H. Schlegel, the latter says that Holberg had a strong liking for Elias Schlegel; the frequent references to Holberg and his works in *Der Fremde* are usually in terms of unqualified admiration.

In 1743, the year in which Schlegel arrived in Denmark, Holberg's was the only name of importance in the Danish theatre, and Schlegel was at first impressed by Holberg's great prestige. There were points of similarity and contact between the Danish dramatist and the young editor of *Der Fremde*. Both were men of commanding intellect, independent in their views and reserved by nature. In *Der Fremde* Schlegel uses illustrations from Holberg's comedies and borrows types and characters from him.[4] Just as Holberg in his comedies, so here Schlegel attacks the vulgar farces and harlequinades of the wandering German troupes, and thus, in Denmark, Gottsched's pupil was

liebt, und ich das Glück vor ihm gelassen zu werden, welches Rittern von Danebrog und sogar Ambassadeurs abgeschlagen worden, ohne alles Verhoffen durch eine kleine List erlanget habe" (W. Söderhjelm, *op. cit.* p. 13).

1 *Ibid.*, October 26, 1743.

2 *Ibid.*, November 9, 1743.

3 "Holberg beklagt sich über den schlechten Geschmack der Groszen und behauptet, dasz der Mittelstand allhier den guten Geschmack besitze" (September, 1747, *ibid.* p. 14, note 27).

4 Cp. *Der Fremde*, Letter 39, where Holberg is alluded to as "Hans Michelsen Brauer" (under which name he wrote *Peder Paars* and his comedies) and where Schlegel praises the fertility of his invention, the naturalness of his language and his freedom from bombast and low vulgarity.

continuing the fight which Holberg had begun.[1] During the years after 1745 Schlegel retains in some measure this attitude of admiration of and agreement with Holberg and his ideas. In his *Gedanken über das Theater und insonderheit das dänische* (1747) Schlegel advocates for the Danish stage many features of which Holberg's plays offered outstanding examples. He demands variety in the characters so that all classes may be represented; he justifies the vulgar and democratic element in Holberg's plays as a necessary "propaedeutic" for the education of the masses; and he demands that the follies and weaknesses shown on the stage should be native follies and weaknesses. Schlegel admires the simple action of Holberg's plays and the successful way in which he avoids, on the one hand, the confused intrigue of the French plays and, on the other hand, the lack of action of the German comedy of the period. He demands that every character should speak according to his condition and that these characters should be familiar to the audience. Schlegel sees in the national spirit of Holberg's plays a better tonic for the theatre than Gottsched's false classicism.

But Schlegel did not regard Holberg's farces and comedies as the final goal of the Danish drama. A refined theatre, he says, refines a nation's manners; and he urges that the theatre should gradually rise from comedies dealing with the lower classes to those dealing with the middle classes, and thence to the court and high tragedy. The regularly constructed French classical tragedy is still Schlegel's ideal of dramatic form, though he demands native themes. When later Holberg fought, and not altogether successfully, against French comedy, Schlegel's inclinations were on the side of the French. It is possible that his attitude helped to spread the idea that Holberg's plays were a collection of rather vulgar popular farces[2]; but in his *Gedanken zur Aufnahme des dänischen Theaters* he is careful not to express such ideas too openly. Schlegel's criticism of Holberg we do

[1] But with Gottsched's pedantry and discouragement of youth and its enthusiasms Schlegel was by no means in agreement.

[2] O. Skavlan, *Holberg som Komedieforfatter*, Kristiania, 1872, p. 308.

not find in his theoretical writings subsequent to 1745,[1] but in his letters to Bodmer. In one of these[2] he says that the famous Holberg does not enjoy in Copenhagen the reputation which his translators and imitators claim for him, and that his comedies are admired only by the lower classes, from which he gathers his material. In another[3] he says, evidently in answer to an enquiry, that most people in Copenhagen think with Bodmer that Holberg should write comedies of a higher type and more refined style, and that his works are regarded by some as a mere collection of platitudes. Holberg's moral treatises are rather *jeux d'esprit* than the fruit of deep thought, although they contain, he admits, much good sense and truth; and in a letter,[4] also to Bodmer, speaking of the small number of original authors in Denmark, Schlegel says that the Danish court has no liking for Holberg's comedies.

But the debt which Schlegel owed to Holberg was by no means a small one. The comedies of Schlegel's pre-Copenhagen period had at least one serious fault: their characters lacked real life. He realized this and, with his habitual thoroughness, he set himself to remedy this shortcoming; and the masters whom he studied were Holberg and Molière. *Der Fremde* is full of little portraits of characters and types on the model of Holberg and Molière. To two works of Holberg, which seem to have made a deep impression on him, to *Peder Paars* and *Niels Klim*, Schlegel makes frequent reference. One letter[5] is, like *Peder Paars*, an attack on those learned people, who, in ordinary social intercourse, preserve carefully their pedantic manners. The "Sexton of Bergen" spoken of by Schlegel, was the name by which Niels Klim was known.[6] In the twelfth letter Schlegel is replying to some criticisms of former letters in *Der Fremde*. He

[1] With two possible exceptions: in *Die Langeweile* (1747), written for the Danish theatre and in the *Gedanken zur Aufnahme des dänischen Theaters* (*Werke*, III, pp. 261 ff.), in both of which works Schlegel attacks vulgarity on the stage, without, however, mentioning Holberg's name.

[2] Dated October 8, 1746, in G. F. Stäudlin, *op. cit.* pp. 39 ff.

[3] September 19, 1746. See W. Söderhjelm, *op. cit.* p. 15.

[4] March 31, 1749, *ibid.*

[5] *Der Fremde*, Letter 8. *Werke*, V.

[6] *Ibid.* Letter 10.

had evidently been accused of having borrowed from Holberg, and he denies that the printed papers of Niels Klim quoted by him had been taken from Holberg's work. One letter[1] contains a satire in verse, "nach Art der Verwandlungen des Herrn Holbergs", and another[2] a letter from the Political Tinker to the eloquent barber, Master Gert Westphaler. Schlegel's thorough study of Holberg's comedies is reflected in the plays which he wrote in his Copenhagen period. The middle and the lower classes he now brings from the "moralische Wochenschriften" on to the stage. In the construction of plot and in the drawing of low comic characters Schlegel is now much more mature. To see this one needs only to compare *Die Pracht zu Landheim*[3] with *Der Geheimniszvolle* (1747).

Schlegel's emigration to Denmark had brought a new and strong influence to bear on his literary development. The Danish art of the theatre was not so old as that of France or England, but it was the first in the North, and it was fully developed at a time when the German theatre was still in its "Wanderjahre". Holberg's democratic theatre showed Schlegel that the theatre must make its appeal to a wide audience, and that there should be no separation of the "people" from the educated classes. In Copenhagen Schlegel grew away from the blind admiration of Racine and Corneille towards the realization of a really native and national theatre; he sees more and more clearly the impossibility of founding such a theatre on a false classicism. In this development Holberg played an important part; he showed the aspiring young dramatist the truth and wealth of Molière. Schlegel now saw that even farce was justified, since it fulfilled the needs of a certain class. Neither Molière nor Holberg was a master acceptable to the school of Gottsched, but it was

[1] *Der Fremde*, Letter 24.

[2] *Ibid.* Letter 27. Schlegel points out that barbers have unrivalled opportunities for suggesting reforms to statesmen while shaving them, and that, in view of this, barbers should be used as political teachers.

[3] Antoniewicz maintains that *Die Pracht zu Landheim* contains much that is reminiscent of Holberg's *Jean de France*, which had been translated into German by Detharding in 1740. One can hardly call the similarity a very striking one.

through the earnest study of their plays that Schlegel gained as a writer qualities of naturalness and simplicity, and as a critic greater clarity in his ideas as to the needs of the German and Danish theatres.

With the accession to the throne of Frederick V in 1746 a change came over the spirit of the Danish nation, and the possibility of a National Theatre began to be discussed. It is not easy to determine how much the foundation of the Danish National Theatre owed to a personal interest in the theatre on the part of Frederick V, and how much to the influence of the men about him. Certainly he never betrayed any special pleasure in theatrical performances and as soon as he conveniently could, he shifted the financial responsibility for the theatre to the municipality of Copenhagen. It is possible that he took more interest in the plastic arts, for he spent much money on works of art; and his generosity to the library should not be forgotten.[1] Holberg's name was still the only great name in the Danish theatre. The first period of his dramatic activity (1722–8) had been unusually prolific and successful. Holberg was still mentally active, but he was no longer so keenly interested in the theatre, possibly because with the upper classes and court circles his comedies were not popular, and it was to Schlegel that those interested in the revival of the theatre turned. It was probably Schlegel's highly placed friends and patrons, Moltke,[2] J. L. Holstein and Berckentin, who asked Schlegel to give his opinion concerning the foundation of a Danish National Theatre. In a letter to Bodmer Schlegel says that under the new reign the fine arts will get a better opportunity, and he hopes that German comedy will be played on the Danish stage.[3] In another letter to Bodmer,[4] he says that when the new theatre is established he would like to write hints to actors on

[1] For a discussion of Frederick V's attitude to the Danish theatre see Edvard Holm, *Danmark-Norges Historie*, Copenhagen, 1898, pt 2, XXII, pp. 420 ff.

[2] It was to Count Moltke that J. H. Schlegel dedicated his brother's works (1761–70).

[3] Dated October 8, 1746. G. F. Stäudlin, *op. cit.* 1794, pp. 34 ff.

[4] Dated September 18, 1747, quoted in J. E. Schlegel, *Ästhetische Schriften*, ed. Antoniewicz, p. 150.

the choice of good plays and on other things concerned with the theatre. The two works in which Schlegel carried out this intention were *Zur Errichtung eines dänischen Theaters* and *Gedanken zur Aufnahme des dänischen Theaters.*[1] *Zur Errichtung eines dänischen Theaters* was written at the end of 1746 when there was still some doubt of the feasibility of a National Theatre.[2] It is more of a rough plan than a finished essay. Here Schlegel lays down what he considers the necessary conditions and requirements for the success of a permanent theatre in Copenhagen; he does not, however, show a very accurate appreciation of the technical and financial requirements for such an undertaking. He says that during the year there should be 165 performances and 50,000 spectators. The company should be under a director. There are to be twelve actors employed at an annual salary of from 200 to 400 daler; they are to play five times a week and the plays performed are to be in Danish and German alternately.

The *Gedanken zur Aufnahme des dänischen Theaters*, the best German work on drama and theatre before Lessing's *Hamburgische Dramaturgie*,[3] presents a fuller consideration of the means of realizing such a theatre and its proper aims. Schlegel says that since there were so many different people then giving to the actors the benefit of their experience, he himself felt impelled to do so by his love for the theatre and by the constant interest he had taken in it for the past twelve years.[4] He will not, he says, write what will please himself most, but will put himself in the nation's place. The theatre is the best field for the exercise of the finest intellects of a nation,[5] and should instruct not as does a pedant, but easily and indirectly, like a man of the world:

[1] Written in 1746 and 1747 respectively; published together in 1764 in Schlegel's complete works under the title *Gedanken über das Theater und insbesondere das dänische.*

[2] Schlegel, *Werke*, v, Introduction, p. xliv.

[3] H. Hettner, *Literaturgeschichte des achtzehnten Jahrhunderts*, 6th ed., Braunschweig, 1913, III, I, pp. 353, 355.

[4] *Ästhetische Schriften*, p. 193.

[5] *Ibid.* p. 226.

Ein gutes Theater thut einem ganzen Volke eben die Dienste, die der Spiegel einem Frauenzimmer leistet, das sich putzen will. Es zeigt ihm, besonders in dem Äuszerlichen des Umgangs, was übel steht, und was lächerlich ist....Es verbreitet den Geschmack an Künsten und Wissenschaften; es lehrt auch den geringsten Bürger Vernunftschlüsse machen, und höflicher werden.[1]

Schlegel points to the Athenians, whose manners and politeness improved as their theatre developed; the theatre and the people, says Schlegel, are like two stones grinding and refining one another.[2] He remarks that whereas in many countries the theatre in its beginnings had to suffer much at the hands of worthless strolling players, the Danish theatre has received a better start and has not had to suffer so much in that respect.[3] He pays a tribute to the decency of the Copenhagen stage and declares that the Danish women show a greater dislike of vulgarity than is to be observed in most other countries.[4]

The idea in the *Gedanken zur Aufnahme des dänischen Theaters* which Schlegel emphasizes most strongly is that the material and manners of both tragedy and comedy must be national. He does not wish to exclude from tragedy all subjects which are taken from the histories of foreign nations, but he makes a strong plea for native manners and native wit, and says that a National Theatre should produce the works of native playwrights. Foreign pieces, which are unsuitable to Danish tastes, should be excluded, and dramas more French than Danish in spirit should not be represented at all. Every nation, says Schlegel, if it is to have a theatre which will please it, prescribes through its native manners certain rules, and a play made for one nation will seldom please another.[5] The simple action, characteristic of Holberg's plays, should be used in plays for the Danish theatre. There have been, says Schlegel, native Danish writers who have called their own nation steady and almost dull,[6] but the Danish stage should not on that account confine itself to extreme farces only. "Wit", which has both truth and delicacy, should be introduced and he cites the great success enjoyed by

[1] *Ibid.* p. 205. [2] *Ibid.* p. 206. [3] *Ibid.* p. 193.
[4] *Ibid.* p. 200. [5] *Ibid.* p. 194. [6] *Ibid.* p. 199.

Holberg's *Maskerade* and *Den honnette Ambition.*[1] The object of a National Theatre at all times should be to give pleasure to all classes of spectators. The public are to be educated gradually and without their being aware of the fact. Their taste is to be made more refined, better able to appreciate the subtleties of something above mere farce. Schlegel never seemed to regard comedy, even the higher type of comedy, as the ultimate aim of any great playwright. Poetic tragedy was, in his idea, the highest form of dramatic art, and he has not altogether freed himself from Gottsched's idea, that farce and comedy have to do with the lower classes, and tragedy with the nobility and the court. Schlegel proposes that in a National Theatre one might begin with comedy and the lower classes, and proceed through the "bürgerliche Trauerspiel" and the "weinerliche Lustspiel" to tragedy of a higher aristocratic type.

To avoid the vicissitudes incidental on changes in the occupation of the throne, Schlegel demands for the Danish National Theatre the appointment of a salaried official, well versed in theatrical matters. Such an official would superintend the engagement of actors and actresses and the selection of plays. The actors are to be in receipt of a steady salary, and Schlegel proposes that the proceeds of the fifth performance should go to the author.[2] Prizes should be offered by those patriots interested in literature in order to encourage native talent.[3]

The *Gedanken zur Aufnahme des dänischen Theaters* was not published until 1764, but Schlegel was in close touch with many men of influence, who were interested in the theatre, and it is not improbable that the Danish National Theatre did owe something to the ideas which he put forward. The king provided a theatre and in 1748, the Royal Theatre, built by N. Eigtwed, was opened in Copenhagen on Kongens Nytorv. Its direction was placed in the hands of the city. Copenhagen had already had a court theatre, but a theatre of this kind, under artistic

[1] *Ästhetische Schriften*, p. 200.

[2] *Ibid.* p. 226. Gottsched had already proposed that the author should receive a share of the takings.

[3] *Ibid.*

direction, was something new. It was successful in the beginning, but later the directorship fell into the hands of incapable amateurs. As Schlegel had recommended, Holberg's comedies, as well as plays by other native writers, formed the basis of the repertory.

In addition to these theoretical writings, Schlegel wrote several German comedies and tragedies[1] for production on the Danish stage. Of the comedies, *Die Langeweile* was translated into Danish under the title *Kiedsommelighed* and published in Copenhagen[2]; *Der Triumph der guten Frauen* was also translated but not published. The German originals of these two plays, together with *Die stumme Schönheit*, were published in 1748 under the title *Beyträge zum dänischen Theater*. These comedies, like *Der Fremde*, treated in the main of small incidents in everyday life and they are, no doubt, a faithful reflection of life in the Copenhagen of the time. Schlegel's *Canut* is the first dramatic result of his studies in northern history, the fruit of his interest in Denmark's literature and theatre. As its name indicates, it is on a Danish subject, and in Canut's love of peace and self-sacrifice for the good of his subjects, we may see the traits which, in the first years of his reign, made Frederick V so popular a king. *Canut* was intended for representation on the Danish stage and was translated into Danish; but in spite of its favourable reception, especially in Danish court circles, it was never played. Berckentin tried to get it translated into French and sent it to Bernstorff in Paris.[3] Both Berckentin and Bernstorff hoped that, if Schlegel continued to develop in this *genre* of tragedy, German literature would have a Corneille to boast of, although they could hardly hope to make of him a Racine,

[1] The plays of Schlegel's Copenhagen period with dates of publication were: *Der gute Rath*, 1745, in *Der Fremde*; *Canut*, 1747; *Der Geheimniszvolle*, 1747; *Der Gärtnerkönig*, 1747; *Die Langeweile*, 1747 or 1748 (see note 2, *infra*); *Die stumme Schönheit*, 1748; *Der Triumph der guten Frauen*, 1748; *Gothrika* and *Heinrich der Löwe* were never finished.

[2] The year of publication of *Die Langeweile* is doubtful. It was either December 18, 1747, or December 18, 1748. See N. M. Petersen, *op. cit.* IV, p. 467.

[3] Letter from J. E. Schlegel to Bodmer, April 15, 1747 in G. F. Stäudlin, *op. cit.* p. 47.

since, in their opinion, the German language did not lend itself to the Racinean type of tragedy.[1] Schlegel's idea of writing another tragedy drawn from northern history was to have been realized in his *Gothrika*, but this play was not finished.

In 1748 Schlegel, who, since his arrival in Denmark, had been resident most of the time in Copenhagen, transferred the scene of his activities to Sorø Academy, to the staff of which he had been appointed as Professor extraordinarius. This Academy, first founded in 1665, was re-established on July 7, 1747. On its re-establishment several influential men looked to Schlegel, as to one who might do much to strengthen the reputation of the revived academy.[2] In 1747 a fourth professor was to be appointed. Three names were proposed, those of Jens Schielderup Sneedorff, Martinus Hübner and Christian Frederik Wadskiær. The Secretary of the Chancellery was ordered to write to Holberg to ask his opinion of the merits of the three candidates. Holberg replied, and in a letter[3] dated July 3, 1747, addressed to Councillor von Holstein, gives his vote, not for any one of the names submitted, but for Johann Elias Schlegel. Holberg states that the latter desires to enter the academic profession, that his knowledge of history and law is known to all, and, furthermore, that he knows of no one better fitted to lecture on modern history and the present state of Europe. He admits that he is a foreigner, but says that he may be regarded as a nationalized Dane, and emphasizes the fact that he has a thorough knowledge of the Danish language. He therefore begs to propose Schlegel as Professor of History and Constitutional Law. In spite of this recommendation, an unusually warm one for a man of Holberg's cool temperament, C. F. Wadskiær was appointed. Later in the year Schlegel accepted a post as secretary to the Saxon legation in Copenhagen, but his real interests were in academic life, and he had not given up hope of securing a post in Sorø. On April 6, 1748, Schlegel sends in a petition[4] to the Danish

[1] Letter from Bernstorff to Berckentin.

[2] *Genealogisk og biografisk Archiv*, I, 1840, p. 260.

[3] Cp. *Museum*, 1893, VII, pp. 35 ff.

[4] *Ibid.*

king. After a long preamble, he beseeches the king to appoint him Professor of Constitutional Law and Political Science, and, since the existing chairs in Sorø were now filled, he would be content to become a Professor extraordinarius at a yearly salary of 300 daler, until he could obtain the same salary and position as the Professores ordinarii. On May 3, 1748, Schlegel was appointed to the position he desired.[1] Apart from Schlegel's undoubted qualifications for the post, the appointment was made partly through the influence of Moltke and Berckentin, and, possibly also, to please Holberg, who was expected to leave the rest of his fortune to Sorø Academy.

According to one writer,[2] who wrote about the middle of the eighteenth century, there were not many students at Sorø at the time of Schlegel's appointment. Count R. F. von Lynar is the only German student mentioned by name, and most of the lectures were delivered in Danish, although all the students and professors could both understand and speak German. The professors, in addition to their official lectures, gave from five to eight private lecture hours a week, so that a hard-working student could get through the academy in from two and a half to three years. Some of the professors would lecture from thirty-six to forty-two hours a week.[3] As to the subjects which Schlegel taught at Sorø, various accounts have been given,[4] but it seems certain that Political Science and Constitutional Law

[1] In a letter from J. A. Cramer to Ramler, dated August 12, 1750, Cramer tells Ramler, evidently in answer to an enquiry from the latter, that the late Elias Schlegel's salary in Sorø was not over 400 daler a year, and that living in Sorø was fairly dear. In the summer of 1750 Ramler was offered the chair at Sorø made vacant by Schlegel's death; but he was dissuaded by his friends from accepting it. Cp. *Vierteljahrschrift für Literaturgeschichte*, IV, pp. 59–61.

[2] *Soransk Tidsskrift*, 1865, I, p. 205.

[3] A. F. Büsching, *Nachrichten*, Copenhagen and Leipzig, 1754–7, II, pp. 352–3.

[4] According to A. F. Büsching, *ibid.* p. 358, and *Museum*, 1893, Heft VII, p. 36, his subjects were Political Science and Constitutional Law; in the *Vierteljahrschrift für Literaturgeschichte*, IV, *l.c.*, it is stated that he also gave lectures on "deutsche Wohlredenheit"; and Bricka, *op. cit.* XV, p. 171, and *Genealogisk og biografisk Archiv*, I, 1840, p. 260, mention Constitutional Law, Modern History, and Commercial Science ("Handelsfaget") as his subjects.

were among them. At that time the Professor of Political Science and Constitutional Law taught all branches of Public and Private Law, as well as the constitutions of individual European states, International Law as it existed in Europe, and the maxims which ruled between the states in time of peace and war; Schlegel lectured also on Montesquieu's *L'Esprit des Lois* and on the "Hofschreibart".[1]

On his duties at the Academy Schlegel entered with great zeal. In a letter to Bodmer dated March 31, 1749, he speaks of delivering from six to eight hour lectures a day. In addition to his scheduled lectures, public and private, he gave courses on art, and it was in this subject that he founded a debating society among the students.[2] He planned critical articles, as well as tragedies and comedies; and was also working on a new edition of Bayle.[3] His interest in poetry was not neglected; there is record[4] of a poem written by him at Sorø Academy on the occasion of the birth of Crown Prince Christian. He also continued his researches into the history of the German Middle Ages and of northern antiquity. In addition to all these various activities Schlegel was librarian at the Academy, probably by reason of his previous experience in such work in Copenhagen, and there is every probability that he reorganized the library at Sorø.[5] Under the pressure and intensity of this work his health, never too robust, gave way. He died in 1749 at the early age of thirty, and was buried in the churchyard of Sorø Academy.

Such of Schlegel's works as were published in Denmark in his lifetime do not appear to have made much stir, to judge by the literary periodicals of the time. We find generally no more than a mention of their publication. Schlegel's death was recorded, but created little interest. P. F. Suhm did, however,

[1] A. F. Büsching, *op. cit.* p. 351.
[2] *Genealogisk og biografisk Archiv*, I, 1840, p. 260.
[3] Letter to Bodmer, March 31, 1749.
[4] A. F. Büsching, *op. cit.* p. 358.
[5] The disastrous fire of 1813 at Sorø destroyed most of the Academy buildings and among them the library; it is thus impossible to trace Schlegel's connection with it.

write a memorial which excited Dass's ire, against the German-born Schlegel:

Klagetalen over Prof. Schlegel vilde jeg heller en Tydsk skulde have skrevet. Vi have længe nok gjort mere af Fremmede end af vore Egne. At Danmarks Historie kunde have ventet adskillig Forbedring ved ham, derpaa synes hans udgivne Conjectura ei at vise saa stor Prøve. Jeg mærker og ikke, at mange her gjøre saa meget af ham...Endelig, lad de Tydske parentere over deres Tydske.[1]

Nor have Schlegel's literary activities in Denmark in their relation to Danish intellectual life been treated of in any detail by the Danish literary critics of later generations. They have admitted that Schlegel did do something towards improving literary taste in Denmark. One critic[2] points out that Schlegel, foreigner as he was, received an unusual, although well-merited honour, when he was appointed to Sorø, and declares that, although Schlegel was German by birth and in his works, yet he was Danish in spirit, and his coming to Denmark was a gain to Denmark and to Sorø. But another Danish critic[3] regards Schlegel as a foreigner in spirit, although he recognizes the influence of his theoretical writings on the theatre and of *Der Fremde* on Danish literary taste.

It is true that Schlegel was a foreigner, but there were very few Danes of the time who took so keen an interest in the Danish language and literature as he did. Even so patriotic a northerner and so critical a judge of men as Holberg, acknowledges this. In Denmark Schlegel had found what had been denied to him in his own country, friendly encouragement and material help; and he was not slow to attempt to repay the debt. His comedies, influenced as they were by Holberg, symbolize the literary union between Denmark and Germany in the earlier eighteenth century. He strengthens the literary relations between Hamburg and Copenhagen; and Klopstock, by his frequent sojourns there,

[1] Letter from Benjamin Dass to Suhm, dated June 5, 1756. See P. F. Suhm, *Samlede Skrifter*, Copenhagen, 1798, XV, p. 245.

[2] C. Molbech, *Om Sorø Akademie, dets Skiebne og dets Fremtid*, Copenhagen, 1847, p. 15.

[3] N. M. Petersen, *op. cit.* v.

developed this intercourse. Schlegel continued what Holberg had begun, the work of bringing Denmark into contact with the restless spirit of eighteenth-century Europe. He was one of the founders of the Danish National Theatre. With *Der Fremde* he prepared the way for the German circle in Copenhagen, by creating a public for the writers of this circle. He helped to make of Copenhagen a literary centre. About the middle of the century, at the time of the death of Holberg, there is to be noticed a sudden change in Denmark's literary atmosphere. Klopstock's coming to Copenhagen marks the turning point; the critical sobriety of Holberg gives way to the enthusiasm of Klopstock; and in this change, Schlegel played an important part.

J. E. Schlegel is the first, after Vitus Bering, Ole Borch and Reenberg's adaptations of Horace and Boileau, to break with the old ideas and make of pleasure the chief goal of art. Before his time, outward form, modelled by pseudo-classical rules, was regarded in Denmark as the really important element in poetry. Now faint stirrings were evident of a desire to judge poetry no longer by classical authority, but by a more subjective standard. Schlegel brings into Danish literature the idea of taste as the criterion of literature. This taste was not to be narrow or pedantic, founded on worn-out rules, but was to be a natural growth from the national character and a necessary element in the creation of a national literature and theatre. This purification of literature, arising from the new demand for naturalness in thought and expression, was first clearly expressed in Denmark in *Der Fremde*. It is significant that the first writer in Denmark to make a real contribution to aesthetic questions was not a Dane but a German.

In his ideas for the creation of a national literature and theatre Schlegel was more patriotic than ministers such as Berckentin and Bernstorff. But the national literature he called for was not to be a narrow or a stationary one. It was to reflect its own century and the new ideas of the time. Here Schlegel is a true son of the eighteenth century, cosmopolitan and broad in his sympathies and interests. He saw, too, that a national literature, in order to have a foundation, must cast back to the past and understand and appreciate what had gone before. Hence his criticism in *Der Fremde* of Danish writers: a criticism to the point and revealing a well defined and aesthetically justified point of view. Hence, too, Schlegel's interest in the old northern literature and history. He declares them to be particularly rich in characters and great events; and he himself desired to "pluck flowers in a field, which literature had, up till then, left almost untouched".[1] This new interest of Schlegel was not inspired by any desire to create a false and imitative bardic literature. Like Herder, he found in all true and natural expression of a national spirit something worthy of admiration; whether in Shakespeare, in the classical literature, or in the bards. The classically trained taste which he brought to bear on the Danish writers and on northern antiquities was not narrow and pedantic, and he succeeded in rousing among the Danes an interest in their own literature, and in beginning what was later in Germany to form part of the revolt against classicism.

The national element in the works of such later Danish writers as Sneedorff, Tyge Rothe and Ewald may be partly traceable to the "national" idea of Schlegel. Schlegel thus continues the movement which had been begun by Gram, Langebek and Holberg, that of popularizing knowledge among the lower and middle classes; as he so often points out, one should teach, not like a pedant, but as a man of taste, without giving the appearance of teaching. This surprisingly democratic *savant* declares that anyone may be a judge of literature if he has sufficient delicacy of feeling and is free from prejudice. Learning is not necessary. In this assertion of the rights of ordinary men to be interested in literature and art, matters which, up to then, had been considered the preserve of a few scholars, Schlegel plays a very considerable part in Danish intellectual development.[2]

[1] *Ästhetische Schriften*, p. 161.

[2] Holberg had already expressed ideas as to the educative power of the theatre in the Preface to *Den danske Skueplads* (1723), but there is no evidence of Schlegel having borrowed from this work.

One quality marks all Schlegel's work, namely, courage; he had the courage indispensable to the true pioneer. He did not come to Denmark as the exponent of the pseudo-classical literature advocated by Gottsched. Schlegel knew that the ultimate path of development for a modern nation's literature could not lie there. It was rather as the champion of new ideas that he came; ideas which were later to have a profound influence on all literary Europe. That Denmark received its share of these ideas is in large part Schlegel's work.

CHAPTER TWO

KLOPSTOCK in DENMARK

It was in 1749 that Johann Elias Schlegel, the forerunner of the German circle in Copenhagen, died. In 1751, the year after Voltaire went to Sans Souci, Klopstock, who was to become the central figure of the circle, arrived in Denmark. Conditions in Germany at that time were not favourable to native writers. Had Frederick the Great so chosen, he might have been a Maecenas to his own country; he preferred instead to help and encourage French literature, for whose tradition, unity and prestige he had a great respect. Klopstock, by reason of his fervent patriotism, had seemed well fitted to become the singer of Frederick II's great deeds. In the ode, dedicated to Bernstorff and Moltke, a poem of no great literary value composed on the journey from Zürich to Copenhagen, Klopstock expresses his admiration for Frederick the Great, and the regret which he felt at leaving the Fatherland. He deplores the fact that the victorious king does not think of keeping within the German frontiers those poets who now seek, in countries other than their own, the opportunity of singing of the Christian faith. But let us turn, he says, from such sad thoughts, and sing instead of Frederick of Denmark, a glory to humanity. The patriotic and democratic author of the *Messias*, however, soon finds in Frederick the Great's contempt for German literature, in his thraldom to the French,[1] in his absolutism and free-thinking, sufficient reasons for changing his attitude to one of active and fearless hostility to the Prussian king: an attitude made more intense by Voltaire's mockery of, and Frederick the Great's indifference to, his *Messias*.[2] In his praises of Frederick V of

[1] D. A. Schmidt, "Klopstock der Vater unserer Vaterlandsdichtung" in *Preuszische Jahrbücher*, XCVII (1899), p. 474.

[2] O. Tschirsch, "Ein Angriff auf Friedrich den Groszen in Klopstocks Gelehrtenrepublik" in *Forschungen zur brandenburgischen und preuszischen Geschichte*, 1891, IV, pp. 586–91.

Denmark Klopstock usually throws a condemnatory glance at the Prussian king. He warns Gleim against writing patriotic poems for Frederick.[1] In *Kaiser Heinrich*[2] Klopstock gives a picture of Frederick the Great sleeping forgotten and unsung in his marble coffin. In the poet's dedication of his *Hermannsschlacht* to Joseph II there is a vigorous attack on Frederick the Great, which, however, was not published.[3] Also the *Gelehrtenrepublik* was intended as a protest against Frederick's foreign tendencies, and it was so regarded by Klopstock's contemporaries.[4] With advancing years the bitterness of Klopstock against the Prussian king increased.

In Copenhagen, for nineteen years, Klopstock spent a pleasant and sheltered existence. During these years, the most fruitful of his literary life, Klopstock stood at the summit of his reputation. Before he left, German literature had developed beyond him.

The circumstances, which led to Klopstock's coming to Copenhagen, are interesting enough to be recapitulated briefly here.[5] In 1750, when Count Bernstorff[6] was on the point of leaving France, where for the preceding six years he had acted as diplomatic representative for Denmark, his legation minister, Schreiber, gave him the first portions of Klopstock's *Messias*.[7] After reading Klopstock's work, Bernstorff, full of a spontaneous admiration, resolved to help the author, and wrote to his friend in Copenhagen, the Danish minister Schulin, asking him to use his influence to get an annual pension for Klopstock. Before Bernstorff left Paris, however, he received

[1] *An Gleim*, *Werke*, I, pp. 109–11.

[2] *Ibid.*, p. 173.

[3] F. Muncker, *F. G. Klopstock, Geschichte seines Lebens und seiner Schriften*, Berlin, 1900, pp. 417 ff.

[4] J. C. C. Rüdiger, *Neuer Zuwachs der Sprachkunde*, 1782, I, p. 16.

[5] See Aage Friis, *Bernstorfferne og Danmark*, 2 vols., Copenhagen, 1913–19.

[6] Born in Hanover 1712; goes to Danish Court 1732; Danish legate in Dresden, Regensburg and Paris 1732–50; Minister of State in Denmark 1751–70; dismissed 1770; retired to Hamburg where he died in 1772.

[7] Aage Friis, *op. cit.*, I, p. 239. Muncker declares that it was the German preacher in Paris, Klüpfel, who had first made Bernstorff acquainted with Klopstock's writings, but Friis' account is probably the correct one.

the news that Schulin was dead and he himself was offered Schulin's post as Minister for Foreign Affairs. On his way to Copenhagen Bernstorff stayed with his brother, Andreas Gottlieb, at Gartow, where he met Klopstock's cousin, Leisching. From Leisching Bernstorff learnt of two invitations, which had been already extended to Klopstock, one from Abt Jerusalem in Braunschweig and one from Bodmer in Switzerland. In a letter to Ebert dated June 17, 1750,[1] at Quedlinburg, the author of the *Messias* indicated his own perplexity:

Aber was meinen Sie von Bodmer? Er hat mir dreihundert Thaler geschickt, und ich soll sie als ein Geschenk annehmen. Ich hatte ihm schon versprochen, zu ihm zu kommen, eh mir der Herr Abt die Stelle anbot. Was soll ich machen?

A letter[2] of the same date from A. G. Bernstorff to Bernstorff, enclosing a letter from Klopstock, gives us some further details:

Bref, je vous l'envoie telle qu'elle est, et j'ajoute pour éclaircissement que ce Botmer allégué lui a offert non seulement table et logis franc, mais même trois cents écus de pension, uniquement pour l'avoir auprès de soi et lui laisser le loisir nécessaire de finir son poème: mais il l'a refusé puisque ce savant généreux passe en même tems d'être d'un humeur bizarre, sombre et intraitable, also dasz dessen tägl. Umbgang und Dependenz von ihm das Vergnügen der Ruhe wieder würden gestöhret haben.

Bernstorff wishes Leisching to tell Klopstock not to pledge himself to either, since there were possibilities in Copenhagen of a pension, and perhaps after the completion of his *Messias*, of a post as court preacher or as professor.[3] In the letter of June 17 to Ebert,[4] Klopstock had spoken of the Copenhagen proposal:

Der Herr von Bernstorff hat sich von selbst erboten, mir eine Pension bei seinem Könige auszuwirken. Wo ich hinginge, sollte ich mich nicht auf lange Zeit engagiren. Meine Gegenwart würde bald in Koppenhagen nöthig sein. Eine Pension und volle Musze.

[1] J. M. Lappenberg, *Briefe von und an Klopstock*, Braunschweig, 1867, p. 38.

[2] *Bernstorffske Papirer*, ed. Aage Friis, 3 vols., Copenhagen, 1904–13, I, p. 33.

[3] Klopstock, *Sämtliche Werke*, herausg. von H. Schmidlin, Leipzig, 1839, I, Nr. 14.

[4] J. M. Lappenberg, *op. cit.* p. 38.

And on August 1, 1750, Bernstorff writes[1] to his friend von Larrey, the Dutch ambassador in Paris, that Klopstock has been called to Copenhagen:

> Le roi a apellé dans le royaume l'autheur du Messias et lui a accordé une pension de quatre cents écus sans autre obligation que celle d'achever son poème. Voilà, vous en conviendrés, un trait dans le goût de Louis XIV.

In a letter from Zürich, dated September 10, 1750, to Marie Sophie Schmidt,[2] Klopstock announces his acceptance of the Danish pension:

> Ich habe bisher zween Freunde gefunden, den König von Dänemark, und einen hiesigen jungen Kaufmann, den ich über den König setze. Der König giebt mir ein jährliches Gehalt von vier hundert Thaler, den Messias zu vollenden. Es ist dies durch die Vermittlung zweener Minister geschehen, die mehr als nur Minister sind, den Baron von Bernstorf, und den Grafen von Moltke. Ich habe Wahrscheinlichkeiten, diesz Gehalt zu vermehren, und mich nur selten in Coppenhagen aufzuhalten.[3]

He then proceeds to speak of the young merchant, a certain Herr Rahn, who has invented a process of printing on white silk. Rahn wishes Klopstock to join him in commercializing the process. Klopstock was to share the profits but was to contribute to the venture merely his good taste.[4] Klopstock seems to be more interested in this commercial venture than in the Danish offer. He declares his intention of remaining the winter in Zürich and of not going to Copenhagen until the following spring. It is not a very grateful letter. Evidently Klopstock is averse to leaving his many friends, and, in spite of the fact that his Danish pension began on July 1, 1750,[5] he spent the winter in Zürich and during that time composed the fourth and

[1] *Bernstorffske Papirer*, ed. Aage Friis, II, p. 320; cp. Magon, *op. cit.* p. 63.

[2] The "Fanny" of Klopstock's Odes.

[3] J. M. Lappenberg, *op. cit.* pp. 51 f.

[4] This Hartmann Rahn, through Klopstock's influence, obtained in 1751 permission to start a silk factory at Lyngby, near Copenhagen. It was to receive a state subsidy. It was not a success, and although Rahn married Klopstock's sister in 1754, the warm friendship between the two men eventually cooled off.

[5] *Reventlowske Papirer*, ed. Louis Bobé, Copenhagen, 1895 ff., IV, p. 319.

fifth cantos of the *Messias*.[1] Near the end of 1750 he writes the dedication ode to Frederick V, which was to stand before the new edition of the work.[2] In February, 1751, Klopstock forsook Zürich for Copenhagen. During the journey between Schaffhausen and the Suabian frontier he composed the second ode to Frederick V,[3] and dedicated it to his two benefactors, Bernstorff and Moltke. He praises the Danish king, the noble Protector of German letters, and compares him to Frederick of Prussia, who would seem to deny the language of his fathers and shows no favour save to French men of letters.[4] Klopstock travelled by way of Gartow, where he met Bernstorff's brother, Andreas Gottlieb Bernstorff, on whom he makes a very favourable impression.[5] It was about the middle of April, 1751, when he finally reached Copenhagen.

The strong pietistic movement, one of Germany's gifts to her northern neighbour, had brought in its train a very large number of Germans across the border. The writers whom Klopstock was able to attract to the land of plenty were but a few drops in the great German stream flowing toward Denmark.[6] The German language was much used in private and in official life.

> Naar man ved dette tidspunkt søger at danne sig et billede af Københavns aandelige fysiognomi, faar man et underligt og ikke ganske glædeligt resultat. Hvor man vender sig hen i Danmarks hovedstad, vrimler det af fremmede ansigter og navne. Man finder dem i haandværkerstanden, blandt fabrikanterne, som skønaander i selskabslivet, i hærens uniformer, paa universitetets katedre og paa ministertaburetterne. Og næsten alle disse fremmede ansigter frembyder en bestemt type og taler et bestemt sprog: det tyske.[7]

[1] "Ich habe den fünften Gesang, dessen Inhalt viel Schwierigkeiten, besonders in Betrachtung der Religion, hatte, nunmehr ganz vollendet. Und der vierte, welcher der längste des Gedichts seyn wird, ist nun auch bald zu Ende" (J. M. Lappenberg, *op. cit.* pp. 57–8. Letter to Fanny, Zürich, November 20, 1750).

[2] F. Muncker, p. 243.

[3] *Ibid.* p. 245.

[4] Klopstock, *Werke*. Leipzig, 1844, IV, p. 66.

[5] "Klopstock a été ici, et il est reparti hier, il a trouvé de l'approbation, et il vous plaira, Dixi" (*Bernstorffske Papirer*, I, p. 36).

[6] *Ibid.*

[7] F. Rønning, *op. cit.* I, pp. 144–5.

Count Bernstorff, for twenty years (1750–70) at the helm of the Danish state, always, as we have seen, spoke and wrote in either German or French, never in Danish. The poverty of literary production among the Danes themselves, the favourable impression with regard to German men of letters, created by J. E. Schlegel and his periodical *Der Fremde*, the strong pietistic element in the Denmark of that time and the wide-spread knowledge of German among the upper and middle classes, particularly among the clergy, helped to create for Klopstock, immediately on his arrival, a prestige, which his attractive personality and poetic powers soon augmented, except among the most irreconcilable of Danish patriots and the most reactionary of his scoffing literary adversaries.

It was as the author of the *Messias*, as a religious poet, that Klopstock was called to Denmark. For the first time in the eighteenth century a German poet was recognized and honoured as such.[1] Before Klopstock's time the position of a poet in society was not a very high one. In Denmark Holberg himself had had to apologize for his comedies on the ground of their tendency to improve morality and manners.[2] Klopstock did not in any way underestimate the importance of his calling or the high destiny to which he was summoned. Always he felt that he was the appointed singer of Things Divine; on him the poetic mantle had fallen, and from all he expected, and usually obtained, due respect. This was rather a new conception for eighteenth-century Denmark. Pioneer as Klopstock was in this respect, his pretensions seemed at times almost comic to his contemporaries. But such amusement, had he known of it, would in no way have disturbed his grave dignity. During his stay in Copenhagen, where he was in close and constant contact with court circles, and during the whole of his long life, his attitude towards his superiors in worldly rank was one of conscious strength and proud reserve. He feared the cold condescension

[1] A. Köster, *Die deutsche Literatur der Aufklärungszeit*, Heidelberg, 1925, p. 116.

[2] L. Magon, *op. cit.* I, p. 83.

of the great, and if any of them wished to woo his favour, they had always to come more than half way to meet him.[1]

It was not long after his arrival that Klopstock realized that the country to which, after much hesitation and doubting, he had come, was no arid polar region. Copenhagen, at that time a town of 70,000 inhabitants, was conspicuous among the capitals of Europe, as it still is, for the beauty of its surroundings. Less than a month after his arrival, Klopstock, in a letter to Fanny, headed "Friedensburg, vier Meilen von Koppenhagen, den 11. Mai, 1751", says:

> Ihre kleine anakreontische Taube kam mir gestern, an einem Frühlingsabend, den der volle Mond noch schöner machte, und in einer Gegend zugeflogen, die so reizend, als irgend eine in Sachsen, ist. Die Nachtigallen singen hier so schön, als bey Ihnen,[2]

and in the succeeding letters he gives a splendid description of northern nature. It was on the invitation of the king that Klopstock spent his first summer in Fredensborg, in the king's own summer residence. There he led a quiet and busy life, occupied with the *Messias*. He loved to saunter through the solitary glades of the park, where he found a peaceful place for meditation on his high subject.[3] Before Klopstock came to Copenhagen he had hoped that an occasional short stay in Denmark would be all that was necessary to qualify for his pension. The kindness of Frederick V and of Bernstorff, the beauty and the peace of Fredensborg and Lyngby, soon changed his ideas and desires.

Klopstock's high conception of the dignity of his calling and of the consideration due to a poet might have led to difficulties in his new environment, had it not been for the appreciation of his *Messias* in a pietistically minded community and the personal kindliness of the democratic Frederick. Klopstock was no court poet. Such poems as he did write for the court, the ode *Friedensburg* (1751), the ode on the death of the young Queen Louise (1752), and his *Elegie bei der Erinnrung Friedrichs des Fünften* (1766), were prompted by his real affection for the

[1] H. P. Sturz in *Deutsches Museum*, November 1777, pp. 459 ff.
[2] J. M. Lappenberg, *op. cit.* pp. 89 ff. [3] *Ibid.*

king, whose kindness and consideration never failed him.[1] Between Goethe's position at Weimar and that of Klopstock at the court of Frederick V there was little similarity.[2] Goethe was a minister, and yet was not entirely free from obligations as a poet. The sole obligation which rested on Klopstock was that of completing the *Messias*.[3] In a letter to Giseke, dated May 4, 1751,[4] Klopstock gives us an interesting account of his first interview with the king. Frederick, charming as he invariably was, quite won the poet's heart. The king expressed his great admiration for the *Messias* and referred to Klopstock's ode to himself, which he thought to be too flattering. He spoke with regret of Johann Elias Schlegel's early death, and said that one should prize men of learning higher than gold. He asked whether it were true that the best German style was to be found in Saxony, which enquiry gave Klopstock an opportunity to speak of the little encouragement given to literature there. In concluding his account of the interview, Klopstock says: "So viel ist gewisz, dasz der König Einer der liebenswürdigsten Männer ist, die jemals verdient haben, nicht in den Hübnern, sondern in der Geschichte wählender Geschichtschreiber vorzukommen." The youthful spirit, the charm of manner, the enthusiasm of Frederick V, found a ready echo in Klopstock's heart; and the changes which had come to Denmark with Frederick's accession, the re-opening of the theatres, the discouragement of all narrow bigotry, the encouragement of the arts and sciences, the more humane attitude reflected in law and politics, were all calculated to rouse the sympathies of the generous-minded Klopstock. Before he had ever met the king, Klopstock had addressed him in one of his odes as "an honour

[1] Frederick V granted Klopstock an annual pension of 400 daler from July 1, 1750 and in 1754 an extra amount of 200 daler a year. Klopstock seems at first to have expected somewhat more generous treatment than he received. Andreas Gottlieb Bernstorff writes to his brother, J. H. E. Bernstorff, Klopstock's patron, in a letter dated May 8, 1751: "Si Klopstock n'était pas content, ce serait uniquement sa faute, et il a bien dû l'être" (*Bernstorffske Papirer*, I, p. 36).

[2] L. Magon, *op. cit.* p. 86.

[3] J. M. Lappenberg, *op. cit.* pp. 87 ff.

[4] *Ibid.* p. 90.

to mankind", a "reflection of the Deity": in his letters to Fanny, after having met him, he calls him the best and most humane man in Denmark.[1] There is no doubt that Klopstock's feelings for the Danish king were deep and sincere.

The relations between Frederick V and the poet were not confined to formal occasions. In pleasant Fredensborg Frederick had many long conversations with Klopstock. It was on the latter's advice that many appointments in church, state and school were made, generally of German candidates. Klopstock's influence with the king becoming known, many Danes of position at court tried to induce Klopstock to intercede for them with Frederick.[2] In practical matters, on which, too, Frederick consulted Klopstock, the poet, unpractical as he was, could hardly have been of very much assistance. The Lyngby silk factory, established through the kindness of Bernstorff, under the direction of Klopstock's friend, Hartmann Rahn, and aided by a state subsidy, was a failure. A project, discussed frequently by the king and Klopstock and later taken up by the "Selskab til de skjønne og nyttige Videnskabers Forfremmelse", that of establishing a printing-press, where the best authors could get their works printed free, was not carried into effect.

The sometimes extravagant praise of his royal patron would seem to lend some colour to the reproach, levelled at Klopstock, that he was a flatterer and not free from the fault of servility.[3] Why, it was asked, does Klopstock represent Frederick as a model of all the virtues, his court as an abode of peace and purity, while the real facts were so very different? The excesses at the Danish court at that time, it was said, were sufficient to merit as ruthless and bitter an attack on court life as was made by Lessing in his *Emilia Galotti*. But Klopstock was no Lessing

[1] J. M. Lappenberg, *op. cit.* p. 90.

[2] *Germanisch-Romanische Monatsschrift*, XII (1924), p. 264.

[3] Klopstock's ode, *Für den König* (1753), was prompted by the irritation felt by Klopstock on hearing that his friends in Germany suspected him of flattering Frederick V. He replied to their suspicions by this ode of eighteen strophes. It is full of an extravagantly expressed gratitude. In the ode, *Fürstenlob* (1775), Klopstock turns this charge of flattery against the admirers of Frederick the Great.

and his "kampfloses Dasein" was very different from Lessing's courageous, battling existence. Perhaps it would have been better for Klopstock's development had he not remained so long in Copenhagen, but gone to London as he at one time intended.[1]

It was only after he left Denmark that his outlook widened. He was a young man of twenty-seven when he arrived in Copenhagen, and he spent nineteen happy years in an atmosphere of adulation and respect from the very highest in the land. He could not forget the warm welcome which Frederick V and Denmark had given him at a time when his own king and country offered him so little. The warm friendliness, the personal charm of the Danish king, made at the outset an impression on the poet, always susceptible to such qualities, an impression which no court gossip could efface; and Klopstock was by no means alone in this feeling of deep personal affection, which Frederick V was at all times able to inspire in those about him.

From the time that Klopstock made the acquaintance of the royal family he regarded it as his duty to become mentor to the young princes. He exhorts them to be kind, pious and just, generous and humane. In his hymn *Das neue Jahrhundert* he reminds these princes that the Revolution of 1660 had founded freedom on right; and he points out that the flame of patriotism can only burn in the air of liberty.[2] Klopstock contributed no doubt to nourish that generous spirit of humanity in Denmark, which later in the century resulted in the abolition of feudal service by the lords of the soil, the renunciation of their hereditary privileges, and in the perpetuation of the spirit of liberalism, traditional in the Danish royal family.

It was to Count Bernstorff that Klopstock owed his call to Denmark. The generous appreciation of Klopstock's works, expressed by Bernstorff before he had ever met the poet,

[1] *Preuszische Jahrbücher*, XCVII (1899), p. 474.

[2] The famous scene (Act iii, Sc. x) in Schiller's *Don Carlos* where the Marquis Posa describes the duties of a king to his people, shows a strong similarity to those expressed in the odes of Klopstock, celebrating the virtues of Frederick V; see E. Bailly, *Étude sur Klopstock*, Paris, 1888, p. 270.

was never lacking during their long and intimate association, and was, no doubt, to some extent inspired by the pietistic and religious nature of the Danish statesman. But Bernstorff soon learned to esteem and like Klopstock on more personal grounds,[1] and there was nothing that he liked better than to pass an evening with the poet and other members of the German circle in his own house. A man of unusual social gifts and wide reading, Bernstorff was always able to stimulate interesting conversation and to sustain in it a worthy part. Countess Bernstorff had as real an admiration and affection for Klopstock as had her husband, and in 1768, when Bernstorff was to accompany the young king, Christian VII, on his journey to foreign countries, the countess asked that Klopstock might stay to bear her company.[2] Only during the years of his marriage to Meta (1754–8) did Klopstock maintain his own town house. After her death he lived for the most part with Bernstorff,[3] although he had a small country house of his own at Lyngby, near Copenhagen. Many of his summers he passed on the count's estate, "Bernstorff", which lay a few miles from Copenhagen.[4] In Bernstorff's well-stocked library Klopstock spent much time. Here, as he tells us, he learned English by reading Young; here he studied Germany's ancient history and the northern mythology. Many long and interesting conversations Klopstock and Bernstorff held in the latter's ministerial room, adjoining the library[5]; and these conversations were not always confined to literature, but extended to more practical and actual things. Their talks on politics are reflected in Klopstock's contributions to *Der nordische Aufseher*.[6] Bernstorff's interest in

[1] In 1763 Bernstorff succeeded in getting for Klopstock a legation councillorship in the hope that the new dignity might soften the heart of the father of Sidonie Diedrich, for whose hand Klopstock was then suing; cp. *Bernstorffske Papirer*, II, p. 342.

[2] *Ibid.* II, p. 490.

[3] R. Kayser, "Deutsches Leben in Dänemark" in *Preuszische Jahrbücher*, CXXXII, pp. 230 ff.

[4] Aage Friis, *Bernstorfferne og Danmark*, I, pp. 301, 303, 310.

[5] F. Muncker, *op. cit.* p. 262.

[6] See for example *Nachricht von einem dänischen in dem Ackerbau sehr erfahrnen Landmanne*, where Klopstock declares political reforms necessary for Danish farmers and peasants; cp. *Der nordische Aufseher*, III.

German literature was stimulated by Klopstock, and in a letter to Giseke,[1] headed Copenhagen, and dated May 4, 1751, Klopstock says:

> Bernstorf...wird die Beyträge, von denen ihm nur der letzte Theil bekannt war, jetzt ausdrücklich lesen, und ich werde ihm die Namen der Verfasser über die vornehmsten Stücke setzen. Er ist recht im eigentlichen Verstande ein Kenner, sein Geschmack geht aber vorzüglich aufs Ernsthafte.

Many of Klopstock's works were read by Bernstorff in manuscript,[2] and Klopstock dedicated his first collection of *Odes* in 1771 to his patron. The intimate relationship with a man of such polish and distinction as Bernstorff gave to Klopstock a fineness of manner and a dignity, which increased as the years went by, so that Goethe, when he met Klopstock, saw in him a man with a bearing almost ministerial and diplomatic.[3]

The poet's relations with Count Moltke, the king's favourite minister, were not of the same intimate order as with Bernstorff. But Moltke had done much to secure Klopstock's appointment to Copenhagen, and he later showed Klopstock great kindness. Like Bernstorff, Moltke was of North German origin and, as Klopstock himself tells us, he evinced a real understanding of the *Messias*:

> Moltke habe ich neulich den ganzen fünften Gesang auf einmal vorgelesen. Ich habe es sehen können, dasz er ihn ganz verstand. Er unterbrach mich oft, und klagte dasz er mich unterbräche: aber er könnte sich nicht enthalten, mir zu sagen, wie sehr es ihm gefiele.[4]

In 1751, when Klopstock arrived in Denmark, he found but few German artists and writers there. Christian VI, who died in 1746, had been more concerned with introducing German theologians, who might more effectively expound the pietistic

[1] J. M. Lappenberg, *op. cit.* p. 87. Klopstock is referring here to the *Bremer Beiträge*.

[2] R. Kayser, *op. cit.* pp. 230 ff.

[3] P. Döring, *Der nordische Dichterkreis und die schleswiger Literaturbriefe*, Sonderburg, 1880.

[4] *Reventlowske Papirer*, ed. Louis Bobé, VIII, Anh., p. 31. Letter from Klopstock to Gleim dated May 24, 1751.

doctrines, which he so warmly espoused.[1] Through his influence with Bernstorff, who did not wish Klopstock to be deprived of the congenial society of his fellow-countrymen and literary confrères, Klopstock was enabled to bring to Denmark many friends and relations, though not always for the good of the state. In letters dated June 5 and June 11, 1751, and addressed to Giseke,[2] Klopstock asks the latter whether he would like to be appointed to the late Johann Elias Schlegel's chair in Sorø.[3] Klopstock had spoken both to Moltke and the king about Giseke and Frederick had said that Klopstock's recommendation would be quite sufficient to obtain the position for him. If Giseke prefers a living as a clergyman in Denmark, he is to write to Klopstock a letter, which the latter can show to Count Moltke. Giseke, however, did not come to Denmark. Meta Klopstock writes on January 2, 1754, that she wishes that the rest of their friends would follow them to the "Beyträgerinsel".[4] In 1757 Gellert refused the post of tutor to the son of Frederick V; Rabener, too, Ramler and Ebert all refused invitations, so that J. A. Cramer, who, through Klopstock, was appointed court preacher in Copenhagen in 1754, was the only one of the circle of the "Bremer Beiträger" and of the Leipzig friends, who followed Klopstock to Denmark. But the number of Germans brought in through Klopstock's influence was considerable enough without these. Mention has already been made of Hartmann Rahn, Klopstock's friend and later his brother-in-law, who by royal favour set up a silk factory in Lyngby. To its direction Klopstock's brother, August Philipp, succeeded in 1755, and later became the proprietor.[5] In 1753 Klopstock brought Basedow as professor to the Academy at Sorø. In 1767, through Klopstock's influence, F. G. Resewitz came as second preacher to the German Petrikirche. J. C. Leisching of Gartow, a cousin of Klopstock, and the intermediary between Klopstock

[1] L. Magon, *op. cit.* p. 205.

[2] J. M. Lappenberg, *op. cit.* pp. 93–4.

[3] Klopstock estimated the chair as worth 500 daler a year with house and some extras.

[4] *Blätter für litterarische Unterhaltung*, 1893, pp. 113 ff.

[5] *Reventlowske Papirer, ed. cit.* v, p. 280.

and the Bernstorffs in 1750, was appointed to the German chancellery in Copenhagen.[1] In 1765 Karl Christoph, brother of Klopstock, became Danish legation preacher in Madrid.[2]

In addition to the ministers, Bernstorff and Moltke, Klopstock was acquainted with Holstein and Berckentin. J. E. Schlegel's friend, Count von Spener, he knew too. He would occasionally visit the house of the young Count von Rosenberg, Imperial ambassador at Copenhagen, and that of Count Rantzau, a man of much wit and learning; a free-thinker, it is true, but a strong admirer of the English, and a devoted reader of Young.[3] Of von Berger, the king's physician, Klopstock becomes an intimate friend.[4] With H. P. Sturz, H. W. von Gerstenberg, J. A. Cramer, F. G. Resewitz, G. F. E. Schönborn, then private secretary in Bernstorff's house, and with the young Karl Friedrich Cramer, Klopstock's relations were of a cordially intimate character. These were all people of German origin, as were the Stolbergs, who came to Copenhagen in 1755. The intermarriage of the Stolbergs with the Bernstorffs brought Klopstock into close contact with the whole Stolberg family, and the two young Counts Stolberg were among the poet's most devoted friends and admirers. When the elder Count Stolberg died in 1765, he confided his sons' education to Klopstock, Cramer and Gerstenberg.[5]

Klopstock's happy nature, his gaiety and love of fun contributed much to the enjoyment of this circle of friends. From H. P. Sturz, who also was a member of the German circle in Copenhagen, we get an interesting account[6] of Klopstock during his Copenhagen period, more particularly as regards his personality and his place in the life of the circle. Sturz was by no means in agreement with Klopstock in all things. His admira-

[1] *Bernstorfferne og Danmark*, II, p. 305.
[2] *Reventlowske Papirer*, V, p. 204.
[3] E. Bailly, *op. cit.* p. 266; see also J. M. Lappenberg, *op. cit.* Klopstock's letters during the years 1751–2 tell us much of his social intercourse during these years.
[4] F. Muncker, *op. cit.* p. 271.
[5] C. F. Bricka, *Dansk biografisk Lexikon* (1895), IX.
[6] *Deutsches Museum*, November 1777, pp. 459 ff.

tion and affection for the poet cannot be explained on this ground. In his views on patriotism and freedom he differed materially from Klopstock, and his insistence on the need of criticism in literature was entirely opposed to Klopstock's views on the subject; but the time that he spent in Bernstorff's house in the company of Klopstock and of the rest of the German circle he regards as the happiest time of his life, "den heitren Morgen einer trüberen Zukunft"; and of this happy band of friends, Sturz always speaks of Klopstock as the central, most magnetic figure. According to Sturz, Klopstock had a genius for friendship: "Gegenwärtig, ferne von ihm, oder im täuschenden Schatten, er verkennet seine Freunde nie. Hat er einmal geprüft und geliebt, so währt es ewig, lass' auf sein Urtheil Wahrscheinlichkeiten und künstlich erlogene Tatsachen stürmen". In conversation Klopstock is genial and brilliant: "Klopstock ist heiter in jeder Gesellschaft, fließzet über von treffendem Scherz, bildet oft einen kleinen Gedanken mit allem Reichthum seiner Dichtergaben aus, spottet nie bitter, streitet bescheiden und verträgt auch Widerspruch gern". Of the musical evenings at Lyngby in Gerstenberg's house, where Klopstock was a frequent visitor, Sturz says: "Wir eilten zum einsamen Haus und verlieszen Paläste, wie man durch Le Nôtres Gärten nach dem kunstlosen Hain eilt". Nor were outdoor sports neglected. The advantages of the natural life so highly extolled later in the century, were practically realized by Klopstock. He revived the love for sport and nature. All his life Klopstock was an enthusiastic sportsman, and riding and skating were his favourite recreations: "In dem Eislauf", says Sturz, "entdeckte sein Scharfsinn alle Geheimnisse der Schönheit...Die Holländer schätzt er gleich nach den Deutschen, weil sie ihre Tyrannen verjagten und...die besten Eisläufer sind". Five of his odes Klopstock wrote on the subject of skating. In the environs of Copenhagen Klopstock found a splendid opportunity for the exercise of his favourite art.[1] With

[1] Klopstock marked on a map of the country round Copenhagen the sheets of water, which were usually the first to be frozen. He organized frequent

Klopstock as leader, whole families of members of the German circle and of their friends made merry excursions into the country. Children were not excluded, for Klopstock was very fond of children and of all young people, as one can see from his relations to the brothers Stolberg and to Karl Cramer. By all this circle Klopstock was held in the greatest respect and affection: "Klopstock ist wie sein Engel. Niemand kann eine Stunde mit ihm umgehn, ohne von ihm eingenommen zu seyn. ...Wer Klopstock nicht bewundert, der hat kein Genie; und wer ihn nicht kennt und nicht liebt, der hat kein Herz".[1] That Klopstock did not exercise this power of attraction merely over his fellow-countrymen is indicated by Jens Baggesen's account of his meeting with Klopstock near Altona, many years after Klopstock had left Copenhagen.[2]

The death in 1766 of Frederick V, who had called almost all the members of the German circle to Copenhagen, shook the circle to its foundations, and was the beginning of its approaching dissolution. In the letters of his last years in Copenhagen Klopstock never mentions the name of Struensee, who succeeded Bernstorff after the latter's fall. From such a free-thinker Klopstock could not expect any appreciation of his poetry.

Klopstock's coming to Copenhagen meant for Danish literature much more than even his most ardent contemporary Danish disciples suspected. It was the point from which Danish literature began to move forward to a new and fuller development.[3] It is true that Klopstock's literary productions did not meet in Denmark, any more than they did in Germany, with a reception always enthusiastically favourable. Klopstock, quite as much as any writer of the eighteenth century, had his irreconcilable

skating excursions from Copenhagen to Lyngby. On one occasion he was found poring over a map of Germany, and he explained to a friend, that he was thinking how splendid it would be if all the waterways of Germany were linked up, so that one could skate through the whole country.

[1] G. B. Funk, *Schriften*, Berlin, 1821, II, p. 312.

[2] "Saa kendelig den øverste Himmel er i hans Digte, saa ganske fremlyser det bedste af Jorden i hans Væsen....Hans Sjæl er opstanden, før hans Legeme døde" (J. Baggesen, *Labyrinthen*, ed. Louis Bobé, p. 55).

[3] K. L. Rahbek, "Über Klopstocks Verdienste um die dänische Litteratur", *Kieler Blätter*, 1819, II, p. 235.

opponents. But these, both in Germany and Denmark, were fighting a losing battle; it was to Klopstock and to his claims for the needs of the heart and the imagination, that the future belonged. Klopstock never sought to exercise any influence on Danish literature. It was by their mere existence, by their novelty, that his works exercised a challenging influence on the adherents of an older literary taste[1]; and it was from the controversy over Klopstock's works, and particularly over the *Messias*, that a more intelligent criticism was developed in Denmark. From the very opposition to Klopstock came a greater clearness in Danish literary ideas.

In 1751 there was but little life in Danish literature. The period 1746–51 was hopefully regarded as a spring after a long hard winter. But great as the promise was, there was but little fulfilment. It is a matter for surprise, in view of the widespread and very sincere feeling of grief, felt by the whole nation on the death of Queen Louise, that there was not one single Danish line of poetry on the subject, which could be regarded as even tolerable.[2] Holberg was no longer the living force which he had been among the people; with court circles he had never had much influence. Falster and Tullin, it is true, were producing their works; and on December 18, 1747, the Danish National Theatre had been opened, but it was a German, J. E. Schlegel, who had contributed most to its establishment, and it was with a prologue of this writer that it was opened. Literature in Denmark was, for the most part, sunk in a sleepy lethargy under the rule of pietism. The religious hymn, of which H. A. Brorson was the chief exponent, was the favourite mode of literary expression. Although Gottsched's ideas were known in Denmark and Norway, where the controversy between Zürich and Leipzig had been followed with interest, yet there was no united body of supporters of Gottsched's theories.

It has been pointed out by competent Danish critics[3] that had

[1] L. Magon, *op. cit.* p. 155.
[2] Rahbek and Nyerup, *op. cit.* pp. 232, 242–3.
[3] *Ibid.* p. 63.

Klopstock never come to Denmark, his works would have made just as deep an impression on Danish minds and would have contributed just as much to the refining and developing of literary taste in Denmark. One might criticize such a view, perhaps, on the grounds that, in that case, Ewald would probably never have met the author of the *Messias*, who gave him in the short period of their acquaintance help and encouragement, and at a time when he received little or none from his fellow-countrymen; Klopstock's influence was important not merely to Ewald himself, but through him to the course which Danish literature was later to take towards Romanticism.[1] The same critics go on to say: "Han levede og aandede her allene i sin tydske Hofkreds, og som han aldrig nedlod sig til at gjøre Bekjendtskab med dansk Sprog eller dansk Litteratur, kunde han heller ikke for vordende danske Digtere være det som en Carstens siden blev".[2] Worms tells of having asked Klopstock several times for information as to dates in his life for insertion in his *Lexikon*, but Klopstock never gave them to him.[3] With the Danish people, whose quiet, sober, moderate temperament he liked, Klopstock had the most superficial acquaintance. He moved chiefly in court circles, where his ignorance of the language presented no bar to easy intercourse. We have no record of any meeting between Holberg and Klopstock. The former, asked as to his opinion of the *Messias*, simply replied that he did not understand the poem; and Klopstock moved among people who regarded Holberg's plays as appealing only to the lower classes.[4] Baggesen, in describing his meeting

[1] "Men det var først ved Ewalds Fremtræden, at der mellem dansk og tysk Poesi sluttedes den Aandskjede, der blev ubrudt helt ned til Romantikkens sidste Tid" (Just Bing, "Klopstock og den klopstockske Kreds i Danmark" in *For Kirke og Kultur*, v, p. 606); and L. Magon, in an article entitled *Aus Klopstocks dänischer Zeit*, published in the *Germanisch-Romanische Monatsschrift*, XII (1924), p. 277, remarks that the Romantic movement, which began in Denmark in 1803, brought Klopstock's art to honour; it filled the shadowy figures of Germanic mythology with life; and it was through Ewald that the Romantic movement in Denmark found Klopstock.

[2] Rahbek and Nyerup, *op. cit.* p. 63.

[3] J. Worms, *Lexikon*, I, p. 531.

[4] F. Muncker, *op. cit.* p. 259.

with Klopstock in Hamburg towards the end of the century, comments on Klopstock's ignorance of the Danish language and literature, and says that since Ewald's time he had read no Danish poem, and that he knew nothing of Pram or Rahbek. Nowhere, says Baggesen, does one see in Klopstock's writings any enthusiasm for Denmark or things Danish.[1]

In his ignorance of Danish language and literature and in his lack of any desire to know the Danish people Klopstock affords a striking contrast to his young predecessor, Johann Elias Schlegel. But Klopstock came to Copenhagen at a more mature age than Schlegel, with a reputation already to some extent made. He was by nature ill-fitted to adapt himself to new modes of thought and life, and his attitude towards Denmark and the Danes was generally characterized by a benevolent condescension.[2] In justice to Klopstock it might be pointed out that he was first and foremost a poet and creator. He did not join, as did Elias Schlegel and Gerstenberg, in the critical examination of ideas which were then stirring in European literature. He was always the enthusiast rather than the critic. During his stay in Copenhagen only one Danish poet, comparable to himself in power of expression and imagination, declared himself, and to Ewald Klopstock did give encouragement and sympathy in very generous measure; while without the practical help and encouragement shown by Cramer and Klopstock to the new "Selskab til de skjønne og nyttige Videnskabers Forfremmelse", that society would hardly have had so great a measure of success.

That Klopstock's works did arouse in Denmark an interest in literature such as had not been evident in that country for many years, is indicated by the words of a contemporary writer:

[1] J. Baggesen, *op. cit.* p. 61. Such odes of Klopstock as *Unsre Sprache* and *Mein Vaterland* show clearly what country he regarded as his Fatherland, and the odes which are Danish in subject (e.g. *Friederich V*, *Königin Luise*, *Für den König*, *Rothschilds Gräber*) are so general that they might have been written for any other country or king. See N. M. Petersen, *op. cit.* V, I, p. 224.

[2] See Klopstock's answer to a letter in *Der nordische Aufseher* proposing the foundation of the Danish Society, *ibid.* II, Article 115.

Hvor man kommer i Byen, saa føres der straks paa Banen om den rimfrie Poet, hvilket hos mange gør lige saa stor Opsigt, som det var et usædvanligt Phænomen, der havde ladet sig til Syne. Hele København kan paa nærværende Tid inddeles i: Klopstock- og Anti-Klopstockianere, og saa vidt jeg formærker, er det sidste Slags den herskende Sekt.[1]

The controversy, waged in the Danish literary world around Klopstock and his works, has been so fully treated of by Danish historians, that it is unnecessary to discuss it at any great length here.[2] The older basis of Danish literature had been in the main that of the Gottschedian school, the expression of clear and reasonable ideas in correct rhyme and verse; but here was a poet, who dispensed with rhyme, and whose ideas were vague and confused, to be comprehended by no man of ordinary common sense. These innovations meant, so Klopstock's opponents thought and maintained, the breaking-down of the whole carefully built-up edifice of poetry. The fashion of unrhymed poetry, which developed quickly in Denmark and which did much to debase literary taste, exposed poetry to the intrusion of any untrained amateur and bungler; such people, it was said, could assume the outward dignity of a poet without being one in any measure.[3]

The feeling of opposition and criticism which Klopstock's works and his *Messias* in particular aroused among Danish writers, produced a literature which was, at any rate, concerned with the actual needs and aims of poetry. Gerhard Treschow, a clergyman, who had written hymns in the reign of Christian VI, attacks Klopstock on the occasion of the latter's ode to Frederick V in the introduction to the first volume of the *Messias* (1751). He reproaches Klopstock with his darkly vague, extravagant style, and for discarding rhyme:

[1] F. K. Schønau, *Lærde Fruentimre*, 1753, pp. 1227 ff.

[2] Rahbek and Nyerup in their *Dansk Digtekunst* (1819) give a full account of the controversy. See also F. Rønning, *op. cit.* I, pp. 186 ff.

[3] N. M. Petersen, *op. cit.* 1871, v, 2, p. 192. "Først gjorde man Nar ad dem, derpaa efterlignede man dem; og det blev ligesom Poesiens 'to be or not to be': Rim eller ikke Rim" (*ibid.* p. 186).

Nu skal det holdes for det høje og sublime
I Digtekonsten, at den er urimelig.
Nu maa de gjerne Folk med tomme Ord afspise
Og sige meget, naar kun Intet bliver sagt.[1]

Stenersen defended Klopstock's rhymeless verse,[2] and Nannestad, who had returned in 1750 from studying under Baumgarten in Halle, answered the charges of vagueness and extravagance.[3] In 1751 Nannestad attempted to show by a simple Danish paraphrase of Klopstock's *Ode an den König* how clear Klopstock's thoughts and expression were. It was not, however, a very successful defence. Nannestad pointed out that many passages in Horace, Virgil, Milton, Addison and Haller were not clear, but an anonymous antagonist[4] answered that, in the case of the classical writers, this was due to our ignorance of the language and of the life of the period. The discussion was continued through 1752. Klopstock's opponents, having got the worst of it in their criticism, began to use the weapon of parody, for the most part of the *Odes*. On the occasion of the death of Queen Louise Klopstock wrote his second *Ode an den König*. In this, while speaking of Queen Louise dying, hearing the sound of the wings of death, the poet calls on his song to keep forever immortal the memory of the queen's last smile. Treschow, with rather questionable taste, replied with his *Ode til Bispen*,[5] where he speaks of the bishop thus:

Hvor smiler Bispen nu!
Sig da, min Sang! at du i Dag har haft den Lykke, at Bispen haver smilt.

Klopstock's first ode to Frederick V (1751) Treschow also ridicules: and Michael Reineken's *Ode an den Menschen*[6] (1753) is a shameless parody of Klopstock's ode *An Gott*. Klopstock, in his *Drei Gebete eines Freygeistes, eines Christen und eines guten*

[1] Appeared in *Lærde Tidender*, 1751, No. 36, under the title *Afskeed med Parnasso*.

[2] *Ibid*. 1752, No. 9, under the title *Critiske Tanker over de rimfrie Vers*.

[3] *Ibid*. 1751, No. 50.

[4] *Ibid*. No. 51.

[5] "For at vise det latterlige i den Klopstockske rimfrie Poesie er der paa dansk udkommen adskillige Oder. Oden til Bispen er bedst gjort af dem alle, og i alle Maader klopstockiansk" (Schönau in *Lærde Fruentimre*, p. 1232).

[6] Gottsched's *Neuestes aus der anmuthigen Gelehrsamkeit*, 1753.

Königs, had warned the king against free-thinking at court, and it was not long before there appeared the parody, *Drey Gebete eines Antiklopstockianers, eines Klopstockianers und eines guten Kritikus*.[1] Every ode of Klopstock which treated of anything Danish was followed by hostile criticism or travesty.

The reception given to the *Messias* in Denmark does not seem to have been very different from that with which it met in Germany. There were many people in Germany whose literary taste was not sufficiently mature to appreciate it; this was also in even a greater degree the case in Denmark.[2] At home the *Messias* had a bewildering effect on people's minds; it was bitterly blamed or enthusiastically praised; it was parodied and imitated. So too in Denmark, where so little in the way of native literary productions could be opposed to Klopstock's work. The popularity of the works of Hagedorn and Gellert, the high reputation of Elias Schlegel in Denmark, would seem to have prepared the way for Klopstock. But Klopstock lacked the "common touch" of Gellert; his seraphic poetry made its appeal merely to a few chosen literary souls. Among the less educated classes he was regarded with a dazed and uncomprehending astonishment:

> Klopstock kom, og med ham en ny Poesie, en ny Smag, en ny Verden, en anden Himmel og Jord. I de højere Kredse vandt han Beundring, de lavere forundrede sig, Digtere og Kunstdommere studsede...men begribe ham kunde de færreste: Messias var for dem en Uting, de rimløse Oder en Ophævelse af Poesie.[3]

On one occasion when Klopstock was waiting upon Frederick V at Fredensborg, he met in the ante-chamber a courtier with whom he had some conversation. When the latter was told with whom he had been talking he exclaimed: "Hvad Djævelen! er De Klopstock! De taler jo ganske forstaaeligt; man havde sagt mig at man slet ikke kunde forstaa Dem".[4] Oehlenschläger says of his mother that she did not care for Klopstock. She found him

[1] A. F. Büsching, *Nachrichten*, II, p. 63.
[2] Rahbek and Nyerup, *op. cit.* pp. 236 f.
[3] N. M. Petersen, *op. cit.* V, 2, p. 182.
[4] K. F. Cramer, *Klopstock: in Briefen von Tellow an Elisa*, 1777, p. 122.

exaggerated in style. Gellert spoke more to her heart.[1] Johann Elias Schlegel had sought to show that literature and art were things that the man of ordinary good sense could understand. But from Klopstock's *Messias* the Danish people got the idea that poetry was something sublime, a kind of speech of the celestial court, far removed from ordinary things and people, a language that only the initiated could understand. Klopstock's Danish admirers had hoped that from the elevated style of the *Messias*, written as it was in a language closely related to the Danish, more polished and elegant elements might find a way into their own language. It was reserved for a later generation in Denmark to conceive the idea of improving and strengthening the language through borrowing from the older Danish vocabulary.[2] J. O. Thiesz, who denied to Klopstock any influence on Danish literature, pointed out that there was no Danish translation of the *Messias*.[3] This, however, was not true to the facts. Rahbek tells us that he himself had the manuscript of such a translation begun by Ewald[4]; and part of another translation by Hans Pontoppidan, probably not begun until the 'sixties,[5] and dedicated to the second wife of Frederick V, Princess Juliane Marie of Braunschweig-Lüneberg, was printed in a Copenhagen journal in 1787.[6]

It was Sneedorff's appearance at the end of the 'fifties and the beginning of the 'sixties, which marks the beginning of the Klopstock movement in Denmark.[7] The battle which Sneedorff waged on behalf of the "skjønne Videnskaber" contributed in no small measure to the strengthening of Klopstock's influence. Most of the Danish authors, who imitated Klopstock, reproduced merely his affectation and vagueness and his high-

[1] Oehlenschläger, *Erindringer*, I, p. 2.

[2] See *Germanisch-Romanische Monatsschrift*, XII (1924), p. 273.

[3] J. O. Thiesz, *F. G. Klopstock*, Altona, 1805, p. 61.

[4] K. L. Rahbek, *Kieler Blätter*, II, p. 240.

[5] The manuscript of this translation is in the Royal Library at Copenhagen. See Appendix. Goedeke gives the date of this translation as 1766. See *Grundrisz*, 3. Auflage, IV, I, p. 166.

[6] *Minerva*, November, 1787. The part published was taken from the fifth canto.

[7] L. Magon, *op. cit.* p. 232.

sounding phrases. It was reserved for Ewald during the 'sixties and 'seventies to show that Klopstock's poetry had appealed to at least one Danish poet, who had real poetic power, the imagination to comprehend Klopstock's full range, and the ambition to do for Danish literature what Klopstock was trying to do for German literature by his revival of an interest in northern mythology. Klopstock's influence on Ewald was undoubtedly strong, but it is not easy to estimate it. Ewald, like Klopstock, had a genuinely poetic nature, and was no mere imitator; he is rather an independent apprentice and spiritual kinsman of Klopstock. Their personalities and ideas are very different. There is in Ewald a sense of clearness and proportion, which is not at all times characteristic of the more visionary Klopstock. Ewald prefers rhymed alexandrines to unrhymed hexameters, and the dramatic form to the epic, since in the former the characters are clearer and the action more plainly defined.[1] With Klopstock's ideas of the dignity of a poet's calling Ewald was in entire accord, and he was one of the very first in Denmark to proclaim himself a poet and nothing more.[2] Between the two men there existed a real affection and regard, tempered on Ewald's side by an admiration and respect for the older and more famous poet. Many years after Klopstock had left Denmark he still spoke of Ewald with respect and affection.[3] The interest taken by Klopstock in Ewald may be inferred from the plan concerted by Bernstorff and himself to send the Danish poet, accompanied by a composer, to Scotland, the Orkney Islands and Iceland, in order to collect the old songs, which they might hear sung by the inhabitants. Klopstock indeed did procure for Ewald the loan of two books from Langebek's library, the first volume of an *Archaeologia Britannica* and a Celtic dictionary.[4] Owing to Ewald's ill-health, however, the plan was not carried out.

[1] A. D. Jørgensen, *Johannes Ewald*, Copenhagen, 1888, p. 192.

[2] "Wenn Ewald als erster Däne es wagte, ganz und ausschlieszlich nur Dichter zu sein, so hat ihm das Beispiel Klopstocks dazu Mut gemacht" (*Germanisch-Romanische Monatsschrift*, XII, 1924, p. 275).

[3] J. Baggesen, *op. cit.* I, p. 146.

[4] J. Ewald, *Samlede Skrifter*, Copenhagen, 1814–24, I–VI, pp. 375 f.

Ewald was as strong and as true a patriot for his own country as was Klopstock for his. In the list of Danish poets who have contributed to the expression of the national spirit and to the strengthening of this spirit among the people, Ewald can claim a place. He is Holberg's successor in the line of national writers. Holberg had castigated the weaknesses and vices of his fellow-countrymen. Ewald holds up before them the example of a glorious past. The method is different, but the aim in both cases is the same. Holberg was the Moses and he brought deliverance, but Ewald was the Joshua, who led his people over the Jordan into the Land of Promise.[1] And the Land of Promise, where the Danish people gained strength and pride of nationality, was the land of northern antiquity. Here Ewald cleared the way for Oehlenschläger's great work, and started the movement which eventually made the old heroic sagas a living reality for the Scandinavian peoples.

H. W. von Gerstenberg, another member of the German circle in Copenhagen, was the first to see the potentialities of this new source of inspiration. It was from Gerstenberg, as Klopstock states, that he received the impulse which gave him a real interest in Scandinavian mythology: "Einige von unsern Kopenhagener Freunden, oder vielmehr alle, die sich darum hatten bekümmern wollen, wuszten, dasz ich die Mythologie unserer Vorfahren erst angenommen hatte, seitdem Sie es im Skalden gethan hatten".[2] To the movement Klopstock contributed chiefly his name and prestige. Gerstenberg's *Gedicht eines Skalden* (1766) first showed the author of the *Messias* that the northern mythology might furnish inspiration and material for a national literature, and Klopstock hoped to find there a background for German literature, similar to that which Greek literature possessed. No doubt, as with Gerstenberg, Klopstock's environment in Denmark had the effect of heightening his interest in Scandinavian mythology, and in such bardic odes as

[1] A. D. Jørgensen, *Johannes Ewald*, Copenhagen, 1888, p. 226.

[2] Letter from Klopstock to Gerstenberg; first published by F. Muncker in *Lessings persönliches und litterarisches Verhältnis zu Klopstock*, 1880, Anhang III, p. 224. See also R. Batka in *Euphorion*, VI, pp. 72 ff.

Der Eislauf (1764), *Braga* (1766) and *Die Kunst Tialfs* (1767) Klopstock introduces scenes characteristically northern. But Klopstock's attitude towards this new source of literature was a narrowly German one. With little or no justification he assumes Ossian to be of Germanic extraction and the whole Scandinavian mythology he attempts to transplant to German soil, in which it could not have any natural growth. That he did not seek his inspiration in the living present, in the great deeds of Frederick the Great, but in the past, is partly due to the attitude of Frederick the Great towards German literature. Except for reproaches which he levels at Gleim[1] for continuing to use Greek gods in his poems, Klopstock writes nothing theoretical to support the influence of this new mythology. In later years he lost all interest in bardic poetry, and from 1771 to 1796 only a few of his odes show traces of Scandinavian mythology. Although this new inspiration in Danish literature (an inspiration which later was to strengthen the patriotic movement in Denmark against the German influence in the country) did not really come from Klopstock, but from Gerstenberg, yet Ewald never mentions the latter's name, although he speaks gratefully of Klopstock's influence.[2]

Ewald's first work of any importance, *Adam og Eva* (1769), shows unmistakably the influence of Klopstock's religious poetry.[3] It roused much attention at the time of its publication.[4] It was the first serious attempt in Danish literature to treat of a great poetic subject in the grand style. Before writing it Ewald had read the *Messias* through three or four times,[5] and this imitation of Klopstock by Ewald was the first real fruit of Klopstock's eighteen years in Denmark.

[1] In a letter to Gleim, spring, 1771.

[2] J. E. Ewald, *Samlede Skrifter*, Copenhagen, 1914–24, III, p. 243, in the preface (1772) to the German translation of *Rolf Krage*.

[3] Ewald himself, speaking of *Adam og Eva*, says: "...og enhver, tænker jeg, vil finde, at jeg i dette Stykke i det mindste har viist Lyst nok at danne mig efter den store Klopstock, om jeg og ei har havt Evne dertil" (Ewald, *Samlede Skrifter*, *ed. cit.* III, p. 247, Introduction (written 1780).

[4] It was read to a select audience by J. A. Cramer in the house of Etatsraad Professor J. K. Kall; cp. C. Molbech, *Ewalds Levnet*, Copenhagen, 1831, p. 88.

[5] *Ibid.* p. 93.

It was after writing *Adam og Eva* that Ewald met the author of the *Messias*, probably through Gerstenberg.[1] Klopstock, in numerous conversations with Ewald, suggested that the latter should turn for his next subject to Danish legendary history. Hence arose *Rolf Krage* (1770), the first attempt in Danish literature to treat Danish antiquity in a serious drama, and a work which gave the first impulse toward the national movement in the literature of Denmark. The subject is taken from Saxo. In the preface to one of the German translations of *Rolf Krage*, after alluding to Shakespeare and Ossian as the two great new influences in his life, influences which Gerstenberg was at the time introducing into Danish and German literatures, Ewald pays a generous tribute to Klopstock: he says that his greatest desire is to be recognized as a follower of the inimitable Klopstock, who had seen *Rolf Krage* before it was printed and had approved of it.[2] He goes on to say:

> Jeg havde samme Tid den Lykke at blive kjendt, og taalt, og yndet af den store Klopstock, og man kan ikke tvivle paa, at jo denne Mands Omgang var mig en ny Kilde....Det første Stykke af Betydenhed, som jeg skrev efter denne Tid, var Rolf Krage. Enhver opmerksom Læser vil finde min forandrede Smag heri.

Ewald had determined to discard the French verse-form, and *Rolf Krage* is in prose. In spite of Klopstock's praise of the work, he did not hesitate to say that the action loses a good deal of its fire in the two last acts, a criticism which Ewald himself mentions[3]. No doubt it was flattering to Klopstock to think that, while he himself was helping by his *Hermannsschlacht* (1769) to create a new interest in the German past, a young Dane, his protégé and pupil, was attempting to do the same for the Danish past. It was Klopstock who sent *Rolf Krage* to the "Selskab til de skjønne og nyttige Videnskabers Forfremmelse" with a strong recommendation. It was submitted to them at a meeting on February 8, 1770. J. A. Cramer warmly

[1] Jørgensen mentions J. A. Cramer as the intermediary. See A. D. Jørgensen, *op. cit.* p. 78.

[2] Ewald, *Samlede Skrifter*, III, p. 248.

[3] *Ibid.*

supported its claims; but the judges, among whom were Luxdorph, Carstens, J. H. Schlegel and Justitsraad Nielsen, voted against its publication. Urged, however, by Cramer, they consented to award a special prize of fifty daler to encourage the author, a figure which was later increased to sixty daler, since both Klopstock and Cramer had raised Ewald's hopes of receiving at least this sum.[1] It was the German members of the society who were Ewald's supporters; indeed most of the early encouragement given to Ewald had come from members of the German circle in Copenhagen. The society's decision has been regarded as a blot on its record. It may, possibly, have been influenced by the fact that the Klopstockian elements in Ewald's poetry roused a certain measure of opposition among patriotic Danes; the anti-German party was beginning to gain power at that time.[2] The majority were unable to see through the superficial faults of Ewald's piece, such as his neglect of recognized poetic rules, to its real strength and power. A society which could afford to publish the empty comedies of Charlotte Biehl, comedies of which Luxdorph speaks in rapturous admiration, might well have published Ewald's *Rolf Krage.*

Balders Død (1773), though retaining some traces of Klopstock's influence, breaks away to a large extent from that influence. With some justification Klopstock could say that he had "lured" *Rolf Krage* from Ewald[3]; but he could not say the same of *Balders Død.* Ewald's feet are now set securely and strongly on the new road and he is travelling along it alone. The subject of *Balders Død,* like that of *Rolf Krage,* is taken from Saxo, but *Rolf Krage,* in spite of its antique subject, shows a contemporary spirit and tone, a reproach which could not be levelled against the deeper and more genuine *Balders Død.*

In the second volume of *Der nordische Aufseher*[4] there is

[1] A. D. Jørgensen, *op. cit.* p. 83.

[2] P. Hansen, *Illustreret dansk Litteratur Historie,* 2nd ed., Copenhagen, 1902, II, pp. 225 ff.

[3] "aflokket": see J. Baggesen, *op. cit.* I, p. 146.

[4] Article 115.

quoted a letter from one or more Danish writers,[1] proposing the formation of a Danish Society for encouraging the production of works of genius by offering prizes, two every year, fifty daler for a poem and forty daler for a sermon or other prose piece. The recent interest roused by a poem[2] of Tullin encouraged the proposers to suggest the formation of such a society, which would give young Danish authors a chance of obtaining a judgment on their literary attempts from some other tribunal than public opinion. The periodical of the proposed society is to contain a certain number of translations of foreign masterpieces; one volume of publications is to be issued every year. The letter concludes: "Wir verbitten aber alle Gelegenheitsgedichte (sie müszten denn der Ode an Bräutigam und Braut gleichen), wie auch alle niedrigen Satiren und Scherze über Wein und Liebe".[3] In declaring the objects of the society, Tyge Rothe writes somewhat naïvely: "Stolte er vi af en Tyge Brahe, en Rømer, af Wormer, og Bartholiner; men vi ville kunne nævne danske Sophocler, Virgiler og Horatser. Hvorfor skulle vi ikke og faae dem?"[4] Klopstock, who replies to the proposal, does so in a favourable, but somewhat condescending manner. He points out that the supporters of the proposal should be content to discover *one* work of genius. The society must not be too lenient in its judgments. The masterpieces, which are to be translated, should be proved ones, might include works of a religious tendency,[5] and should be carefully translated. It is probable that Tyge Rothe and Sneedorff, seeing that they might not be able to realize the scheme without the help of people more influential at court than themselves, applied in this way to Klopstock and Cramer.[6] Cramer probably obtained Count Moltke's support

[1] There are the same number of asterisks in the signature as in Sneedorff's name. Tyge Rothe and Sneedorff are commonly regarded as the sponsors of the scheme.

[2] *Maidagen.*

[3] *Der nordische Aufseher*, II, Article 115, p. 475.

[4] K. L. Rahbek, "Om Selskabet til de skjønne og nyttige Videnskabers Fremme dets Stiftelse og Stiftere" (*Dansk Minerva*, III (1816), p. 240).

[5] Klopstock seems here to be thinking of his own *Messias.*

[6] N. M. Petersen, *op. cit.* V, 2, p. 184.

and Klopstock the king's. Frederick V promised to help to defray the expenses of the society,[1] but did not fix the amount of his gift. Pleased at the kindly reception given to their idea in *Der nordische Aufseher*, Sneedorff and Tyge Rothe, having already in their manifesto expressed a desire to have in the new society men of letters who, although not able to judge of the beauties of Danish works of literature, could yet appreciate the qualities of such works in other languages, asked both Klopstock and Cramer to be members, an invitation which was accepted.

Up to the time of their departure from Copenhagen both Klopstock and Cramer took an active part in the proceedings of the society.[2] It received the name of "Selskabet til de skjønne og nyttige Videnskabers Forfremmelse"[3] and was formed on the model of the "Bremer Beiträger" in Leipzig, of which both Klopstock and Cramer had been members, and to which German literature owed the stimulus to a new development. Whether Klopstock was formally recognized as one of the founders of the society or not, is not of great importance, in view of the material help which he gave towards its foundation and the active interest which he subsequently took in its proceedings. Sneedorff, Tyge Rothe, Cramer, Carstens and Luxdorph were all among the founders. On the committee sat literary, academic and business men, both German and Danish. The secretary to the society was J. H. Schlegel, brother of J. Elias Schlegel; he was appointed to the post in 1763. Not all the names of the members of the society were known to the outside public, and, since all announcements were made over the name of J. H. Schlegel, the impression quickly gained ground that the society was chiefly a German one.[4] In a letter[5] to Suhm, dated

[1] Shortly after Klopstock's arrival in Copenhagen Frederick V had discussed on several occasions with Klopstock the possibility of founding a printing-press for publishing literature of merit at the expense of the State, the author to receive all the profits. See *supra*, p. 65.

[2] K. L. Rahbek, "Über Klopstocks Verdienste um die dänische Litteratur" in *Kieler Blätter*, 1819, II, p. 238.

[3] Founded 1759.

[4] L. Magon, *op. cit.* p. 271.

[5] Quoted by N. M. Petersen, *op. cit.* v, 2, p. 184.

March, 1760, and written from Luxdorph's house, where he was then staying, Dass writes: "Det ny smagende Selskab har endnu intet udgivet i Trykken. Man vil sige, at de indbyrdes skal være temmelig uenige, og at det tyske[1] og franske Parti vil have Overhaand, saa at Etatsraad Luxdorph skal være færdig at gaa ud derfra".

P. C. Stenersen (1723–76) can hardly be compared to Ewald for poetic power and originality. But he was one of Klopstock's chief followers and admirers in Denmark in the 'fifties, and had always fought for the ideas of the Swiss School and opposed Gottsched's rigid rules. In this regard he is one of the pioneers of a more enlightened literary criticism in Denmark. In his *Critiske Tanker over de rimfrie Vers* (1752), he praises[2] the *Messias* and defends unrhymed verse, seeing in it a liberation of poetic thought. His Ode, *Ved min Søsters Ægteforbindelse* (1754), an imitation of Klopstock in the choriambic metre, was his best ode, the finest Danish poem up to that time in the Klopstockian style, and the first in that particular metre.

In 1770 Struensee, the royal doctor at the court of Christian VII, Frederick V's successor (1766), brought about the fall of Klopstock's patron and friend, Count Bernstorff, and in the same year Klopstock, together with Bernstorff and Schönborn, left Copenhagen, where he had found for so many years a hospitable home. They went to Hamburg, which now became a new centre for the northern circle.

It is true of Klopstock, as a French critic[3] says in speaking of his relations to his devoted admirers, the Stolbergs: "Klopstock leur apparaissait non seulement comme un dieu de la poésie, mais encore comme le représentant du génie de la patrie sur une terre étrangère, où l'influence allemande excitait les mêmes jalousies que l'autorité des écrivains français à la cour de

[1] Dass is probably thinking here of Cramer, Klopstock and Carstens.

[2] "Da man begynder snart overalt at holde det for et Tegn paa Dumhed eller Bedrageri at være en Kristen, kan en Poesie som Messias være bekvem til at gjøre det høje, det heroiske i vor Religion føleligt til Spotternes Beskjæmmelse."

[3] E. Bailly, *op. cit.* p. 367.

Berlin". Klopstock was very German. His patriotism was not marked by much sympathy with the national aspirations of other peoples, and he had not the desire to learn and to develop, the adaptability and the tact of an Elias Schlegel; neither had he the wide reading, nor the cosmopolitan viewpoint of a Gerstenberg—qualities which might have rendered his Teutonism more acceptable to the Danish writers and people. In Cramer's periodical, *Der nordische Aufseher*,[1] he had the opportunity to display such qualities, but his contributions consisted mainly of essays on language, poetry, and art, and his moral essays in this periodical are not particularly entertaining.

Ewald, Stenersen and the "Selskab til de skjønne og nyttige Videnskabers Forfremmelse": this does not seem a very long list of the different directions in which Klopstock influenced Danish literature during his stay of eighteen years in Copenhagen. But one cannot measure and limit the influence of Klopstock in so immediate a manner. In Denmark as in Germany his *Messias* gave a freedom to the imagination, which, until then, no writer had been bold enough to take, nor powerful enough to utilize. His influence, preserved by Ewald, was real enough many years later to affect the Danish romantic movement and to justify the tribute paid to him by one of the foremost Danish critics of his time:

> So lange es eine dänische Litteratur, eine dänische Sprache und eine dänische Nation giebt, wird auch der Name Friederich Gottlieb Klopstock in dem Pantheon, das unser dankbares Vaterland seinen groszen Männern weihet, tief verehret und verehrungswürdig unter den Namen jener seiner erhabenen Freunde und seiner dankbaren Zöglinge, unverdunkelt glänzen.[2]

[1] *Der nordische Aufseher* belongs to a consideration of Cramer's relation to Danish literature rather than of Klopstock's.

[2] K. L. Rahbek, "Über Klopstocks Verdienste um die dänische Litteratur" in *Kieler Blätter*, 1819, II, p. 242.

CHAPTER THREE

GERSTENBERG and DANISH LITERATURE

"GERSTENBERG tilhører med hele sit Liv og sin literære Produktion Landene norden for Elben".[1] This opinion of one of the most distinguished of living Danish critics would seem to warrant this attempt to estimate the part which Gerstenberg played in the stimulating and developing of Danish literature at a time when it was sorely in need of help and enlightened encouragement. The task has not been an easy one; partly because of the paucity of material concerning Gerstenberg's period in Denmark,[2] and partly because Gerstenberg, fertile in valuable ideas for literary development as he was, possessing as he did an extraordinary divinatory gift as to the new sources from which literature was to take its inspiration, does not present in his life and writings a picture of steady growth and development. A lethargy, curiously mingled with periods of irresistible enthusiasm, prevented him from following his ideas to their conclusion. His life and work are marked by a passionate and feverish unrest. He is a typical and unhappy representative of a period of transition, victim alike of his own instability and of the quickly-moving times, in which he lived.[3] His fate was dark and unhappy. Gerstenberg, this "leicht

[1] L. Bobé, *Reventlowske Papirer*, VI, p. 583.

[2] Gerstenberg's manuscripts were left to C. Redlich of Hamburg. Individual letters were permitted to be published and the manuscripts were subsequently scattered. See L. Bobé, Introduction to *Reventlowske Papirer*.

[3] "Immer wieder zeigt sich Gerstenberg als Mensch zwischen den Zeiten; er kann sich noch nicht entschlieszen, ausschlieszlich dem Gefühl zu folgen... hin- und hergeworfen zwischen Herz und Verstand, Anschauung und Logik, bleibt nichts als auszubiegen in Unbestimmtheit und Verwaschenheit, eine Art von Flucht vor sich selber, die für sein späteres Leben so charakteristisch ist" (A. M. Wagner, *Heinrich Wilhelm von Gerstenberg und der Sturm und Drang*, 2 vols., Heidelberg, 1920–24, II, p. 96).

erhitzbarer Kämpfer für seine Ideen",[1] this "schönes aber bizarres Talent",[2] had ceased to be an active force in literature fifty years before his death. His reputation had almost vanished during his lifetime. In 1810, thirteen years before Gerstenberg's death, Hofrat von Morgenstern included in a collection of letters of deceased writers, one belonging to Gerstenberg.[3] The complete collection of Gerstenberg's works was not published until 1823, when the literary movement had gone far beyond him. Had he had the energy, the steady driving force in the same degree as he possessed a warm enthusiasm for the ideas and writers whom he supported, he might have taken his place beside the greatest names in German criticism of the eighteenth century. He was rooted in the movement of Rationalism; was one of the founders of the "Sturm und Drang"; during the classical age of German literature he buried himself in the philosophy of Kant and died ten years before Goethe, feeling a deep grudge against the victorious Romantic movement.[4] Persistent endeavour and steady development were alike impossible to Gerstenberg. The causes which he so warmly espoused, he soon left coldly aside. To twenty years of fertile and varied production there succeeded a long period, in which he produced almost nothing. At the time of the "Sturm und Drang", of Lessing's *Emilia Galotti* and *Nathan*, of the beginnings of Goethe and Schiller, Gerstenberg grew silent, and remained so until 1785, the year in which he published his unsuccessful *Minona*. The ten years of his sojourn in Copenhagen (1765–75)[5] formed the most effective period of his life. During these years

[1] H. W. von Gerstenberg, *Rezensionen in der Hamburgischen neuen Zeitung*. 1767–71 (*Deutsche Literaturdenkmale des* 18. *and* 19. *Jahrhunderts*, No. 128), ed. by O. Fischer, Berlin, 1904. Introduction, p. x.

[2] A. M. Wagner, *op. cit.* I, p. 1.

[3] *Morgenblatt für gebildete Stände* (1810), p. 737.

[4] A. M. Wagner, *op. cit.* I, p. 2.

[5] C. Redlich in the *Allgemeine deutsche Biographie*, IX, p. 62, gives the date of Gerstenberg's going to Copenhagen as 1763, but 1765 appears to be the correct year. See *Westermanns illustrierte deutsche Monatshefte*, XLIV, pp. 50 ff., A. M. Wagner, *op. cit.* I, p. 197, note 61, and letter from Gerstenberg to K. L. Rahbek, dated April 20, 1819, and quoted by L. Bobé in his *Johannes Ewalds Levnet og Meninger*, Copenhagen, 1911, p. 319.

all his works of significance were written. Before he left Copenhagen, so early as 1771, his writings showed a marked deterioration. Klopstock's departure, the break-up of the German circle and Gerstenberg's unhappy financial position contributed, no doubt, to this result.

Born in 1737 at Tønder in Slesvig, son of an officer in the Danish army,[1] Gerstenberg was educated in Germany and German was his mother tongue.[2] He was thus well fitted for his rôle as intermediary between the literatures of Germany and Denmark. His first school was at Husum. In 1754 he went to the Altona Gymnasium; in 1757 to the University of Jena, where he was a member of the "Deutsche Gesellschaft".[3] In 1759 he returned to Holstein, where he studied English and ancient northern history.[4] In 1760 he entered the Danish army and during the following years paid frequent visits to Copenhagen with his general.[5] From 1765 he resided in or near the Danish capital. In 1766 Frederick V of Denmark died and Gerstenberg's patron, Marshal Saint-Germain, retired. In 1771, disappointed in his hopes of advancement, Gerstenberg retired from the army with the rank of Rittmeister and became a Danish civil servant in the German chancellery. In 1775 he left Copenhagen to become Danish Resident in Lübeck, where he remained until 1784. After a short stay in Eutin (1784–6) he moved in 1786 to Altona, where he died in 1823 at the age of eighty-seven.[6]

[1] Gerstenberg's father was German-born. See article by K. L. Rahbek in *Hesperus*, 1819, pp. 1–17.

[2] According to Grimm, Gerstenberg's knowledge of the Danish language was not very thorough. Baggesen, however, says that Gerstenberg could both read and speak Danish tolerably well; see J. Baggesen, *Labyrinthen*, ed. L. Bobé, p. 73. Gerstenberg himself confesses that he never really mastered the Danish language and emphasizes the fact that his education was altogether German; see A. M. Wagner, *op. cit.* I, p. 10.

[3] Klopstock, Mylius, Lessing, H. P. Sturz, and Matthias Claudius were all members of this society, or associated with its members.

[4] Gerstenberg sketched the outlines of several dramas from Scandinavian history.

[5] A. M. Wagner, *op. cit.* I, p. 50.

[6] For further details of Gerstenberg's life see article by C. Redlich in *Allgemeine deutsche Biographie*, IX, pp. 60–66.

Gerstenberg's works include: *Idyllen* in the style of Geszner and ana-

As early as the autumn of 1762 Gerstenberg had written to C. F. Weisze informing him that he intended to spend the following winter in Copenhagen, but that he would continue to write for Weisze's *Bibliothek*, and might be able to get some contributions for that periodical from Klopstock and Cramer.[1] He continues:

Klopstock und Cramer, nebst Schlegeln und Funk hatten vorigen Winter eine poetische Zusammenkunft festgesetzt, wozu sie mich gleichfalls hatten aufnehmen wollen, wenn ich nach Copenhagen gekommen wäre, welches verschiedener Abhaltungen wegen damals nicht geschehen konnte. Sollte dieses itzt aufs Tapet kommen, so können Sie leicht erachten, dasz ich etwas Gutes daraus für die Bibliothek zu stiften Gelegenheit nehmen werde. Vielleicht bleibe ich überhaupt künftig länger in Copenhagen, als bisher geschehen ist.

The first years in Copenhagen were the happiest in Gerstenberg's life; he was contented at home and was surrounded by many stimulating and appreciative friends. He knew all the members of the German circle and was intimate with Klopstock, J. A. Cramer, Matthias Claudius[2] and Schönborn. His interest in psychology and child education brought him into contact with Basedow. Resewitz, Funk, Sturz, J. H. Schlegel, Bal-

creontic poems in the style of Gleim, known as *Tändeleyen* and published in Leipzig in 1759; contributions to C. F. Weisze's *Bibliothek der schönen Wissenschaften* (vol. v, Article 2, contains a criticism of Lessing's *Philotas* by Gerstenberg); articles contributed in 1762 to F. J. Schmidt's weekly periodical, *Der Hypochondrist, oder die holsteinische Wochenschrift*; 1763, translation of d'Espagnac's *Versuch über den groszen Krieg*; 1763, *Handbuch für einen Reuter und Kriegslieder eines kgl. dänischen Grenadiers bei Eröffnung des Feldzuges* 1762; (in 1762 Peter III of Russia invaded Mecklenburg with the idea of seizing Holstein. Denmark raised both a fleet and an army to resist the Russian forces, but no active hostilities ensued); 1765, contributions to the *Samling af de adskillige Skrifter til de skjønne Videnskabers og det danske Sprogs Opkomst og Fremtarv*, commonly known as the *Sorøske Samlinger*; 1765, translation of Beaumont and Fletcher's *The Maid's Tragedy*; 1766, *Gedicht eines Skalden*; 1767, Cantata *Ariadne auf Naxos*; 1767, *Ugolino*; 1766–7, contributions to the *Briefe über Merkwürdigkeiten der Litteratur*, known as the *Schleswiger Briefe*; 1785, *Minona oder die Angelsachsen*, a tragic melodrama.

[1] A. M. Wagner, *op. cit.* I, p. 60.

[2] Matthias Claudius had known Gerstenberg in Jena and always felt for him a very great affection. In 1768 Claudius went to Hamburg to the *Hamburgische neue Zeitung*, of which paper he later became editor. It was, possibly, on Claudius' recommendation that Gerstenberg was asked to write for that journal.

thasar Münter, von Berger, Oeder, J. M. Preisler, the two young Counts Stolberg, Friedrich Leopold and Christian and the young Karl Friedrich Cramer, were all among his friends or acquaintances. Like Klopstock, Gerstenberg used to visit frequently Bernstorff's summer residence, "Bernstorff", and had the entrée to the count's house in Copenhagen.[1] The evenings passed in stimulating company at Bernstorff's house, and the excursions of the German circle,[2] with Klopstock as leader, into the country around Copenhagen were healthy diversions to a mind like Gerstenberg's, too much accustomed to morbid introspection. The musical evenings at his own house at Lyngby were regularly attended by Klopstock, J. A. Cramer, Resewitz, Funk, Sturz and J. H. Schlegel. Both Gerstenberg and his wife were excellent pianists, and the latter sang well. Gerstenberg's circle of friends was by no means confined to members of the German circle. He cultivated the society of those Danish writers who wished to bring their country into contact with new ideas. K. L. Rahbek, the Danish literary historian, quotes a letter from Gerstenberg to himself, dated April 20, 1819, in which Gerstenberg stated that in Copenhagen he had known Sneedorff, Tyge Rothe and Ewald personally.[3] He mentions, too, a young poet named Hammer,[4] a great admirer of Young's *Night Thoughts*, whom he had met at Klopstock's house, but not subsequently. In 1772 Gerstenberg entertained the idea of becoming a naturalized Dane and assuming a Danish name,[5] despite the fact that he had no very high opinion of the kind of intellectual activity which he found in Copenhagen on his arrival there. "Gerstenberg glaubt (und

[1] Aage Friis, *Bernstofferne og Danmark*, II, pp. 301, 303, 310. When, in 1768, Gerstenberg was in difficulties through the resignation from office of his patron Marshal Saint-Germain, Count Bernstorff procured him a position in the Danish civil service.

[2] It was on one of these excursions that Gerstenberg discovered on J. A. Cramer's estate at Sandholm the grave, which gave him the idea of writing his *Gedicht eines Skalden*.

[3] L. Bobé, *Johannes Ewalds Levnet og Meninger*, Copenhagen, 1911, p. 319.

[4] In the *Forsøg i de skjønne og nyttige Videnskaber samlede af et patriotisk Selskab*, 1761, Article I, issued by the Danish Society, there is a poem by Hammer entitled *Søfarten*.

[5] *Allgemeine deutsche Biographie*, IX, p. 61.

Schönborn sagt dasselbige), das hiesige Klima sey dem Denken zuwieder, die Nation ist eine Menge lebendiger Zeugen dieser Wahrheit".[1] Like the other members of the German circle, Gerstenberg seems to have entertained an ardent admiration for their royal patron, Frederick V, and after his death speaks in enthusiastic terms of the late sovereign's generous character.[2]

It was through Klopstock that Gerstenberg came to Copenhagen.[3] Gerstenberg's attitude to Klopstock during the time in Copenhagen was one of unqualified admiration. It had not always been so. While still under Gottsched's influence, he had expressed a scornful criticism of Klopstock's "verworrene und unklare" ode on the Lake of Zürich. But before he came to Copenhagen his attitude had changed, and Klopstock's influence was doubtless not without its effect in causing Gerstenberg to give up his earlier anacreontic style.[4] Their common love of music was a strong bond between the two men. Like all Gerstenberg's friends of the German circle, Klopstock feared that Gerstenberg's creative activity would soon be exhausted.[5]

The *Sorøske Skrifter* or the *Samling af adskillige Skrifter til de skjønne Videnskabers og det danske Sprogs Opkomst og Fremtarv*, to which Gerstenberg contributed, and in which he was the moving spirit, was edited and printed in Sorø, from which place Jens Schielderup Sneedorff had issued his *Den patriotiske*

[1] Letter dated December 11, 1773, from F. L. Stolberg to J. H. Vosz (*Briefe F. L. Stolbergs und der seinigen an J. H. Vosz*, ed. by Otto Hellinghaus, Münster, 1891, pp. 8 ff.). But elsewhere Gerstenberg gives a warning against such generalizations: "...dasz die Norweger eine der schätzbarsten, fähigsten und muntersten Nationen in der Welt sind. Glauben Sie mir, nichts ist abgeschmackter, als diese allgemeinen Urtheile über ganze Völker, die durch die geringste Bekanntschaft auf einmal ihren ganzen Werth verliehren" (*Schleswiger Briefe*, ed. Weilen, Stuttgart, 1890, Letter 11, p. 65).

[2] In the *Briefe über Merkwürdigkeiten der Litteratur*, Letter 13, p. 209, Gerstenberg speaks of "der ganze Werth des guten Herzens, von dem es vielleicht in der Geschichte der Menschheit kein so einleuchtendes Beyspiel giebt, als in der kurzen Geschichte des verstorbenen Königs von Dänemark".

[3] A. M. Wagner, *op. cit.* I, p. 81. Klopstock and Gerstenberg were regarded by German writers as the outstanding names in the German circle in Copenhagen. It was chiefly of them that Herder thought on his sea-journey from Riga to France in 1769.

[4] W. Herbst, *Matthias Claudius*, Gotha, 1857, p. 43.

[5] J. M. Lappenberg, *Briefe von und an Klopstock*, Braunschweig, 1867.

Tilskuer (1761–3). *Den patriotiske Tilskuer* was a weekly moral periodical, the successor of *Der nordische Aufseher*, but it was written in Danish, and it made a more popular appeal. Sneedorff had a very great interest in language and in literary criticism, in which subjects the *Sorøske Samlinger* continued his work. Gerstenberg knew Sneedorff personally, and it is quite possible that the latter was influenced to some extent by Gerstenberg's ideas.[1] The Sorø publication appeared in 1765.[2] Only one volume in three parts appeared, although several volumes were intended. The ambitious plans which the journal was to fulfil were never carried out. All the articles are in Danish. The object was to present in translation the best of foreign literature, as well as some original works, and to lay the foundations for a sound critical sense.[3] In the choice of translations Gerstenberg exercised a controlling influence, while in criticism he was able to bring to his subjects a width of reading, a catholicity of ideas and a bold originality of viewpoint, rare in Danish literature at that time.

Gerstenberg's collaborators were Peter Kleen, who had been his school-companion in the Altona Gymnasium and had collaborated with him in 1762 in the periodical *Der Hypochondrist*, and Etatsraad Christian Fleischer. In a letter from Gerstenberg to K. L. Rahbek, dated April 20, 1819, Gerstenberg claims to be the real originator of the *Sorøske Samlinger*, but emphasizes the popularity of Councillor Fleischer's essays, which contained, as Gerstenberg expresses it, the most important leaven for the Danish language. Fleischer looked after the printing and issuing of the journal. Gerstenberg acknowledges that when he wrote in Danish, Fleischer corrected it for

[1] Sneedorff died in 1764. Wagner is of opinion that Gerstenberg communicated to him his ideas on "Volkstümlichkeit" and originality. See A. M. Wagner, *op. cit.* I, p. 88.

[2] Bode, publisher of the *Ugolino*, attempted with the help of Dusch, Sonnenfels, Klopstock, J. A. Cramer and Herder to issue a continuation of the Sorø publication in 1770. Only one volume appeared, to which Klopstock and Schönborn each made one contribution; see *Allgemeine deutsche Biographie*, 1879, IX, p. 63.

[3] See Preface by Gerstenberg to *Sorøske Samlinger*, dated March 1, 1765.

him, and when he wrote in German, Fleischer would translate it into Danish. In the same letter Gerstenberg says that Kleen only understood as much Danish as one could get on with; but Kleen, as well as Fleischer, felt a strong love for Denmark and showed a keen interest in Danish literature. The preface to the first part of the *Sorøske Samlinger* is by Gerstenberg and probably also the prefaces to the two later parts.[1] As regards the rest of Gerstenberg's contributions to the journal, there is a letter from him to Rahbek a few years before his death, in which he says that he himself has written whatever else there is in the *Samlinger*, in development of the ideas expressed in the preface. Before collaborating with Gerstenberg, Fleischer had already translated into Danish Gerstenberg's *Poems*, Lessing's *Fabeln* and C. F. Weisze's *Richard III*. In a letter to Nicolai dated December 5, 1767, Gerstenberg speaks of this translation of *Richard III*:

Der Etatsrath Fleischer hat auch vor kurzem Herrn Weiszens Richard III in reimlose fünffüszige Jamben übersetzt, welches der erste Versuch dieser Art in Dänemark ist; und wenn er nicht, so wie er ein Sammler von Vögeln, Insecten und Mineralien ist, die kleine Grille hätte, auch altnordische Wörter zu sammeln, und bey jeder Gelegenheit an [den] Mann zu bringen, so würde diese Übersetzung auch auf dem Theater reüssiren können. Die Grazien nebst andern Kleinigkeiten von mir hat er sehr vortrefflich übersetzt.[2]

At Gerstenberg's suggestion Fleischer translated, for the third part of the *Sorøske Samlinger*, Nicolai's *Abhandlung über das Trauerspiel*. In the letter to Nicolai, from which we have just quoted, Gerstenberg says:

Ihre Abhandlung vom Trauerspiel hat der Etatsrath Fleischer, der Hauptverfasser der Samlinger etc., ins Dänische übersetzt, und ich gestehe Ihnen, dasz ich selbst ihm diese Übersetzung angerathen habe, weil ich mich nicht besinne, mehr gute Anmerkungen in einer so kurzen Abh. beysammen gefunden zu haben, ob ich gleich nicht mit allem einig bin.[3]

[1] Wagner points out that in writing of the *Sorøske Samlinger* in the *Bibliothek der schönen Wissenschaften* Gerstenberg praises all the contributions except the Prefaces; see A. M. Wagner, *op. cit.* I, p. 61.

[2] "Gerstenbergs Briefe an Nicolai", ed. R. M. Werner in *Zeitschrift für deutsche Philologie*, XXIII, p. 59.

[3] *Ibid.* p. 59.

The idea of translating such a work as this into Danish would seem to confirm the interest which Gerstenberg took in Danish literature and his appreciation of its real needs. Nicolai's treatise offered for the first time to the Danish public a consideration of the nature and purpose of tragedy and an analysis of the requirements for a good tragic style.[1] Danish literature had at that time no tragedy to show.[2] Whether Ewald was influenced by this work of Nicolai, it is not easy to say. It is possible that he took his ideas from Corneille directly. The first part of the *Sorøske Samlinger* contained Fleischer's Danish translation of Möser's *Harlekin*, the second part a translation of Riccoboni's *L'Art du Théâtre*, and the third part contained one of Noverre's *Lettres sur la Danse et sur les Ballets*.

Gerstenberg had always been keenly interested in matters concerning language. His knowledge of modern languages was above the ordinary. Latin, French and English he knew well. Of Danish he had a certain command; Spanish he had studied. With the English moral periodicals, especially *The Tatler*, with Milton, Shakespeare and the English dramatists he was familiar. French comedies and tragedies he knew, partly in their original form and partly from the *Deutsche Schaubühne*. He possessed in a high degree the gift of feeling the spirit of a language, and he doubtless gave valuable encouragement to Fleischer, whose contributions on the Danish language are among the most important parts of the *Sorøske Samlinger*. This interest in language was not a new thing in Denmark. The journal was continuing a movement for the rejuvenation and improvement of the Danish language, which had been begun in Denmark in the 'forties, a movement to which Sneedorff had contributed. It was part of a patriotic movement, in which Holberg played a part, to resist the foreign influences, chiefly German, which threatened to engulf Danish nationality. That the bitter struggle between the German and Danish elements in Denmark in the 'seventies ended in a victory for the Danish party is to be in part attributed to the spirit of patriotism, developed by such men

[1] L. Magon, *op. cit.* p. 237.

[2] *Sorøske Samlinger*, Article 2, p. 80.

as Holberg, Sneedorff, Fleischer and Ewald in the preceding years. Similar linguistic discussions had been going on in Germany, and Gerstenberg had followed them with keen interest.[1] There was no work in the 'sixties in Denmark, which made so valuable a contribution to the theory of language as the *Sorøske Samlinger*, a rather curious fact when one considers that not one of the three collaborators spoke Danish as his mother tongue; but Fleischer, who contributed six articles on language, was well fitted by his reading and interests to write on this subject.[2] He represented a new school of thought; he realized that the Danish language could hope for no new strength or vitality from the borrowing of words from other languages and he calls for the expulsion of all foreign words, the meaning of which could be expressed equally well by native words. He would retain many living Danish words, commonly regarded as vulgar, and would revive words falling into disuse. If there must be borrowing, then, says Fleischer, let it at least be from allied languages such as the Norwegian and Swedish. An anonymous work of 1766, *Tanker om det danske Sprogs nye og gamle Tilstand og Forbedring*, continues these ideas of Fleischer and advocates the collection of old words from the ancient laws, folk-songs and literatures of Norway, Sweden, Denmark and Iceland, as well as from the psalm-books of the Reformation, and puts forward the idea of a Danish etymological dictionary. The author makes particular reference to Iceland, where the old language is preserved.

In the 'sixties of the eighteenth century, Denmark was still without native literary criticism of any real value. Suhm in his classification of literature divided books into good books and bad books; Fielding's novels are good, since they are not long, and make for virtue; *La Pucelle d'Orléans* is among the bad

[1] *Sorøske Samlinger*, Article 2, p. 166.

[2] Fleischer's articles treated of such subjects as the improvement of language in respect of synonyms, and the use of archaic and new words. There was also an article in the collection dealing with J. H. Schlegel's treatise on the Danish language.

books, since it is immoral and blasphemous.[1] Except for Ewald's treatise of 1766, there was nothing original in the ideas of Danish writers of the 'sixties on the nature of poetry. In the prefaces to the *Sorøske Samlinger* Gerstenberg expresses ideas which were then stirring in Europe, but which were new to Denmark at that time. He was more nearly in touch with the literatures of other countries than any other writer in Denmark, and his contributions to the journal are characterized by all the enthusiasm, power and clear-sightedness of his early critical writings. For a proper understanding of Gerstenberg's critical ideas the Preface of March 1, 1765, is important. Here Gerstenberg acknowledges the rights of those who are not experts to derive pleasure from literature, and he distinguishes between "Elskere" and "Kiendere":

> Vi for vor Deel indbefatte under det dømmende Publiko dem, som selv have giort sig bekiente med de bædste Smagens Verker af alle, eller dog de meest berømte Nationer. Vi kalde dem Elskere, saa længe de blot lade sig nøye med Følelsen af det Skiønne, uden at opsøge dets Grunde, og vi kalde dem Kiendere, naar de forbinde med deres Læsning en ret antrænget Eftertanke over Naturen af det Skiønne.[2]

He allows that public taste should be considered, and blames the pedant, who thinks more of rules than of genius. He defines the true critic as: "...den Kritikus som vel kiender Kunstens Regler, men, med uafvendte Øyekast fra sin øverste Dommere, mere følger sin Følelse, og tillige raadfører sig med alle Tiders Erfaringer, hvorfor det har behaget, og hint har mishaget".[3] Gerstenberg follows Sneedorff in his demand for a free, fearless and unprejudiced criticism.[4] He makes a valuable contribution towards impressing on the Danish literary public the real necessity for an enlightened school of criticism and the very

[1] P. F. Suhm, *Tronhjemske Samlinger* (1761–4), and quoted by F. Rønning, *op. cit.* Copenhagen, 1886, I, p. 252, note 2.

[2] *Sorøske Samlinger*, Preface, pp. 5 ff.

[3] *Ibid.* "Babues Svar paa nogle Breve."

[4] Possibly there may be an echo here of the Langebek-Pontoppidan controversy in 1745, in which Bishop Pontoppidan was able to extort an apology from the less influential Langebek for the latter's criticisms of a work of his.

real help which such criticism could give to the building up of a national literature. He declares that real genius cannot be suppressed and that intelligent criticism helps it: since Elias Schlegel's death in 1749 until the *Sorøske Samlinger* in 1765 no member of the German circle, with the possible exception of J. A. Cramer, had betrayed so strong an interest in the aspirations of the Danish writers towards developing and defining their nationality. Through his journal Gerstenberg did give valuable encouragement to these patriotic writers, and made a real contribution to Danish critical literature. His influence as well as that of Sneedorff may be traced in two Danish periodicals, both of which appeared in 1768, J. Baden's *Kritisk Journal* and B. G. Sporon's *Breve i Anledning af udkomne Skrifter*.[1]

The *Schleswiger Litteraturbriefe* or *Briefe über Merkwürdigkeiten der Litteratur* continued the new type of literary periodical, which Gerstenberg had introduced with the *Sorøske Samlinger*. In the *Schleswiger Briefe* Gerstenberg was, however, entering a wider field than in the earlier journal, in which he had dealt with questions particularly interesting to a Danish audience. There are indications that his Danish contemporaries considered that in the *Schleswiger Briefe* he was setting up standards of criticism which were too high as yet for the struggling Danish literature to reach, pointing out directions which it was as yet unable to take. But Gerstenberg saw the danger of Danish literature becoming too provincial and too narrow, and, like Holberg, he tries to open the Danish windows on western Europe. As he had already said in the earlier journal:

> En Nation, som indsvøber sig bestandig i sig selv, aldrig sammenligner sig med Fremmede, drømmer sig lettelig de Fuldkommenheder til, den aldrig besidder. Den er alletider en nyttig Borger iblandt dem, som anstiller Sammenligning, og, uden at lade sig bortføre af den almindelige Hvirvel med Kækhed raaber til sit Folk; Vi ere endnu ikke det vi skulde være.[2]

[1] See L. Magon, *op. cit.* p. 239.
[2] *Sorøske Samlinger*, Preface.

And this "useful citizen" Gerstenberg may fairly claim to have been. The *Schleswiger Briefe* occupy an honourable place among the periodicals which foreshadow the main directions of literary development. *Der Fremde*, *Der Hypochondrist* and *Der nordische Aufseher* preceded the *Schleswiger Briefe*, but the latter answered the new desires of the literary public for a more critical organ. In a letter to Nicolai from Copenhagen, dated August 2, 1766, Gerstenberg writes that his intention at first was to take only a small part in the *Schleswiger Briefe*.[1] He was, however, the general editor, and probably contributed nineteen of the twenty-six letters of the first three collections,[2] and his letters form by far the most valuable part of the periodical.[3] The first two collections were issued in 1766; the third, beginning with Letter 20, in 1767, in which year the letters came to a close. The journal was resumed in 1770 under the title *Über Merkwürdigkeiten der Litteratur*, but not in letter form; this latter publication is not so interesting nor so important as those of 1766 and 1767.

Already, before the *Schleswiger Briefe*, Gerstenberg had written articles on Danish literature, which appeared in the *Bibliothek der schönen Wissenschaften*: on *Der nordische Aufseher*[4]; on Tullin's *Maidag* and *Reden über die glückselige Regierung Friedrichs V*[5]; *Über Johann Elias Schlegels Werke*[6]; on J. A. Scheibe's translation of *Peder Paars*[7]; on existing conditions of the Danish theatre[8]. These articles were all written by Gersten-

[1] "...nur einen entfernten Antheil zu nehmen dachte."

[2] See A. M. Wagner, *op. cit.* I, p. 64.

[3] G. B. Funk, at that time house tutor to J. A. Cramer, to whose *Nordischer Aufseher* he had contributed, made some few contributions to the *Schleswiger Briefe*. Funk was born in 1734 in Saxony; studied at Freiburg and Leipzig; 1756–69 in Copenhagen; 1769 went to Magdeburg, where he died in 1814. See Jördens, VI, p. 124 ff. P. Kleen probably contributed the sixth letter (omitted in the Weilen edition). Kleen was born in 1732 in Glückstadt; in 1758 he became clerk in the Army commissariat in Copenhagen, where he died in 1766. He translated into German prose Tullin's prize poem, *Om Skabningens Ypperlighed*, under the title *Die Schönheit der Schöpfung* (Copenhagen, 1765).

[4] V, 2, p. 273.

[5] VII, 2, p. 364.

[6] VIII, 1, p. 101 and IX, 1, p. 59.

[7] XII, 1, p. 114.

[8] XII, 2, p. 348.

berg from Copenhagen, as he states in a letter of April 20, 1819, to Rahbek.[1] The nineteenth of the *Schleswiger Briefe* is among the most interesting and important, particularly from a Danish point of view. Gerstenberg declares his belief in the future of Danish literature in optimistic fashion: "So viel ist wol gewisz, dasz jetzt der Periode für die schöne Litteratur in Dänemark herannahet, und sich durch alle Cabalen seiner Gegner nicht wird verdrängen lassen, bis er von selbst Abschied nimt. Er geht seinen Weg mit starken Schritten".[2] Gerstenberg gives us an interesting account of the new Danish Society[3] and of its publications, showing all through the letter his very thorough knowledge of current Danish literature. He quotes the avowed objects of the society: "die Sprache und den Geschmack zu verbessern", and "eine noch gröszere Absicht zu erreichen—die Absicht, emsige und brauchbare Bürger zu bilden".[4] He stresses the fact that the Danish Society enjoys many advantages which the German societies do not possess. It had for its patrons Frederick V, who had promised the society financial help, and subsequently his successor, Christian VII. Gerstenberg hints that from the latter additional help might be forthcoming. The members of this society, as Gerstenberg points out, were mature men of varied interests and occupations, and the competition for the society's prizes was not confined to the members. All works submitted to the society for prizes or publication were judged severely without fear or favour.[5]

Gerstenberg then proceeds to speak of the works which had been published by the society,[6] in particular of Tullin's contributions to the first part of the first volume, his two prize poems, *Søfarten* and *Den nye Edda*. Gerstenberg gives a detailed criticism, illustrating and justifying it by quotations from the works. He praises the former of these poems very

[1] This letter is now in the Royal Library in Copenhagen.

[2] *Briefe über Merkwürdigkeiten der Litteratur*, ed. A. von Weilen, Stuttgart, 1890, p. 168.

[3] Founded in 1759. See *supra*, pp. 86 f.

[4] *Briefe über Merkwürdigkeiten der Litteratur, ed. cit.* p. 169.

[5] *Ibid.* p. 168.

[6] *Ibid.* pp. 169 ff.

highly and places Tullin between Young and Pope. He comments on the philosophic depth of the poem, but is of opinion that the five-foot verse of the English poets would have been better than the alexandrine form of verse chosen by Tullin, since it would have been better suited to the brevity and energy of the Danish language. Despite the fact that Tullin had chosen the five-foot verse for the second of the poems of *Søfarten*, Gerstenberg does not rank it so highly. To Tullin's *Den nye Edda* Gerstenberg gives high praise. He finds that Tullin has known how to absorb the spirit and style of the older *Edda*: "Der Verfasser hat sich vortreflich in die Idee der alten Edda zu setzen gewuszt; seine Schreibart ist edel, reizend, körnigt und blumenreich; und seine Allegorie so schön und unterhaltend, dasz Sie sie sicher den besten Addisonschen an die Seite setzen können".[1] Tullin's poem, *Om Skabningens Ypperlighed*, Gerstenberg also praises highly.[2] In concluding his criticism of Tullin's works he pays a warm tribute to the Norwegian writer:

> Tullin ist nicht correct; dies hat er mit Young gemein; seine Versification ist blühend, seine Ideen sind malerisch und systematisch; diesz hat er mit Popen gemein: er erlaubt sich mehr lyrische Schwünge als Pope, mehr Simplicität als Young: diesz zeichnet ihm seinen Weg zwischen beiden aus. Sie können leicht denken, dasz ich eine grosze Meynung von ihm haben müsse, wenn ich ihm einen so glänzenden Rang anweise; ich läugne es nicht; ich halte ihn für einen der gröszten philosophischen Dichter, die ich kenne.[3]

The Danish Society had awarded the prize for a poem on the Creation to Benzon, a Dane, and Gerstenberg finds fault with the award, declaring that literary societies generally commit the fault of rewarding taste rather than genius: "Genie geht nach der Ordnung der Natur vor dem Geschmack her. Dieser Ordnung sollte die Kritik folgen".[4] The Danish translation of part of Voltaire's *Mérope* in the second part of the society's publications Gerstenberg compares unfavourably to a previous Danish version of the same play.[5] In criticizing a satire,

[1] *Ibid.* p. 173.
[2] *Ibid.* p. 175.
[3] *Ibid.* pp. 175 f.
[4] *Ibid.* p. 176.
[5] *Ibid.* p. 173.

which he entitles *Die Glückseligkeit der Thoren*, Gerstenberg advises more restraint, and more variety and originality in expression.[1] The criticism by Severus of this same poem in the third part Gerstenberg does not find justified.[2] *Lykkens Tempel* by Ewald he praises.[3] Schiermann, who had made the *Mérope* translation, just alluded to, had contributed a verse translation of Pope's *Essay on Criticism*, and to this Gerstenberg gives moderate praise.[4] Of the free Danish translations of a small poem by Sedaine,[5] Gerstenberg expresses approval. He then discusses[6] the introduction by J. H. Schlegel, secretary to the Danish Society, to the fourth part of the Society's published works. Schlegel had complained of the too severe criticism[7] by a "private society" of the publications of the Danish Society, and had said that in a country where literature is still in an early stage of development, the critical office should be exercised forbearingly. Here, in the *Schleswiger Briefe*, Gerstenberg defends criticism but expresses himself more suavely than he had done in the *Sorøske Samlinger*:

> Der Wind erhöht eine starke Flamme, und tödtet die schwache. Dieselbe Wirkung hat auch eine strenge Kritik in Absicht auf die schönen Wissenschaften. Sie musz sich nothwendig nach dem Zustande des Landes richten lernen, wenn sie nicht, ihrer Bestimmung zuwider, mehr schaden als nutzen soll.[8]

But Gerstenberg goes on to point out that the Danish Society itself has been just as severe in its own judgments of the writings of its members. Near the close of the nineteenth letter Gerstenberg gives some of the ideas, which inspire the Danish Society: "damit Sie sehen, dasz vernünftige Leute in allen Ländern durch die Uebereinstimmung ihrer Ideen eine Art von Republik unter einander ausmachen".[9] This nineteenth letter, together with the twenty-fifth and twenty-sixth letters, gives

[1] *Briefe über Merkwürdigkeiten der Litteratur, ed. cit.* p. 173.
[2] *Ibid.* p. 176. [3] *Ibid.* p. 177. [4] *Ibid.* p. 178.
[5] *Ibid.* p. 179. [6] *Ibid.* p. 177.
[7] By P. Kleen. The criticism was published in Copenhagen in 1765.
[8] *Ed. cit.* p. 177. And Gerstenberg adds: "...eine spröde Kritik steht mit den ersten Versuchen einer Nation in keinem guten Verhältnisse."
[9] *Ibid.* p. 177.

us an insight into the condition of Danish literature of the time. There can be no doubt but that the nineteenth letter afforded Danish literature particular encouragement at a time when it was sorely needed. Gerstenberg's high praise of Tullin's works could not fail to inspire the younger Danish writers. In matters of literary criticism Gerstenberg would admit no narrow national frontiers, and the comparison of Tullin to such well-known writers as Young, Pope and Addison, and the broad international viewpoint adopted by Gerstenberg, formed a new mode of criticism for Denmark.

Letters fourteen to eighteen of the *Schleswiger Briefe*, entitled *Versuch über Schakespears Werke und Genie*, give to this periodical its historical importance. It was not the first time that Shakespeare had been mentioned in Danish critical literature.[1] Already Gerstenberg himself had done so in the preface to his translation of *The Maid's Tragedy* of Beaumont and Fletcher, entitled *Kritische und biographische Abhandlungen über die vier gröszten Dichter des ältern brittischen Theaters*. In letters twenty-one and sixty-nine of *Der nordische Aufseher* (1758–61) Cramer had criticized Shakespeare. He had declared that the English dramatist would have done better to have followed a prescribed path, rather than his own wild fancy. From this position to the unbounded admiration which Gerstenberg expressed for Shakespeare was a long step forward. If to Ewald's dramas the chief credit should be awarded for revealing to the Danes the possibility of utilizing the wealth of dramatic material, which lay buried within Scandinavian antiquity, it must not be forgotten that it was Gerstenberg's letters on Shakespeare, which indicated a new and more suitable form for the treatment of this material. The Shakespearean elements in *Ugolino* were recognized by Danish critics, and in spite of its revolutionary character, Jacob Baden gives it great praise in his *Kritisk Journal*, the foremost critical periodical in Denmark at that time, and he claims Gerstenberg as a Danish-born subject:

[1] J. E. Schlegel's essay, *Vergleichung Shakespears und Andreas Gryphs*, was written in 1741, but can hardly be regarded as belonging to Danish literature.

Gerstenberg ikke alene opholder sig i Danmark og er i dansk Tjæneste, men ogsaa er en født dansk Undersaat....Man kan ikke nok beundre Forf.'s frugtbare Geni, der, uden stor Forvikling, uden Episoder, har vidst af sit simple Subjekt selv at uddrage al den Materie, han brugte, har vidst at variere Karaktererne saa mesterlig....Dialogen er i vore Tanker uforbederlig....Vi ønskede det maatte finde en god Oversætter hos os: ti det var dog Skade, om vi skulde have en Shakspear iblandt os, uden fuldkommen at kunne skönne paa hans Talenter, fordi han ikke skriver i vort Modersmaal.[1]

Towards the end of the 'sixties the name of Shakespeare begins to appear with greater frequency in Danish critical literature; but in spite of the interest roused in Shakespeare by the *Schleswiger Briefe* and by *Ugolino*, it was not until 1777 that a Danish translation of one of Shakespeare's plays, *Hamlet*, appeared. The translator was J. Boye. The *Kritisk Journal*, in speaking of this translation, praises Shakespeare's play and acknowledges the author's unmistakable genius, but refers to the English dramatist as the "vildeste og uregelmæssigste Geni", and applies to Shakespeare what the latter had said of the world: "...'tis an unweeded garden That grows to seed; things rank and gross in nature Possess it merely".[2]

Gerstenberg's German contemporaries regarded his *Schleswiger Briefe* with great interest. The *Dänisches Journal* in 1767 gave a long account and criticism of the *Schleswiger Briefe*, praising particularly the letters from London and Paris, but finding fault with their too artificial style and their use of foreign words.[3] Herder, in a letter to Nicolai dated February 19,

[1] *Krit. Journal*, 1769, pp. 335 ff., quoted by Rønning, *op. cit.* II, p. 85. Gerstenberg's *Ugolino* was translated into Danish by J. H. Mejer in 1779.

[2] *Ibid.* 1777, No. 28. The following lines from Boye's translation give some idea of the quality of the work: Act I, Scene 3: "O! at dette alt for haarde, haarde Kød vilde smælte, tø op og henflyde i Dug! eller at den Evige ej havde stillet sin Torden mod Selvmorderen! O Gud! O Gud! Hvor langvilligt, slet, afnyttet og ubrugeligt er al denne Verdens Gode for mig! O fy, o fy, den er en uluged Have, der skyder i Frø,..." (quoted by Rønning, *op. cit.* pp. 84 f.).

[3] "Wenn wir zum Beschlusz noch unsere Meynung von der Schreibart unserer Briefe sagen sollen, so ist es kürzlich diese: Sie ist manchmal etwas gekünstelt: fremde Wörter werden zu oft, und ohne Noth, eingemischt; und die Mottos aus andern Schriften sind gar zu häufig angebracht worden. Die Briefe aus London und Berlin dünken uns fast am schönsten geschrieben" (*Dänisches Journal*, I, 1767, p. 445).

1767, says: "Ein Aufseher über Deutschland an den Ufern der Düne ist so eine wunderbare Kreatur, als ein Litteraturschriftsteller auf den Sandbänken der baltischen Halbinsel",[1] and he goes on to say that the Copenhagen circle wishes to form a fourth party, with the intention of opposing the influence of the *Berliner Litteraturbriefe* and of saving something of the Gottschedian influence. He is not sure as to their attitude to the Swiss school: "Sie scheinen...einen skaldrischen Geschmack aufbringen zu wollen, der zur Bildung Deutschlands viel beytragen kann". The change from the tinkling, toying tones of anacreonticism to the thunder of the bards marks a great change in Gerstenberg's ideas. In it he reflects the reaction of his time towards nature, rude primitive nature, which was to replace the "precious", decorative nature of the anacreontics.[2]

Before Gerstenberg, Mallet[3] had done a great service to Danish literature in reviving the interest in northern antiquity; but the Danish bardic productions such as Bredal's lyric drama, *Gram og Signe* (1756) and Katharina von Passov's *Cupido Philosoph* (1757), were poor and uninspiring. Von Passov's play was dedicated to Bredal, whom she addresses as "Nordens Skjaldrers Zir". In the preface the authoress states her intention of using Roman mythology. She was told of Mallet's *Histoire de Dannemarc* and of his Icelandic *Edda*, which had been translated into French, and a further play by her, of little value, was the result.[4]

Gerstenberg's interest in northern antiquity was no new one with him. It dated back to his schooldays in Altona Gymnasium (1751–7). As a seventeen-year-old schoolboy he had

[1] O. Hoffmann, *Herders Briefwechsel mit Nicolai*, Berlin, 1887, p. 8.

[2] In 1777 Gerstenberg and Overbeck proposed to Vosz that they should leave Europe and live a natural and happy life in Tahiti.

[3] *Introduction à l'Histoire de Dannemarc*, Copenhagen, 1755, 1756. It was translated into English by Percy under the title *Northern Antiquities*. Mallet also issued an abbreviated edition of Snorre's *Edda*.

[4] See Rahbek and Nyerup, *Den danske Digtekunst*, pp. 118 ff. In Lillie's *Lærde Efterretninger* it is pointed out that Fru Passov could have read the Resenius version of the *Edda*, and got more from it than from the Mallet version. Neither Gerstenberg nor Klopstock had a high opinion of Mallet's work.

written an ode, *Von der Freudigkeit der alten Celten zu sterben*, in which there is none of the cumbersome and artificial nordic apparatus of names and bardic allusions, but the stern qualities of the northern races are extolled in a more simple manner.[1] When in 1759 he resumed these studies in northern antiquity, Professor Gottfried Schütze, then professor at Hamburg Gymnasium, tried to persuade his brilliant young pupil to continue the work begun by Elias Schlegel. After praising Gerstenberg's intention of "offering a learned sacrifice to the memory of our brave and honourable ancestors" Schütze continues:

> Ich bitte Sie, diesen Vorsatz nicht fahren zu lassen, und wenn ich glüklich muthmaszen kann, so weissage ich Ihnen, da mir Ihre Fähigkeit bekannt ist, ein nicht gemeines, sondern etwas recht beyfalswürdiges Urtheil. Ihnen ist es bekannt, dasz Deutschland und Dännemark den verewigten Schlegel noch immer mit einer Art der Sehnsucht nennet, nachdem er Canut mit Beyfall auf die Schaubühne gebracht hat. Und ich weisz aus eigener Erfahrung, dasz Dänemark Mæcenaten hat, in denen ein dänisches Blut rollet, und die bey dem erneuerten Andenken ihrer Vorfahren nicht gleichgültig sind.[2]

Schütze then goes on to speak of the love of music among their northern ancestors, evidently to increase Gerstenberg's interest in them, and concludes: "Ich stelle mir vor, dass Sie den Saxo Grammat. als ein sehr bekanntes Buch, in Itzehoe leicht zum Gebrauch finden werden. Wo nicht, so erwarte ich fernere Nachricht, was ich zu Ihrem Gebrauch excerpiren soll".[3] But from these earnest exhortations of Gerstenberg's friend and mentor there were no immediate results. The bardic allusions in the *Kriegslieder eines dänischen Grenadiers* (1762) were few and unimportant. In the *Sorøske Samlinger* (1765) there is only one bardic reference.[4]

It may well be that it was the change to Copenhagen which was responsible for the fructifying of Gerstenberg's nordic

[1] This ode was discovered by R. Batka; see his *Altnordische Stoffe und Studien in Deutschland*, p. 65; see also A. Blanck, *Den nordiske Renässansen i sjuttonhundretalets Litteratur*, Stockholm, 1911, p. 131.

[2] *Reventlowske Papirer*, ed. L. Bobé, VI, p. 584; letter from Schütze to Gerstenberg from Altona, November 16, 1759.

[3] *Ibid.*

[4] Article 2, p. 121.

interests.[1] In the German circle and among the friends of the members of this circle there were many who had already evinced a strong interest in northern antiquity. The patron of the circle, Count Bernstorff, had helped with the publication of Mallet's work. Carstens had been Mallet's adviser. J. H. Schlegel's *Geschichte der Könige von Dänemark aus dem Oldenburgischen Stamme* touches on Danish antiquity. J. A. Cramer, too, was interested in the subject.[2] In 1750 Tyge Rothe had attempted a work in Latin on Danish antiquity. Furthermore there had existed for centuries in Danish literature an unbroken tradition of interest in the northern past, an interest which, in the second half of the eighteenth century, was receiving an added force through the developing spirit of nationality. Gerstenberg had already read fairly deeply in the subject of northern antiquity and with his impressionability to national influences and his quick imagination he was no doubt attracted by the idea of giving to Danish as well as to German literature a new inspiration and content; and in this field he gave to Danish literature at least as much as he received. Through his articles in the *Schleswiger Briefe* he pointed out the splendid qualities of the *Kjæmpeviser* and made the general public acquainted with the works of Ole Worm and Peder Syv, writers who, before Gerstenberg's time, had been regarded with a certain amount of awe by unlearned readers.

Mallet's translation of the *Edda* of Snorre was both elegant and tasteful, well suited to the polite world of Copenhagen. But Gerstenberg possessed a power denied to Mallet, that of actually feeling the spirit and power of the northern language and literature of which he writes.[3] His eighth letter in the *Schles-*

[1] Magon is of this opinion. See *op. cit.* I, p. 357.

[2] It was to J. A. Cramer that Gerstenberg dedicated his *Gedicht eines Skalden*.

[3] "Det er Fremskridtet hos Gerstenberg, at han naar frem til en historisk-æstetisk Betragtning af den oldnordiske Digtning, udvikler Lovene for dens Stil og Metrik, ja, lægger et Ord ind til Forklaring og Forsvar for Skaldenes Kenninger...her træffer dog det literære Publikum for første Gang bestemte Henvisninger baade paa den norrøne Digtnings Indhold og paa dens Form" (Just Bing, *op. cit.* in *For Kirke og Kultur*, v, p. 604).

wiger Briefe is entitled: *Memoire eines Irrländers über die ossianischen Gedichte—Reliques of Ancient English Poetry—Dänische Kiämpe Viser.* Gerstenberg begins with a bold declaration of the richness of the treasures, which lie to hand in the northern literatures.[1] He exhorts the Danes to awaken to their own advantages in this respect and points to the old lyric poems, known as *Kjæmpeviser.* He regrets that so many of them have been translated into modern Danish and so lost a part of their significance and power. He points out that there are many Danes who are not aware even of the existence of these folksongs. All through this eighth letter Gerstenberg shows a very thorough knowledge of the northern sagas. The eleventh letter, *Von der alten runischen Poesie*, gives an account of Peder Syv's edition of a collection of old sagas and of Ole Worm's *Danica litteratura antiquissima.* Gerstenberg gives, too, an account of ancient northern literatures. There was nothing new in this, but Gerstenberg expressed, in a form and language which even the unlearned in Denmark and Germany could understand, what up to that time had been buried in two formidably ancient books[2]; and Gerstenberg was able to communicate his enthusiasm to his readers.

In the twenty-sixth letter of the *Schleswiger Briefe*, in referring to Mallet's work and Saxo, Gerstenberg speaks, in language strongly reminiscent of J. E. Schlegel, of northern antiquity as being particularly rich in material for tragedy, rich in great occasions and events, and in the strong, proud, noble character of the ancient Danes, fitting subjects for a great tragic style.[3] It was Ewald, however, and not Gerstenberg, who used a subject from northern antiquity for dramatic treatment; but it may well have been Gerstenberg who first directed the attention of Ewald to Saxo, to whom the young Danish dramatist turned for the subjects of his dramas.[4] In Ewald's dramas Gerstenberg gave back to Denmark what he had received from

[1] *Briefe über Merkwürdigkeiten der Litteratur, ed. cit.* p. 58.

[2] F. Rønning, *op. cit.* I, pp. 205 ff.

[3] *Ed. cit.* pp. 282 ff.

[4] A. M. Wagner, *op. cit.* II, p. 272.

her. Ewald's *Rolf Krage* and *Balders Død* had a considerable influence on the second renaissance of northern antiquity, that of the Danish Romantic movement; it was these dramas which struck the first sparks of the northern poetic fire in the heart of Oehlenschläger.[1] Rahbek, in an article on Klopstock, says: "Klopstock und Gerstenberg, dem Nestor der dänischen wie der deutschen Litteratur, verdanken wir unseren Ewald, den Dichter, der unserer Dichtkunst das war und ist, was Klopstock der Seinigen".[2] Rahbek goes on to speak of Gerstenberg as having been the first to recognize Ewald's genius and says that it was through Gerstenberg that Ewald met Klopstock. Of these things, however, there is no proof, and the degree of intimacy between Gerstenberg and Ewald still remains a matter for conjecture.[3] Ewald never mentions Gerstenberg in his writings, though he does speak in warm terms of Klopstock, Carstens and J. A. Scheibe. In 1766, while Ewald was living at Walkendorff's college, Gerstenberg stayed in the house of Ewald's stepfather. In a letter in 1818 to Rahbek Gerstenberg speaks of his *Ugolino* as having given rise to "theatralische Gespräche" between himself and Ewald; but he goes on to say: "Ich zweifle aber sehr, dasz diese Gespräche irgend einen Einflusz auf das gehabt haben, was späterhin aus ihm geworden ist, um so mehr sogar, da eben diese meine Excentricität weder bey Carstens noch bey seiner Gesellschaft viel Beyfall finden konnte".[4] It was while Gerstenberg was living in the house of Ewald's stepfather that Frederick V of Denmark died, and to J. A. Scheibe, then court organist, was entrusted the task of

[1] "On n'en est plus a répéter timidement Resenius ou Mallet. Les ouvrages, les traductions, les imitations se multiplient, et ces antiquités vont jouer un grand rôle dans le romantique danois qui se forma au début du dix-neuvième siècle avec Oehlenschläger" (P. van Tieghem, *La Mythologie et l'ancienne poésie scandinaves dans la littérature européenne au dix-huitième siècle*, in *Edda*, 1920, p. 59).

[2] *Kieler Blätter*, XIX, 2, p. 239.

[3] "Man ved, at hofpræst Cramer læste 'Adam og Eva' op for professor Kall efterhaanden som det blev trykt. Maaske er det digteren Gerstenberg, der først har henledt Cramers opmærksomhed paa Ewald; og fra Gerstenberg og Cramer var det ikke vanskeligt at finde vejen til Klopstock" (F. Rønning, *op. cit.* II, p. 77).

[4] *Archiv f. d. Stud. der neueren Spr. und Lit.* CXXXVI, p. 25.

selecting a suitable mourning cantata on the king's death. Both Rahbek and Friedrich Münter assert[1] that it was Gerstenberg who persuaded Ewald to write a poem,[2] and induced Kapellmeister Scheibe to give Ewald's poem the preference.[3] Gerstenberg himself states expressly the share which he had in Ewald's success: "Den Auftrag zur Trauer-Cantate erhielt Ewald auf meinen Rath vom Kapellmeister Scheibe, der sie auch aufführte...".[4] In the *Schleswiger Briefe*[5] Gerstenberg mentions Ewald's cantata in very laudatory terms.

The absence of any allusion by Ewald to Gerstenberg or his works is curious. It is difficult to believe that Ewald did not read the *Schleswiger Briefe*. The young Danish writer, conscious of the deficiencies in his own literary education, thirsty for knowledge, desirous at all times of increasing his literary range, must have, more than most of his contemporaries, been able to appreciate the boldness and strength of Gerstenberg's critical ideas, particularly of those on Shakespeare. With his letters on Scandinavian mythology, on nationality in literature and the drama, on Shakespeare—all matters in which Ewald was keenly interested—Gerstenberg must have played a part, directly, or indirectly through Klopstock, in Ewald's development.

In the nineteenth and twenty-first letters of the *Schleswiger Briefe* Gerstenberg gives in German translation his model for the *Gedicht eines Skalden*, Tullin's *Die neue Edda oder Gylphs zweyte Reise*.[6]

With his *Gedicht eines Skalden* (1766) Gerstenberg showed how this northern material could be used not merely for the learned consideration of philologists and antiquarians, but also

[1] Rahbek and Nyerup, *Christian VII*, 1828, I, pp. 47–66.

[2] Jørgensen says that it was the Rector of Copenhagen University who asked Ewald to write the poem. See *Hesperus*, I (1820), p. 12.

[3] Of Scheibe Ewald speaks gratefully. See Johannes Ewald, *Samlede Skrifter*, Copenhagen, 1914–24, V, p. 233.

[4] L. Bobé, *J. Ewalds Levnet og Meninger*, Copenhagen, 1911, p. 320.

[5] *Ed. cit.* p. 105. Gerstenberg, in writing of Klopstock's elegy, *Rothschilds Gräber*, quotes the opening lines of Ewald's recitative.

[6] The opinion has been expressed that Gerstenberg found the source for the *Gedicht eines Skalden* in a poem by O. F. Müller; see A. Blanck, *Den nordiska Renässansen*, Stockholm, 1911, pp. 136 ff.

for the creation of literature possessing a human interest. The *Gedicht eines Skalden* is not a great poem, but it was the first modern poem to handle successfully a subject from northern antiquity. Compared to earlier Danish attempts it strikes a much more genuine and convincing note. The *Dänische Journal* of 1767 praises Gerstenberg's poem highly: "Der Dichter hat in demselben auch die eigentümliche Denkart und Mythologie der alten Bewohner Dänemarks glücklich angebracht, und in den Gesängen wird mit der Versart und dem Sylbenmasze auf eine freie und der Natur der Sache gemäsze Weise abgewechselt".[1] In the description of "Valholl" in his *Gedicht eines Skalden* Gerstenberg pays a generous tribute to Frederick V, the patron of the German circle.

H. F. Abrahamson,[2] the author of *Et Forslag angaaende Kæmpeviserne*,[3] first became acquainted with the northern folk-songs through Gerstenberg.[4] Abrahamson had some knowledge of Icelandic and with Rahbek and Nyerup edited the *Folkeviser* and made the first attempt at a complete Danish *Sprachlehre* for Germans.[5] His enthusiasm for northern antiquity subsequently led him, as was the case with other Danish writers, to turn against the German influence in Denmark; and this, although he was himself of German origin. He regarded it as a hindrance to the development of what was genuinely Danish. With C. H. Pram,[6] too, Gerstenberg was acquainted, although it is not easy to determine what influence Gerstenberg exercised over him. Pram was actively interested in the enlightenment of the people, and his *Stærkodder* (1785) was the first attempt at a national Danish epic founded on northern antiquity.

Gerstenberg's contributions to the *Hamburgische neue Zeitung* are not so interesting from a Danish point of view as the *Schleswiger Briefe*. They treat of German, French and

[1] I, p. 106.

[2] 1744–1812.

[3] *Bibliothek for nyttige Skrifter*, 1772.

[4] F. Rønning, *op. cit.* II, p. 378.

[5] In later years Gerstenberg told his friend Rahbek that Abrahamson was the only critic who had properly understood his *Ugolino* (see A. M. Wagner, *op. cit.* I, p. 94).

[6] 1756–1821.

English works and were written for a German circle of readers.

In 1775 Gerstenberg, through the influence of A. P. Bernstorff, was appointed Danish Resident in Lübeck. While there he was friendly with K. F. Cramer and Vosz, and knew, too, Overbeck, Boie, the Stolbergs, Sprickmann, and Biester. His financial position was a source of great distress to him, and in 1783 influential friends in Copenhagen tried to help him by obtaining permission for him to sell his office in Lübeck. A buyer was found at a price of 20,000 daler. Gerstenberg, however, found it difficult to obtain a new post, and Copenhagen remained deaf to the entreaties of his friends. The younger Bernstorff and Schimmelmann considered him irresponsible in money matters and not very fond of work, and they therefore refused him the appointment then vacant in the Royal Library.[1] From the point of view of literary production Gerstenberg's importance ceased with his departure from Copenhagen. As early as the second edition of *Der Hypochondrist* (1771) there is to be seen that bitterness against his contemporaries, which helped to darken Gerstenberg's later life; when he had realized their greatness his part was played. His was a weak nature, and, his immediate ends accomplished, he ceased to be a force of further significance in his literature.[2] In 1785 his favourite work, *Minona, oder die Angelsachsen*, "a tragic melodrama", was published. Its ill-success embittered the unhappy author still more. His latter years were spent in philosophic studies, particularly of Kant; but the results of his philosophic labours were never published.

That Gerstenberg was regarded as an authority on the Danish literature of his time is indicated by a letter of K. L. Rahbek (1766–1830), the author of *Den danske Digtekunst under Frederik V* (1819). The letter was written to Gerstenberg in 1818 and asked him for information as to the period of Danish literature

[1] See *Allgemeine deutsche Biographie*, IX, p. 65.

[2] O. Fischer, "Gerstenberg als Rezensent der Hamburgischen neuen Zeitung" (1767–71) in *Euphorion*, X (1903) p. 75.

during which Gerstenberg had lived in Denmark. Gerstenberg responded in helpful fashion, and the two writers maintained a friendly correspondence for some time. In 1819 Rahbek in his speech at the "Gedächtnisfeier" for Klopstock in Altona, mentions Gerstenberg as the "Nestor" of German and Danish literatures.[1] *Den danske Tilskuer*, a Danish periodical edited by K. L. Rahbek, bore the following dedication: "Det danske som det tydske Parnassus ærværdige Ældste, Klopstocks, Ewalds og Abrahamsons Ven, H. W. von Gerstenberg ærbødigen helliget".[2]

To Johann Elias Schlegel, the forerunner of the German circle in Copenhagen, Gerstenberg bears in many important respects a striking resemblance. Both men were exceptionally well fitted for the critical work which formed so important a part of their activity. Their wide reading and knowledge of languages gave to their "national" ideas a breadth and an appreciative tolerance, which enabled them to see the good points of the literatures of nations other than their own. They realized that Shakespeare's dramas and the northern sagas were natural outgrowths from the national character. A real interest in, and knowledge of, Danish literature, ancient and modern, were common to them both, as one can see from a perusal of *Der Fremde* and of the *Schleswiger Briefe*. In the old northern histories they saw a new and fertile field for exploitation by poetry and the drama. Elias Schlegel founded the reputation of Copenhagen as a literary centre with *Der Fremde*, and with the *Schleswiger Briefe* he increased the Danish capital's reputation and brought Denmark into the main stream of European literature. Both were greater as theoreticians than as creators. Schlegel had declared that criticism should not be literature's harsh and pedantic stepmother, but rather the sympathetic interpreter, guide and friend, and Gerstenberg emphasized this still more strongly. To the movement begun in Denmark by Gram, Langebek and Holberg, of creating for literature a wider and more generously appreciative public, of popularizing literature

[1] *Kieler Blätter*, 1819, II, p. 239.

[2] *Tilskueren*, II, 1819.

and art with the middle classes, both men made an important contribution. Gerstenberg, by his translations of such works as Nicolai's *Abhandlung vom Trauerspiel*, F. Riccoboni's *L'Art du Théâtre* and Noverre's *Lettre sur la Danse et sur les Ballets*, showed that he, as well as Schlegel, was alive to the necessity of educating the Danish public as to the needs and aims of the theatre and tragedy. Gerstenberg, like Schlegel, was ahead of his contemporaries in regarding comedy as an important educational element and not necessarily inferior to tragedy. French tragedy, with its all-too-prevalent "Verliebtheit", found in both resolute opponents, just as Shakespeare and the English theatre found in them warm supporters. Lessing recognized in Gerstenberg's, as he did in Elias Schlegel's critical works, the truth and vitality of ideas which were later to prove important to the development of German literature.

There was little that Gerstenberg touched, which did not prove fruitful. He had in a high degree the unusual gift of divining in what direction the real development of literature lay, from what source it was to take new inspiration and new life. He had a mind sensitive, impressionable and enthusiastic, yet with an unerring sense of the essential in literature. Had he possessed the tenacity, the balance and the powers of work of an Elias Schlegel or of a Lessing, he would have occupied a greater place. As it was, he reflected almost all the important literary movements of the quickly-moving times in which he lived. He passed from the pre-Kantian anacreonticism to romanticism and made some contribution to all the important literary movements compassed in this development. Few writers make more than one important contribution to critical literature. Gerstenberg made many. His style matched his ideas, suggestive, provocative, fertile and always independent. "Die schöne Begeisterung für alles Tatkräftige", so characteristic of Gerstenberg in his vigorous, hopeful years, an element which had so strong an influence on the "Sturm und Drang" movement in Germany, was not without its effect in Denmark, where, so short a time before, the religious hymn had been regarded as the highest form of literary expression. In stimulating the impulse to the poetic regeneration of the northern mythology and sagas in Denmark, Gerstenberg helped to inaugurate that series of interactions between Danish and German literatures which lasted on into the nineteenth century, through Herder to Grimm and Uhland. Klopstock's genius marked the beginning of a more enthusiastic, a more imaginative note in Danish literature, and Gerstenberg played an important part in interpreting genius to the literary public of Denmark. He continues what Holberg had begun, the work of bringing Denmark into contact with eighteenth-century Europe.

CHAPTER FOUR

J. A. CRAMER'S CONTRIBUTION to DANISH LITERATURE

It was through J. A. Cramer[1] that Klopstock had been introduced to the circle of the "Bremer Beiträger" in Leipzig, and among the friends whom the author of the *Messias* celebrated in his ode, *An die Freunde*, Cramer was one of the closest. After Leipzig their paths lay apart for a few years. When Klopstock went to Copenhagen, Cramer was called to a pastorate in Quedlinburg, where he soon acquired a more than local reputation as a preacher. In the prosperity and congenial surroundings of his new home Klopstock did not forget his friend of the Leipzig student days, and he soon found an opportunity to recommend Cramer to his patron, the Danish minister, Count Bernstorff. In 1753 there was a vacancy as court preacher in Copenhagen and in 1754 Cramer was appointed to the position. There had been a possibility mentioned by Meta Moller, later Klopstock's wife, that a Dane would be appointed: "Ich hatte den Tag vorher eben in den Zeitungen gelesen, dasz ein gewisser Däne zum Oberhofprediger erwählt wäre, und damit war nun meine ganze Hofnung aus! Es gab mir zwar eine nicht kleine *pique* gegen unsern König...".[2] In a letter to Rabener dated March 16, 1754, Cramer says that he has accepted the royal summons to Copenhagen and has received a very gracious letter from Count von Moltke.[3] Büsching tells of meeting Cramer in Hamburg in April, 1754, on his way to Copenhagen.[4]

[1] Born 1723 at Jöhstadt, Saxony; studied in Leipzig; 1745–8 lecturer in the University of Leipzig; 1748 entered the church; 1750–4 pastor in Quedlinburg; 1754–71 court preacher in Copenhagen; died in 1788.

[2] J. M. Lappenberg, *Briefe von und an Klopstock*, Braunschweig, 1867, p. 123; see also pp. 128–9.

[3] G. W. Rabener, *Briefe*, ed. C. F. Weisze, p. 167.

[4] *Beyträge zu den Lebensgeschichten denkwürdiger Personen*, VI, p. 231.

Cramer's intellectual accomplishments, his modest, unassuming character and his unusual social gifts soon attracted both Germans and Danes. At the beginning of his stay in Copenhagen he does not appear to have seen as much of his friend Klopstock, as he desired.[1] Klopstock moved in court circles, to which Cramer, in spite of his position as court preacher, had not as yet an easy entrée. Between Cramer and Gerstenberg there soon developed a close friendship. The steady, severe, but kind and understanding Cramer gave many a useful piece of advice to the restless, wayward Gerstenberg. Hardly a day passed without their seeing each other.[2] Cramer's house in the Petristræde soon became a meeting-place for the German colony and during the first years of his residence in Copenhagen it was with members of the German circle that Cramer came chiefly into contact.[3] Through his appointment to a professorship at the University of Copenhagen he had better opportunities of meeting the Danes, particularly Danish students, and of these opportunities he made full use. Cramer did not feel any of the sense of superiority to the Danish people,[4] revealed by other members of the German circle and by Klopstock in particular.[5] He admired the Danish character[6] and was grateful to the country, which had given him a comfortable and assured living. He frequently alluded to it as his "second fatherland". He was always mindful of the intellectual and literary aspirations and material needs of the Danish people, and there was no other

[1] Letter from Cramer to Rabener, dated May 16, 1756; see Rabener, *Briefe*, *ed. cit.* p. 172.

[2] K. L. von Knebel, *Literarischer Nachlasz*, ed. Varnhagen und Mundt, Leipzig, 1840, II, p. 85.

[3] "Som Fremmed og ved det han hos den afdøde Geheimeraad Bernstorff kom strax i Selskab med de herværende Tydske, varede det noget, inden han lærte at kjende Nationen, og Nationen ham, men tilsidst vandt de begge derved" (P. F. Suhm, *Samlede Skrifter*, x, p. 28).

[4] *Nyt theol. Bibl.* III (1823), p. 10.

[5] See Chapter II, p. 75.

[6] In conversation with Frederick V Cramer expressed this admiration on more than one occasion. "Han elskede de Danske og deres National-Karakter, forsømte ingen Leilighed at forskaffe velfortiente Danske Fordeele og Understøttelse hos den elskværdigste blandt Kongerne; ingen Under, at vi Danske igjen elskede ham, og elske ham og hans Minde endnu efter Døden" (H. J. Birch, *Haandbog for Geistlige*, 1795, II, p. 161).

member of the German circle who enjoyed as much popularity in Denmark with all classes as did Cramer, "den Ejegode".[1] At the frequent meetings of the circle in Bernstorff's town house in the Bredgade and in summer at his country seat, "Bernstorff", Cramer was a regular attender. With the Danish minister himself he seems to have been on terms of close friendship.[2] In summer Cramer lived at Sandholm in the parish of Blovstrød, a mile from Hørsholm. He took a keen interest in agriculture and was the first to introduce the cultivation of potatoes into Denmark.[3]

As a preacher Cramer enjoyed a great reputation. His sermons were regarded by the Danes as models of theological oratory. During his stay in Copenhagen many of them were published, together with some of his poetic translations of the psalms. Bishop Hersleb, who, in Cramer's time, was regarded as the greatest of Danish preachers, was declared by Danish critics to have been much inferior to Cramer both in elegance of expression and in depth of religious feeling.[4] His success as a preacher Cramer did not owe to his manner of delivery. He was not particularly eloquent; his voice was too high-pitched and caused too loud an echo in the church, making him at times unintelligible.[5] His reputation as a preacher was not confined to Denmark. He was probably even better known in this respect in Germany,[6] and during the years after his arrival in Copenhagen he refused several attractive offers from abroad, in particular one from the Duke of Brunswick, who offered him an excellent position and the use of the Wolfenbüttel library. Cramer, preferring to remain in Denmark, refused the offer,

[1] A name bestowed on a popular Danish king of the eleventh century.

[2] On one occasion in Bernstorff's house, Cramer and Bernstorff, to settle a wager, competed with one another in the rapidity of mastering the contents of a book. Each of the two took a copy of the same book to a separate room. Resewitz, who had read the book, examined them and declared Bernstorff the winner. See F. Rønning, *op. cit.* I, p. 153.

[3] C. F. Bricka, *Dansk biografisk Lexikon*, IV, p. 102.

[4] *Nyt theol. Bibl.* III (1823), p. 7.

[5] F. Rønning, *op. cit.* I, p. 151.

[6] J. N. Wilse, *Rejseiagttagelser i nogle af de nordiske Lande*, Copenhagen, 1790–8, III, p. 329.

and received the personal thanks of King Frederick V for having done so. A Danish account of the interview says that at the audience Frederick took Cramer's hand and said: "Nu, min kære Cramer, ser jeg, at De er min sande Ven, da De ikke vil forlade mig. Nu er jeg ikke i Stand til at belønne Dem, men jeg vil sørge for Dem".[1] As an immediate result of this royal approval Cramer's salary at the "Slotskirke" was increased by 600 daler and in 1765 he was appointed to the vacant chair of Theology in the University of Copenhagen, as successor to Professor Otto Bang, in spite of the sixteenth-century law, which declared that no one person should be allowed to hold a chair in the university and be court preacher at the same time.[2]

When Cramer came to Copenhagen the pietistic movement had spent its greatest force. In introducing rationalistic ideas from Germany, Cramer was helping to prepare the way for the "Oplysningstid" in the country of his adoption. Denmark needed at that time theologians who could separate the wheat from the chaff in these new ideas, and for such a task Cramer was well fitted. Before his time it had not been thought necessary for the professors of Theology in the University of Copenhagen to keep in touch with new theological ideas. Suhm relates a conversation which he himself had had with Marcus Wøldike, at that time professor of Theology in the University of Copenhagen. Suhm asked Wøldike whether Cappel or his opponents were right with regard to a disputed point in the Hebrew language. Wøldike answered: "Uden Tvivl, Cappel, men det maatte man ej sige højt".[3] Cramer, however, foreigner as he was, was not fettered by the inherited traditions of the Danish professors. A pupil of Ernesti, Cramer introduced with Bernstorff's approval the new "historical-critical" treatment of theology, begun by J. D. Michaelis in Göttingen and by Semler in Halle. His lectures were chiefly on Exegesis, Church History and Homiletics. They were delivered in German or Latin, for Cramer, although he understood Danish, had, like most

[1] J. K. Høst, *Clio*, II, pp. 77–8. [2] *Nyt theol. Bibl.* III (1823), p. 15.
[3] *Ibid.* p. 17; also quoted by Rønning, *op. cit.* I, p. 272.

foreigners, considerable difficulty in speaking it. He was the first theologian in Copenhagen University to lecture on Church History. Since attendance at these lectures was not necessary to qualify for the examinations, the number of his students was not large. At the last of these lectures there were only two students, and one of them was his eldest son.[1] But that Cramer awakened great interest by his other lectures and was popular with the Danish students is attested by a tribute from J. H. Taber, one of his theological students:

> Den Popularitet, den uplumrede Spejlklarhed i hans Foredrag, forenet med nøje Bekjendtskab med alt det Ny i den theologiske Videnskab og en øvet Færdighed i at have alt det, han havde læst, strax ved Haanden under Forelæsningerne, bandt ham til hans Tilhørerne, især dem, som ikke vare altfor raa eller for lidt forberedte til at forstaa hans ciceronianske Indklædning og platoniske Foredragsmaade.[2]

Cramer started a "sermon club" for students which was continued after his day; the proceedings were in the Danish language. During his time at the university Cramer had a dispute with Professor Holm, senior professor of Theology, on a question connected with Cramer's refutation of some points raised by the English theologian, Taylor. In the course of the dispute Holm accused Cramer of being a friend of Basedow, and declared that Basedow had boasted of their friendship in certain books in which he attacked Christianity.[3]

Cramer had not the same opportunity in Copenhagen of displaying his business abilities as he had later as chancellor of the University of Kiel; but as a member of the faculty of the University of Copenhagen he did a great deal in a financial and legal way, and he was charged with drawing up several petitions and with submitting them to the government. One of these petitions (1771) contained most of the reforms in university and

[1] *Philomususes Lykønsknings Brev til Balle*, Copenhagen, 1772.

[2] Extract from J. H. Taber's diary in *Dansk Maanedsskrift*, I (1865), p. 104. See also "Tabers Autobiographie" in Block, *Den svenske Geistligheds Historie*, II, p. 437.

[3] *Kirkehist. Samlinger*, IV, p. 329.

school during the last half of the eighteenth century in Denmark.[1] The foundation of the pension fund of Copenhagen University was due partly to Cramer's efforts.

As editor of the "moral" periodical, *Der nordische Aufseher*,[2] a journal which was to have a fairly long line of Danish successors, Cramer made a more important contribution to Danish intellectual life than as a preacher or as a university teacher. The moral periodicals did not start in Denmark until a much later date than in Germany,[3] and *Der nordische Aufseher* belongs to the type of moral weeklies in vogue in Germany during the first half of the eighteenth century. Under Frederick V the influence of Germany on Danish intellectual life was at its highest, and in publishing *Der nordische Aufseher*, Cramer could count on a receptive public, which included the Danish court and aristocracy, and on the collaboration of Klopstock and of other able German writers, who were at that time in Copenhagen. The fifth and last volume of Holberg's *Moralske Epistler* had appeared in 1754 and these letters, with their easy, urbane tone and their variety of subject, had already created an audience in Denmark for this type of publication.[4] The reasons, which impelled Cramer to found *Der nordische Aufseher*, are not difficult to divine. The German circle in Copenhagen needed a journal in which to express its views. Already Zürich and Leipzig had their periodicals, and now Berlin had an organ in the *Bibliothek der schönen Wissenschaften und der freyen Künste*. Cramer had already had experience in journalistic work. At the early age of twenty he had edited, with Mylius, a paper entitled *Hallische Bemühungen*.[5] He had contributed to the *Bremer Beiträge*[6] and edited the moral weekly, *Der Schutzgeist*[7] and, with the collaboration of Ebert and Giseke, had brought out *Der Jüngling*.[8]

[1] Baden's *Universitets Journal*, Copenhagen, 1793, II, 2, pp. 49–61.

[2] Continued from January 5, 1758 to January 8, 1761, 3 vols., Copenhagen and Leipzig.

[3] The early Danish periodicals were chiefly translations, as, for example, *Den fordanskede Patriot* (1726) of Joachim Wielandt, a translation of *Der Patriot* (Hamburg).

[4] L. Magon, *op. cit.* p. 192.

[5] 1743. [6] 1746. [7] 1746. [8] 1747.

Most of the articles in *Der nordische Aufseher* were written by Cramer. Klopstock wrote some on language, poetry and art.[1] Funk wrote a few articles on music. Basedow wrote one on the universality of the moral law, an article which Cramer altered before printing. Meta Klopstock and J. F. Barisien were also contributors.

Thirteen years earlier Elias Schlegel had made a similar venture in Denmark with a moral periodical[2] and with marked success; and Schlegel had possessed but few of the advantages with which Cramer launched *Der nordische Aufseher*.[3] Like *Der Fremde*, *Der nordische Aufseher* was written in German. The general use of the Danish language in literature did not at the time of the appearance of *Der nordische Aufseher* seem to have advanced very far[4]; but Cramer feels it necessary to apologize for the use of the German language instead of the Danish:

> Ich schreibe in der deutschen Sprache, weil ich ihrer mächtiger bin, als der Sprache meines zweyten Vaterlandes. Unterdesz sind die Dänen und die Deutschen so sehr verwandte Völker, dasz billig keine Sprache auf die andere eifersüchtig seyn musz.[5]

In introducing *Der nordische Aufseher* Cramer tells his readers that the periodical is written by Arthur Ironside, son of Nestor Ironside, whose family went to England with Canute. Nestor Ironside had been Inspector of Manners in Great Britain, and his son resolves to do for his second fatherland what his father had done for England.[6] Pre-eminent among these services *Der nordische Aufseher* regarded the furthering of the cause of virtue and the improvement of taste; and in spite of the limitations of Cramer's periodical from a journalistic point of view, the articles all express an indefatigable striving towards the general good:

[1] Klopstock contributed twenty moral and literary articles to *Der nordische Aufseher*. The most important of these were: *Von der Sprache der Poesie*; *Gedanken über die Natur der Poesie*; *Von der besten Art über Gott zu denken*; *Beurtheilung der Winkelmannschen Gedanken über die Nachahmung der griechischen Werke in den schönen Künsten*.

[2] *Der Fremde*, 1745–6.

[3] See Chapter I, pp. 36 ff.

[4] N. M. Petersen, *op. cit.* v, 1, p. 23.

[5] *Der nordische Aufseher*, 1, Copenhagen and Leipzig, 1758, Article 1.

[6] *Ibid.* 1, p. 9. It may be remembered that Ironside is the name assumed by Steele in *The Guardian*.

Mein Vorhaben soll seyn, den Fleiszigen in seinem Fleisze zu erhalten: den Bescheidnen in Schutz zu nehmen: den Unverschämten und den Müssiggängern die Schamröthe wiederzugeben, die er verloren hat: den Guten und Frommen zu ermuntern: den Stolzen und Feigen in seiner Blösze zu zeigen, und den Ruchlosen und Boshaften zu schanden zu machen. Dieses alles kann nicht geschehen, ohne mit der vollkommensten Unpartheylichkeit nicht allein die Pflichten, sondern auch die Höflichkeit des Lebens zu beobachten.[1]

The title of the second article, *Von der Freude über das allgemeine Beste*, strikes the note for the whole of *Der nordische Aufseher*. "Das gute Herz" is prized above wit and cleverness. It is assumed that no new truths will be expected.[2] The fight against free-thinking, begun in the *Bremer Beiträge*, is made one of the most important tasks of the Copenhagen periodical. It was, perhaps, unfortunate from a literary point of view that religion bulked so largely in *Der nordische Aufseher*, but Cramer regarded a religious training as a necessary part of the equipment of a good citizen. The importance of the purely religious articles, from the Danish point of view, lay in the fact that there was presented in them a clear account of the religious revolution then taking place. New ideas, many of them from Germany, were brought in and opposed to the old orthodoxy. Cramer advocates the claims of the Bible not only as a moral book, but also as a book which may afford aesthetic pleasure to the reader.[3] He tried to breathe a new enthusiasm into the dry Protestant dogma, and, while stressing the imaginative element in the scriptures, endeavoured to create in Denmark a wider audience for the poetry of Klopstock.

The majority of the social and educational articles in *Der nordische Aufseher* are by Cramer. There are a few by Klopstock, but where the pietistically-minded Klopstock appeals to the feelings, to enthusiasms and ideals, Cramer fights against

[1] *Der nordische Aufseher*, I, pp. 7–8. Even the poems by Klopstock and Cramer in *Der nordische Aufseher* are generally preceded by a prose introduction of a moral or religious character.

[2] "Unter denen Wahrheiten, welche das menschliche Herz bessern sollen, sind die nützlichsten immer auch die bekanntesten, und eben diese können nicht zu oft wiederholt werden."

[3] *Ibid.* Article 57, *Über die Lektüre der Bibel.*

crime and treats of practical social questions, and he is especially interested in the education of children, both in their religious and general moral education. In his numerous articles on these subjects[1] he expresses sound and useful ideas, and gained a place in the history of the pedagogic science, founded soon afterwards by Rousseau, Pestalozzi and by his friend Basedow. In the education of women, too, Cramer takes an interest, but he holds no brief for the emancipation of women, and his ideas on this subject contain nothing new. To science and the arts there is not much space devoted, although painting and music are not altogether neglected.[2]

Since the German circle in Copenhagen was formed round Klopstock, poetry in *Der nordische Aufseher* occupies an important place. Cramer tries to do for Denmark what the "Bremer Beiträger" had done for Germany several years before, to create an audience and to lay the foundations for an independent national literature. Abstinence from criticism had been part of the programme of the *Bremer Beiträge*, and this principle Cramer now applies to his periodical.[3] "Sympathetic and unpretentious" accounts of literary works are promised as well as some observations on the best way of enjoying and judging them, and warnings against works in which genius and wit are used to hurt religion and morality.[4] Essays on Corneille and Shakespeare were published as well as a translation of Young's *Essay on Original Composition*. Cramer expressed the wish that a Dane would translate Batteux' *Les Beaux Arts réduits à un même principe* (1746), with additions suitable to the literary conditions prevailing in Denmark.[5] Thirty-three articles of *Der nordische Aufseher* were devoted to a consideration of twenty different authors. Among them were eight

[1] *Ibid.* Articles 27, 46, 47, 48, 50, 88–93. In Articles 46–48 Cramer gives an account of his own education.

[2] Articles 80, 152, 153 and 179 by G. B. Funk are on music.

[3] Klopstock would hardly have contributed to a critical journal.

[4] *Der nordische Aufseher*, I, p. 14.

[5] In 1773 Jens Hvass translated Batteux' work into Danish and added to it his own ideas on the subject.

German authors, seven English, three French, and two Scandinavians, the latter being C. B. Tullin[1] and J. S. Sneedorff.

With *En Maidag* of Tullin the history of modern Scandinavian poetry may be said to have begun. Article 52[2] of *Der nordische Aufseher* treats of this work. Cramer realized its promise, and he was the first critic to make the merits of the poem known not only in Denmark and abroad, but also in Christiania, Tullin's birthplace. Tullin's poem[3] is a moral work descriptive of nature, on the model of Pope and Young. It was written on the occasion of the marriage of Tullin's friend, Morten Leuch, with Jomfru Collett. *Der nordische Aufseher* expresses pleasure over its appearance and says that, although it is written on a somewhat banal subject, yet it contains so much true poetic beauty that it deserves close attention. Tribute is paid to the liveliness and boldness of its language and to the loftiness and novelty of its metaphors. The critic gives an outline of the story of the poem as well as extracts in Danish, with German translations.[4] Cramer found several faults with the poem. Tullin answers these criticisms and shows that through his ignorance of the Danish language Cramer has not properly understood some passages. But Tullin was grateful to Cramer for his generous appreciation of the poem and acknowledged that he had contributed largely to laying the foundation of his, Tullin's, reputation. It was through this article that Lessing first became acquainted with Tullin's poem, and he agreed with Cramer in his appreciation of its quality.[5]

[1] Born 1728 in Christiania; 1745–8 studied law in Copenhagen; 1748 returned to Christiania, where he died in 1765.

[2] November 9, 1758.

[3] *En Maidag* was published in 1758 in Copenhagen without Tullin's knowledge or consent.

[4] *Der nordische Aufseher*, I, pp. 477–8. The account of *En Maidag* concludes with the words: "Mehr Gedichte in diesem Tone würden dem Genie und dem Herzen des Verfassers und zugleich der Nation Ehre machen, wenn er zumal sich nichts erlauben wollte, was dem verirrten Geschmacke des groszen Haufens schmeichelt und Kennern wahrer Schönheiten niemals gefallen kann" (*ibid.* p. 490).

[5] "Erfindung, Anlage, Einrichtung und Ausführung verrathen einen von der Natur begünstigten Geist, der noch mehr erwarten läszt. Dieses Urtheil

It was, however, in his relations with J. S. Sneedorff[1] that Cramer exercised the most definite and valuable influence on the education of the Danish public. In many important respects the ideas of the two men are similar. With Sneedorff, as with Cramer, morality and patriotic ideas are closely connected in their writings. Although Sneedorff finds in the Danish absolute monarchy the ideal form of government, yet he realizes that the spirit in which a government is administered is more important than its form, and the cultivation of religion and virtue he regards as necessary to the well-being of a state.[2] Hence his complete approval of the ideas expressed in *Der nordische Aufseher*. Cramer was acquainted with Sneedorff's moral writings of the years 1758–60, and he gives a favourable account[3] of his *Fortsættelse af Babues Breve*[4]; he brought Sneedorff's name before a very much wider audience, as that of one of the foremost Danish prose-writers of the eighteenth century. It was from Cramer's periodical that Sneedorff took the idea of a weekly periodical in the Danish language, and to the carrying out of this idea Cramer lent all the weight of his influence and prestige. In the last number of his periodical[5] Cramer announces that a Danish weekly would try to continue the work which he had begun. *Den patriotiske Tilskuer*, for such was the name of Sneedorff's periodical, appeared twice a week from January 20, 1761, to December 31, 1763. It was printed at Sorø and was in Danish, a new and significant feature. Most of the articles were written by Sneedorff himself. His style in *Den patriotiske Tilskuer* is by no means so dryly philosophical as that of *Der nordische Aufseher*. He adopts a more popular tone and shows a wider tolerance. The Holbergian characters in Sneedorff's periodical

ist keine Schmeicheley; denn die Strophen, welche er im Originale und in einer Übersetzung daraus anführt, sind so vortreflich, dass ich nicht weis, ob wir Deutsche jemals ein solches Hochzeitgedicht gehabt haben" (Lessing, *Sämtliche Schriften*, ed. Lachmann-Muncker, VIII, p. 126).

1 Born in 1724 at Sorø; 1739–46 studied at Copenhagen; 1747–51 studied at Göttingen; 1751–61 professor of Legal and Political Science at Sorø Academy. Died in 1764.

2 J. S. Sneedorff, *Skrifter*, Copenhagen, 1775–7, VII, Fortale.

3 *Der nordische Aufseher*, Article 140.

4 Sorø, 1760.

5 *Der nordische Aufseher*, Article 193; Ankündigung vom 8 Januar, 1761.

remind us more of *Der Fremde* than of *Der nordische Aufseher*. But the influence of the latter periodical is clearly perceptible in the articles on the general good and common interest of the state.[1] From *Der nordische Aufseher* Sneedorff inherited a close association with the Danish court and king. The dedication on the first page of *Den patriotiske Tilskuer* is "Til Kongen",[2] and Frederick V helped to defray the cost of production of the periodical. Both Bernstorff and Moltke showed their sympathy with Sneedorff's venture.[3] The success of *Den patriotiske Tilskuer* resulted in a great increase in the number of Danish periodicals in Denmark. In 1766 *Den danske Proteus* appeared; in 1772 *De Fremmede* of J. Ewald (not, however, printed until later), and from 1791 to 1816 K. L. Rahbek's *Den danske Tilskuer*.

Although *Der nordische Aufseher* bears the stamp of the German circle, of which it expresses very faithfully the intellectual direction and influence, yet its editors regarded themselves as good Danish subjects. Many occasional poems in the periodical express loyalty or gratitude to the reigning house. At the close of the second article Cramer speaks of Denmark's happy fate and of the beneficent reign of the good king, Frederick V. Events at court and political celebrations are treated sympathetically. Warm support is given to Bernstorff's moral and religious ideas. There is not much politics in *Der nordische Aufseher*, but what there is, is inspired by Bernstorff's ministry. The improvement of the lot of the agricultural labourer in Denmark, the development of agriculture, the establishment of manufactures and the support of home industries, all of them ideas of Bernstorff, find in Cramer a strong supporter.[4] Inoculation, which Bernstorff was advocating in the face of considerable opposition from the people, doctors and church,[5] was

[1] A. M. Luehrs, *Der nordische Aufseher*, Diss., Heidelberg, 1909, p. 137.

[2] Klopstock's poem on the death of Queen Louise bore the dedication *An den König*; see Chapter II, p. 77.

[3] Sneedorff, *Skrifter*, VIII, p. 428.

[4] *Der nordische Aufseher*, Articles 119 and 127b.

[5] Aage Friis, *op. cit.* II, pp. 44 ff.

supported by *Der nordische Aufseher*, but on moral not scientific grounds. Mention was made of new scientific discoveries which might prove of benefit to Denmark.

From *Der nordische Aufseher* the reader may gain a picture of the social habits and vices of the Denmark of the time. There are articles against gambling,[1] against bad language on the stage,[2] against the thirst for titles and extravagance in dress[3] and against the poor pay of teachers.[4] Throughout we are reminded that the periodical is intended for a Danish audience. In some articles the Danes are addressed directly.[5] The Germans are called "Ausländer".[6] There are allusions to places in or near Copenhagen, such as Frederiksberg,[7] the Rosenborg Garden,[8] and the Wallpromenade.[9] Such Danish words as "Jomfrue" and "Frøken" occur frequently. There is no article in *Der nordische Aufseher* which discusses peculiarly German affairs or conditions. The circulation of the paper was chiefly in Copenhagen, and only in book form did it go abroad. Although Danish literature is only spoken of twice, in the articles on Tullin and Sneedorff, Danish writers and scholars are frequently mentioned,[10] as well as several literary works which had been published in Copenhagen, for example, Basedow's *Praktische Philosophie*, Regenfusz' *Conchylienwerk* and Funk's translation of Du Bos.

It was in 1759 that Lessing first made mention of *Der nordische Aufseher*.[11] His criticism was not altogether unfavourable; he paid due tribute to what he regarded as good in it,[12] and

1 *Der nordische Aufseher*, Articles 14, 20, 32, 45, 53.

2 *Ibid.* Articles 55, 56, 67, 69, 70.

3 *Ibid.* Articles 12, 34, 189.

4 *Ibid.* Article 14.

5 *Ibid.* Articles 8, 63, 66, 116.

6 *Ibid.* Article 52.

7 *Ibid.* Article 70.

8 *Ibid.* Articles 27, 70.

9 *Ibid.* Article 70.

10 *Ibid.* Article 184.

11 *Briefe die neueste Litteratur betreffend*, Nos. 48–51.

12 "Kopenhagen hat bereits an dem Fremden (einem Werke des sel. Hrn. Prof. Schlegels) eine dergleichen Schrift von sehr vorzüglichem Werthe aufzuweisen. Und nun kann es leicht kommen, dasz der nordische Aufseher ein allgemeines Vorurtheil für die deutschen Werke des Witzes, welche in Dänemark erscheinen, veranlassen hilft..." (Lessing, *Schriften*, *ed. cit.* VIII, p. 122). "Was der nordische Aufseher zum besten der unstudirten Liebhaber guter Schriften gethan hat, beläuft sich ohngefehr auf sechs oder sieben neuere Autores, aus welchen er, nach einer kurzen Beurtheilung, besonders merkwürdige und lehrreiche Stellen beybringt" (*ibid.* p. 125).

praised Cramer's article on Tullin's *Maidag*[1] and his satirical report on the new Amazons.[2] He praised, too, some of Klopstock's articles, particularly *Von der Sprache der Poesie*,[3] quoting several passages from it and recommending it to all writers.[4] With some of Klopstock's later poems in *Der nordische Aufseher* Lessing finds fault,[5] although he appreciated his poems in the first volume of the periodical; he does not seem to have been much impressed by Cramer's three odes in the same volume. He declares that Cramer's odes were those of a mere versifier and worthy of no criticism. He attacks Klopstock's article, *Von der besten Art über Gott zu denken*,[6] and finds fault with Cramer for declaring that to be upright one must needs be religious.[7] He is opposed to the latter's ideas on religious training for youth, and charges him with poor pulpit oratory and with using "eternal and schoolboyish parables". Basedow defends his friend Cramer against these charges in his *Vergleichung der Lehren und Schreibart des nordischen Aufsehers*[8]; but neither Basedow's nor Cramer's defence could weaken Lessing's points. In an article replying to Lessing's criticism Klopstock and Cramer collaborated to point out that the fine arts in Denmark might be helped by all literary men working together, and by the production of a non-critical journal on the lines of the *Bremer Beiträge*, although this journal was not mentioned by name. The preface to the third volume of *Der nordische Aufseher* shows the bitterness of the fight.

Lessing's attack on *Der nordische Aufseher* was prompted by the feeling that the tendency of this journal was to subject literature to the influence of a coterie of preachers of somewhat narrow views, and his criticisms from a German, if not from

[1] *Der nordische Aufseher*, Article 52.
[2] *Ibid.* Article 54.
[3] *Ibid.* Article 26. Described by Herder as the most important article in the first volume of *Der nordische Aufseher*; see Herder's *Werke*, ed. Suphan, I, p. 468.
[4] *Litteraturbrief* No. 51.
[5] "Lieder, die so voller Empfindung sind, dasz man oft gar nichts dabey empfindet" (*op. cit.*, p. 140).
[6] *Der nordische Aufseher*, Article 25.
[7] "Rechtschaffenheit ohne Religion sind widersprechende Begriffe" (*ibid.*, p. 127).
[8] Sorø, 1763.

a Danish, literary point of view were largely justified by the importance which literary criticism was then beginning to assume in Germany. For German readers this attack of Lessing destroyed the literary nimbus of the Copenhagen journal. Many of the articles in *Der nordische Aufseher* were inspired by an exaggerated piety and an arrogant orthodoxy.[1] While disclaiming any intention of striking a critical note, the authors did not attain to that easy, urbane, unpretentious style, which characterized *Der Fremde* or *Den patriotiske Tilskuer*. In his philosophical and religious essays Cramer was rather copious and diffuse; his style was often stiff and heavy and savoured too much of the pulpit. The light humorous element and the trivial novelties of the English periodicals, which might have relieved this heaviness, were rigorously excluded from Cramer's, probably because he thought that such lightness would hardly be in keeping with his position in the church. Klopstock's moral essays are not entertaining and his attitude was too often one of too patent superiority to his audience. One looks in vain for new truths in *Der nordische Aufseher*; what novelty there is, is in style and expression.[2] In the accounts of new books, a few general introductory remarks followed by quotations from the author himself make up the article.[3] A comparison between the criticisms of the same book in the *Litteraturbriefe* and in *Der nordische Aufseher* shows the great difference between the moral and critical weeklies.[4]

But Lessing was writing from a German point of view. The change from moral to critical periodicals was not reflected in

[1] In one of Klopstock's articles, *Auszug aus dem Protokoll des Unsichtbaren*, there is a character, Lucinde, who loves a free-thinker and is loved by him. She is not very hopeful of converting her lover and finds herself in a dilemma. Klopstock cannot understand that any woman could be in love with a free-thinker, a man whom she could not hope to meet in the next world, and he even expresses the doubt as to whether it is possible for a free-thinker to be really in love. See E. Bailly, *Étude sur Klopstock*, Paris, 1888, p. 296.

[2] *Bibliothek der schönen Wissenschaften*, v, 3, p. 277.

[3] Cp. *Der nordische Aufseher*, articles 169 and 170.

[4] For example, the criticisms of J. A. Schlegel's translation (1752) of Batteux' *Les beaux arts réduits à un même principe*. See P. M. Luehrs, *op. cit.* p. 79.

Denmark until a much later date than in Germany, and Lessing probably did not realize clearly enough that *Der nordische Aufseher* was making its appeal to an audience which, for the most part, had but little understanding of literary criticism. With his appreciation of the works of Tullin and Sneedorff Cramer makes Scandinavian literature known abroad and encourages the foundation of a Danish national literature. Sneedorff's *Den patriotiske Tilskuer* was the first independent Danish moral periodical which can be compared to the German periodicals, and the best expression of Danish intellectual development under Frederick V. In this development *Der nordische Aufseher* had played a not inconsiderable part. Through the articles on religion and education the Danish people had been brought into touch with ideas then current in countries intellectually further developed than Denmark. Danish literary taste had been improved, and for the first time a moral weekly, published in Denmark, had an influence on the life and manners of the people. Cramer's periodical was the mouthpiece of the pioneers of the new foreign culture, poetic, religious and pedagogic,[1] and from it we gain some knowledge of the life and the intellectual movements of the time in Denmark. That *Der nordische Aufseher* was popular among the most patriotically-minded and enlightened Danes is indicated by the words of Tyge Rothe: "Hver Torsdag ser jeg en Del ret kloge Skyther, der have et Blad i Haanden, hvilket han (Cramer) lader prænte; de ønske at kunne faa et hver Dag i Ugen".[2] Sneedorff, in his reply, says:

> Jeg agter et af hans Blade mer end alle de millioner Bybler, som man til forn har ført her ind fra Ægypten (Germany); hans Landsmænd har vel Aarsag til at misunde os ham. Saadan en Medborger havde hverken vi eller de for faa Aar siden,[3]

and Sneedorff does not lament the fact that *Der nordische Aufseher* is in German and not in Danish. He realizes that the national self-consciousness is not yet thoroughly awakened in

[1] F. Rønning, *op. cit.* I, p. 152. [2] *Breve til Babue*, p. 26.
[3] Sneedorff, *Babues Svar*, pp. 25 and 27 (Rönning).

Denmark.[1] These contemporary Danish opinions are supported by the majority of the later Danish critics. There is hardly a Danish history of literature, which does not give favourable mention to *Der nordische Aufseher*. Rahbek even goes so far as to declare that Klopstock played a greater part in Danish literature by his contributions to that journal than by his *Messias*.[2] Rønning views Cramer's importance for Denmark as having consisted chiefly in the fact that he was editor of the first outstanding literary periodical in Denmark.[3]

In yet another way Cramer attempted to help the development of a national Danish literature, by his share in the foundation of the "Selskab til de skjønne og nyttige Videnskabers Forfremmelse",[4] a society which, for so many years, had an influence, though not always a favourable one, on Danish literary productions. The honour of founding it is usually ascribed to either Cramer or Tyge Rothe. That Cramer's part therein was not unimportant is indicated by the answer made by Professor J. Baden, secretary of the society during the 1780's, to an article by Pram.[5] Pram had maintained that Rothe had founded the Danish society. Baden says:

> Hvad den første Idee til Selskabet angaaer, da er det vanskeligt at sige, hvem der gav dem: den kunde jo vel opstaae hos flere tillige. Men dette kan jeg sige med Vished, at daværende Hofpræst Cramer var den, som enten gav den første Idee til Selskabet, eller optog den, bragte den til Modenhed, og ved den Varme, hvormed han antog sig Sagen hos daværende Overhofmarschall Gehejmeraad Grev A. G. Moltke, tilvejebragte den kongelige Gave: hvorved han ogsaa troligen blev understøttet af daværende Hofskriver nu Conferentsraad Müller.[6]

[1] F. Rønning, *loc. cit.*

[2] *Kieler Blätter* (1819), pp. 237–8.

[3] "Cramers betydning for vor udvikling ligger ikke i hans gærning som præst, men deri, at han blev udgiver af vort förste skönliteraære tidsskrift af nogen betydning" (F. Rønning, *loc. cit.*).

[4] It was in *Der nordische Aufseher*, Article 115, of November 14, 1759, that the announcement of the foundation of the society was made. See Rahbek and Nyerup, *Den danske Digtekunst*, p. 140. For a fuller account of the foundation of the society see Chapter II, pp. 86 f.

[5] *Minerva*, 1789, II, p. 124.

[6] J. Baden, *Svar til Beskyldningen*, etc., Copenhagen, 1789, p. 37.

In 1763 Cramer's name appears as a permanent member of the society. The society modelled its activities on those of the "Bremer Beiträger", and with these Cramer, more than any other German in Copenhagen, was familiar. In all the work, which Cramer did for the society, he never pushed forward the claims of his fellow-countrymen, and he was quite willing to step back when the Danes themselves could carry on. His desire to widen the influence of Klopstock's poetry in Denmark was a natural one, but he was the only supporter of Klopstock within the society. According to Baden, Cramer obtained from King Frederick V through Count Moltke 400 daler a year for the society.[1] From 1764 Cramer does not appear so frequently at the meetings, but sends in his votes in writing.[2] The records of the society show that he appeared in person at the meeting of January 23, 1766, when Christian VII was asked to continue his financial help, and also at the meeting of February 8, 1770, when the fate of Ewald's *Rolf Krage* was decided.[3] In Ewald's work Cramer took a deep interest. He read the separate acts of *Adam og Eva* in the house of Councillor Kall, before they were printed[4]; and it was possibly through Cramer that Klopstock became acquainted with Ewald's work.

The later years of Cramer's stay in Copenhagen were not without their troubles and embarrassments. Cramer was a man with a genius for friendship, loyal and sincere in his attachments. For Count Bernstorff he had always entertained feelings of the liveliest gratitude and affection, and Bernstorff's fall in 1771 was for him a source of deep personal grief. One of his students at Copenhagen University, J. H. Taber, gives an interesting account of Cramer's announcing to his class the news of Bernstorff's leaving Copenhagen for Hamburg:

> En Dag, da Dr. Cramer havde endt sine Forelæsninger om Formiddagen fra 9–10, sagde han, "Mine Herrer maa undskylde mig, at jeg ikke i Dag kan holde mine øvrige Forelæsninger fra 11–12 og fra 1–2.

[1] *Ibid.* p. 76.
[2] Protocol of the Society; see also L. Magon, *op. cit.* p. 217.
[3] *Ibid.*
[4] C. Molbech, *Ewalds Levnet*, Copenhagen, 1831, p. 88.

Jeg skal ledsage min Velynder Bernstorff", og da han udtalte disse Ord, strømmede hans Taarer ned ad Kinderne. Han følte maaske tillige en Anelse om sin egen forestaaende Afskedigelse fra Hofpræstembedet.[1]

Struensee succeeded Bernstorff at the helm of the Danish state. With the new minister, avowed free-thinker as he was, Cramer was but little in sympathy. Under Struensee and Christian VII, the weak successor of Frederick V, the manners at court were notoriously bad. Once before, at the Saxon court, Cramer had seen similar undesirable conditions, and he was not the man to stand silently by and condone existing evils. He spoke out fearlessly, both in his sermons and in private, against the vices of a class with which he had always been extremely popular, although he knew the dangers to which this proceeding exposed him. His friends trembled for him, but Cramer paid no heed to the risk to his own career. In 1771 he was dismissed[2] from his position as court preacher in Copenhagen, and retired to Lübeck, to the great regret of the members of the German circle then in Copenhagen and of a wider circle of Danish friends and admirers. The great esteem and affection in which his students held Cramer may be seen from an entry in Tabers' diary on the occasion of Cramer's losing his appointment as court preacher:

Saasnart Cramer havde læst Sedlen, lod han med en uforstilt Standhaftighed og en fast Karakter sin talrige Børneflok sammenkalde, sagde dem uden kvindagtig Vemodighed, at han nu efterdags ikke kunde koste saa meget paa deres Opdragelse og formanede dem til Flid og Orden. Alle græd, og ingen i det hele Selskab viste mere Fornuft end den mest fornærmede og den af Banstraalen trufne, ejegode Cramer.[3]

After the revolution, which resulted in Struensee's fall, Cramer was recalled and in 1774 made pro-chancellor and first pro-

[1] J. H. Tabers, *op. cit.*; quoted in *Dansk Maanedsskrift*, 1865, I, p. 121.

[2] The Danish government, however, still allowed him a pension of 800 daler a year.

[3] J. H. Tabers, *op. cit.* p. 125. Frederikke Brun too, at that time a mere child, relates how bitterly she wept when she saw the preparations for Cramer's departure going forward in the house opposite. See F. Brun, *Wahrheit aus Morgenträumen*, Aarau, 1824, p. 24.

fessor of Theology in the Schleswig-Holstein University of Kiel. Here he found full scope for his varied abilities. He was successful in increasing the funds of the university, in obtaining an increased grant to the university library, and founding a pension scheme for the widows of professors. He founded a school-teachers' seminary and obtained the appointment of better teachers. He revised the university statutes and did much for the education of young theologians. In 1784 he was made chancellor of Kiel University. He died in 1788.

By reason of his close friendship with Klopstock and of his social gifts Cramer occupied a prominent position in the aristocratic society of the Danish court and in the German circle in Copenhagen. Of this circle he was to the Danes the best-known and certainly the most popular member. Cramer has been praised by both Danish and German critics as a theologian, philosopher and preacher. But in none of these rôles was his influence really significant for Denmark. The real fruits of his eighteen years' sojourn in the Danish capital are to be found in his influence in the "Selskab til de skjønne og nyttige Videnskabers Forfremmelse" and in *Der nordische Aufseher*. Through these two channels he exercised a considerable influence on Danish literature, taste and manners. It was Cramer who revealed Tullin to the outside world and to Danish readers, and Tullin gave to the Danes a new conception of what was possible in their own language. The seeds for the native poetic harvest of the reign of Christian VII were sown in the time of Frederick V, and in this work Cramer did his share. His friendship with J. S. Sneedorff and the generous encouragement which he gave to this patriotic Danish writer had a real influence on the development of Denmark's national literature. With Sneedorff and Tyge Rothe Cramer nursed the weak national literary flame through a period when it was faint and flickering. More than any other member of the German circle of his time Cramer showed a genuine and sympathetic interest in Danish aspirations, and the Danes themselves were not slow to perceive and gratefully to acknowledge this interest.

CHAPTER FIVE

J. B. BASEDOW at SORØ

BASEDOW[1] came to Denmark in 1753. Already before this date he had thought of trying some field more profitable to a man of letters than Germany.[2] It was through his patron, Geheimrat von Quaalen of Holstein, in whose house he had been tutor for three and a half years, and through the Danish minister, Count Bernstorff, that on January 26, 1753, Basedow was appointed professor in the Ridderakademi of Sorø.

The existence of the Academy of Sorø had been marked by many changes and by one long interruption.[3] It was founded in 1150 as a Cistercian monastery and continued as such until 1536. In 1586 it was started as a school and continued until 1623. From 1623 to 1665 it was an academy and school. In 1665 it ceased to exist, but in 1747 it was re-established as a "Ridderakademi", largely through the exertions of Holberg, who gave to it generous donations of lands, books and money. Holberg saw in the revival of the Sorø Academy the possibility of instilling into the minds of the aristocratic youth of Denmark those patriotic ideas to which he himself had given such emphatic expression, but which found little encouragement in the University of Copenhagen, where the foreign elements were particularly strong. At Sorø scholars were to be prepared for the higher offices of state. Foreign journeys, hitherto regarded as indispensable to the proper finishing of the education

[1] Johann Bernard Basedow, born in Hamburg 1723; 1744–6 studied in Leipzig; 1746–9 in Hamburg; 1749–53 tutor in Holstein; 1753–61 professor in Sorø Academy; 1761–71 in Altona; 1771–90 in Dessau; died 1790. For Basedow's life see J. C. Meier, *J. B. Basedows Leben, Charakter und Schriften*, Hamburg, 1791–2; also *Allgemeine deutsche Biographie*, II, pp. 113 ff.

[2] "Basedow will nach Ruszland gehen? und warum? Der groszen Kayserin die Hand zu küssen? Wenn die grosze Kayserin ihn nur dem Vaterlande zurückgiebt! Ich kann es nicht leiden, dasz unsere groszen Leute nicht lieber in ihrem Vaterlande verhungern" (Letter from Gleim to Klopstock; *Jahresberichte für neuere deutsche Literaturgeschichte*, IX, 4, 2, p. 98).

[3] *Blandinger fra Sorø*, 1831, I, pp. 159–67.

of young Danish noblemen, were to be no longer necessary. The curriculum of the academy was adapted to these ends. Modern languages, Danish, German and French, were regarded as more important than the classics, and emphasis was laid on legal and political science, modern history, practical philosophy and the fine arts.[1]

Already before going to Sorø Basedow had entertained the idea of founding a seminary, where he might put into practice his educational ideas, and it appeared at the beginning of his career at Sorø as if he might find there the opportunity he was seeking. It was a new kind of position for Basedow, one not easy for him to fill. A typical representative of the reform fever of the eighteenth century,[2] he was hardly fitted to become a peaceable member of the faculty of a small Danish college. His temper was fiery and turbulent, his manner of address uncouth, arrogant and overbearing. So rough and challenging a character could hardly be sympathetic to the more easy-going Danes. His habits of study were peculiar and he had to fill in gaps of quite elementary knowledge necessary for one in teaching work.[3] His relations with the majority of his colleagues were not of the happiest. The latter were for the most part jealous of the popularity of his lectures on religion and morality,[4] a jealousy which was increased by Basedow's uncompromising demeanour. In J. S. Sneedorff, however, who was at that time on the Sorø staff, Basedow found a sympathetic friend and ally. They had many ideas in common. Both men regarded an

[1] Holberg's expectations were not realized. The academy had but few students and there was little unity among members of the faculty. It was some time before Sorø gained any real contact with new educational developments in western Europe.

[2] F. Rønning, *op. cit.* I, p. 309.

[3] "Basedow var en forstyrret Mand, der selv levede og tillige behandlede de unge Mennesker paa Akademiet paa den mest hensynsløse Maade. Han var raa og halvdannet; men han besad den Evne at gjøre Opsigt, aldrig at blive træt, aldrig at trække sig tilbage, altid at imponere med Frækhed" (N. M. Petersen, *op. cit.* V, p. 26).

[4] "Man kunde ikke tilgive ham den Forvovenhed, at han, en Fremmed, en Tydsker, vilde forlade den gamle Schlendrian, og overgaae de ældre Lærere" (*Minerva*, Copenhagen, February, 1801, p. 125, Article by C. L. Sander).

absolute monarchy as the best system of government[1] and both realized the importance of the introduction of new ideas into Denmark in education, philosophy and theology. Jens Kraft, professor of Mathematics at Sorø, represented the reactionary elements on the staff, and Basedow gave a ready support to Sneedorff in his opposition to this colleague. In practical philosophy and the fine arts, which were among Basedow's subjects, Sneedorff took a deep interest.[2] He recommended Basedow's *Praktische Philosophie für alle Stände* (1758) to Danish readers and announced the approaching appearance of another book by the same author.[3] Sneedorff was broad-minded enough to realize and courageous enough to declare that Danish literature and thought could draw profit from the ideas of such foreigners as Cramer and Basedow. He saw in Cramer a readiness to help in the development of the Danish national literature, and in Basedow the power of bringing Denmark into touch with modern educational ideas.

The range of subjects which Basedow taught at Sorø afforded sufficient scope to his varied talents.[4] In pedagogy, philosophy and religion Basedow was keenly interested, and he possessed the gift of communicating this interest to his students.[5] Many

[1] Cp. Basedow's speech at Sorø on April 1, 1754, on the occasion of Frederick V's birthday, in which he extols the blessings of absolute monarchy under Frederick V; cp. also Sneedorff, *Om den borgerlige Regering*, Copenhagen, 1757.

[2] *Luxdorphiana*, ed. Nyerup, Copenhagen, 1791, p. 29.

[3] *Babues Svar paa nogle Breve*, 1758–9, Letter 3. See L. Magon, *op. cit.* p. 515, note 90.

[4] "Herr Johann Bernhard Basedow, Professor der praktischen Philosophie und der deutschen schönen Wissenschaften, erkläret den praktischen Theil der gottschedischen Philosophie, unterrichtet in den deutschen schönen Wissenschaften und zeigt die Schriftsteller in denselben an, giebt auch Anweisungen zur deutschen Schreibart" (A. F. Büsching, *Nachrichten*, IV, Copenhagen and Leipzig, 1754, p. 337).

Basedow gave every week in the summer of 1754 six lectures on German eloquence, two on moral and critical explanations of German poets, five on "ars germanice perorandi" and two on German spelling; see *Lærde Tidender*, 1754, No. 22 (quoted by F. Rønning, *op. cit.*, I, p. 346).

[5] "Als Basedow seine Lectionen anfing, da spitzte man die Ohren, da hiesz es: 'das ist ein ganz andrer Mann; es ist ein neuer Lehrer, ein Prophet unter uns gekommen'" (J. C. Meier, *J. B. Basedows Leben, Charakter und Schriften*, Hamburg, 1791–2, p. 233).

of the ideas which he presented were not in agreement with church dogma; he did not, however, always present them as his own, but as ideas deserving of examination and consideration. He tried to awaken in his students a love for truth and a desire for investigation.[1] With the students Basedow was at first extremely popular. Nothing like his lectures on philosophy had been heard at Sorø before. His unorthodox manner of lecturing, downright, humorous and interesting, appealed to the students, who had hitherto been accustomed to a heavier, more pedantic manner. His philosophical and theological lectures, although attendance was not compulsory, were the most popular in the academy. The discussion of such subjects as the Christian Religion, Church History and the New Testament roused an interest in religion, which had become dead among the young nobles at Sorø.[2] Basedow's popularity as a lecturer lasted for some considerable time, but his unconventional conduct, his too familiar intercourse with the students, and his contempt for all rules and forms of behaviour soon exposed him to attack. Complaints, some of which originated with students, were made as to Basedow's private life; it was said that his way of living was far from being in accordance with his moral teaching.[3] Furthermore, his reckless utterances against the dogmas of the church were not regarded favourably at Sorø, where the atmosphere was narrowly academic and orthodox.

It was this latter reason, Basedow's unorthodoxy, which was the final reason of his expulsion from Sorø. Basedow had not originally been appointed to lecture on theology, but in 1757 von Haven, who was at the same time parish priest in Sorø and professor of Theology in Sorø Academy, died. Basedow, who

[1] Heinrich Rathmann, *J. B. Basedow*, Magdeburg, 1791, p. 15.

[2] *Ibid.*

[3] "I Sorø Basedow lagde straks baade sine heldige og uheldige Egenskaber for Dagen; hans kraftige om end raa Veltalenhed, hans store Arbejdskraft og den Uforbeholdenhed, hvormed han fremsatte sine Anskuelser, gjorde Indtryk paa Eleverne; men hans Ligegyldighed, ikke blot for Formerne, men for selve Sømmeligheden, og hans ingenlunde pletfri Vandel vakte ogsaa Anstød" (*Kirkehistoriske Samlinger*, IV, p. 328).

was then in poor financial circumstances[1] and wished to eke out his small salary of 400 daler, applied for the post. He had previously studied theology, but knew no Greek, and was really not qualified for the post. Bernstorff, however, supported Basedow's application, and by a royal decree of September 23, 1757, he was appointed to the position. In his introductory lectures, Basedow declared that he stood entirely on the ground of Christianity, but he soon proceeded to deal some shrewd blows at orthodoxy and at the then existing church system.[2] He was, however, merely voicing free-thinking ideas then prevalent in higher circles in Denmark, ideas in which many of the supposedly orthodox clergy believed, but which they were afraid to express openly. In 1760 Count F. Danneskjold-Samsøe became president of Sorø Academy. Danneskjold was a relentless opponent of Count Bernstorff to whose later downfall he contributed, and he was not well disposed to Bernstorff's protégé, Basedow. A man of very orthodox and narrow views, a serious Christian of the old school, the new president soon noticed the heterodoxy of Basedow's teaching. In a conversation with Danneskjold, Basedow said that he rather favoured materialistic doctrines.[3] From that time on Danneskjold kept a close watch on Basedow, and it was not long before he discovered that he was teaching false doctrines to the students.[4] Danneskjold stopped Basedow's lectures on theology and assigned to him in their stead lectures on language and literature. In these lectures Basedow proceeded to express his religious ideas. Danneskjold then stopped his lectures altogether and his salary was continued on the express condition that he was no longer to teach or write in public.[5]

[1] Basedow himself relates that owing to his second marriage and his travelling expenses and illness of his wife he was 150 daler in debt after his first year at Sorø. See R. Diestelmann, *Basedow*, Leipzig, 1897, p. 22.

[2] *Reden über die glückselige Regierung Friedrichs V*, Sorø, 1761, pp. 99 ff. and 109.

[3] *Luxdorphiana*, Copenhagen, 1791, p. 30: *Danneskjold-Samsøes Indberetning til Kongen.*

[4] F. Rønning, *op. cit.* I, pp. 305 ff.

[5] Danneskjold declared that the chair of theology should not be held by one who said openly, "han favoriserede Materialisternes Lærdom, ja roste endog disse falske Lærere some de, der vare bekvemmest til at omvende Naturalister, Deister og Ateister" (*Kirkehistoriske Samlinger*, IV, p. 329).

Bernstorff, who had protected Basedow as long as was possible, had to yield to Danneskjold's insistent demands, and in 1761 Basedow was transferred to Altona Gymnasium as professor of Moral Philosophy. Danneskjold's attack on Basedow had met with a certain amount of sympathy from many of the Germans in Copenhagen, who had blamed Bernstorff for the ready support which he had given to Basedow, and from the Danes, with whom Basedow had never been popular. It had been with regard to Basedow's appointment to Sorø and his activities there that the Danes had complained about the too great number of Germans occupying lucrative positions in Denmark.[1]

The eight years which Basedow spent in Sorø were busy years. In addition to his many hours of lectures he had written many books, delivered numerous speeches and contributed to *Der nordische Aufseher*, taking part in the controversy with the *Berliner Litteraturbriefe* in defence of Klopstock and Cramer. In 1753 he published his *Versuch, wie fern die Philosophie zur Freygeisterey verführe?* and dedicated it to Count von Moltke. In the same year he published his Latin work, *De philosophiae studio a procerum filiis prudenter moderando*. In 1756 his *Lehrbuch prosaischer und poetischer Wohlredenheit* appeared. It was reviewed favourably in Denmark and the reviewer pays tribute to Basedow's reputation as a teacher and thinker.[2] In 1757–8 Basedow's first important work in which he expresses his ideas on religion, philosophy and general education appeared, *Die praktische Philosophie für alle Stände*.[3] This latter work was very popular; it was used as a text-book in Basedow's lectures at Sorø. Two of the chapters in it, entitled *Von der Erziehung und dem Unterrichte der Jugend*, contain most of Basedow's subsequent ideas for the improvement of scholastic instruction. In 1759 Basedow's German grammar, entitled

[1] *Reventlowske Papirer*, *ed. cit.* VI, pp. 508–9; see also Basedow's letters in *Bernstorffske Papirer*, II, pp. 27–47.

[2] A. F. Büsching, *Nachrichten*, II, p. 433.

[3] Published 1777 in enlarged form. In *Der nordische Aufseher*, I, pp. 24 and 29, Cramer expressed a very favourable opinion of this work of Basedow.

Neue Lehrart und Übung in der Regelmäszigkeit der deutschen Sprache and dedicated to Gellert, appeared. During his stay at Sorø Basedow appears to have made a reputation as an orator. A volume of his speeches was published in Copenhagen in 1761.[1] To these speeches contemporary Danish reviewers gave great praise.[2] His speech on the king's birthday (1754) pays an eloquent tribute to the personal character of Frederick V and to the benefits of absolute monarchy.

It was largely through Bernstorff's generous intervention that Basedow went to Altona on such honourable conditions, retaining his pension and rank and title of professor. Altona was at that time a place of refuge for heretics and dissenters, and it was thought that in a smaller place Basedow's eccentricities would do less harm. Basedow's work was now considerably lighter, and he had much more time to devote to the subjects which interested him, than in Sorø.[3] During these years in Altona[4] he continued his inquiries into natural religion and the teaching of the Bible. In his *Unterricht in der nationalen und biblischen Religion*[5] he attacks accepted views on such questions as eternal punishment, communion, baptism and the inspiration of the Bible. His main interest, however, now begins to be centred in education. His *Theoretisches System der gesunden Vernunft*[6] and the *Philalethie*[7] contain his ideas on the reform of the treatment of the philosophical sciences in the

[1] A copy of this book, entitled *Reden über die glückselige Regierung Friedrichs des Fünften*, is in the library of the Sorø Academy. It was dedicated to the Crown Prince of Denmark and the list of speeches is given as follows: (1) *Basedows Rede, am Geburthstage des Königes, von der Glückseligkeit der dänischen Staaten.* (2) *Desselben Rede, am Geburthstage des Königes, von den Belohnungen eines guten Regenten.* (3) *Desselben Rede, am Jubelfeste wegen der hundertjährigen Souveranität.* (4) *Desselben Discours von der Nothwendigkeit und Art theologischer Vorlesungen auf Ritterakademien.* (5) *Desselben Reden, über den frühzeitigen Tod eines tugendhaften und gottseligen Freyherrn.*

[2] See A. F. Büsching, *Nachrichten*, II, p. 517, and *Fortgesetzte Nachrichten von dem Zustande der Wissenschaften und Künste*, II, Copenhagen, 1762, Article 4, p. 375.

[3] Basedow only lectured three hours a day in Altona and towards the end of his stay there he was absolved from all lecturing work, although he still retained the salary; see *Minerva*, February, 1801, p. 125.

[4] 1761–71. [5] 1764. [6] 1765. [7] 1768.

universities. After the publication of these two works Basedow directed his attention to education in schools and to private instruction. As a result of his outspoken theological works he was declared a heretic, his family was excluded from communion and his works were proscribed in Altona, Hamburg and Lübeck. Had it not been for the protection of Bernstorff and Cramer, Basedow must have succumbed to such intolerance and persecution.[1] Among the many opponents of Basedow's ideas there was none more relentless than Count Danneskjold. He had not ceased to pursue Basedow after the latter's departure from Sorø and in 1767 he launches a new attack against him in a petition to the king:

> Udi eders Majestæts Riger og Lande findes een af de skadeligste falske Lærere, der nu lever i Europa, det er Professor Basedow, der nu er Professor i Altona, og tilforn har været Professor i Sorø, som overøset med Naade og Velgierninger af Eders Majestæts højstsalige Hr. Fader, har misbrugt og misbruger endog endnu daglig de milde Regenteres Naade, under hvilke han lever, til at styrte deres Undersaater, saavidt det staaer i hans Evne mundtlig tilforn, og nu skriftlig, i den største af alle Ulykker ved sine falske imod Christendommen stridende Lærdomme.[2]

Danneskjold further points out that the fact of Basedow's teaching in a state institution constituted a serious menace to the loyalty of the Danish nation. He proposes that Basedow retain his pension, under penalty of losing it should he continue to publish. In 1768 Basedow was dismissed from the Danish government service with a pension of 800 daler.[3]

As to Basedow's private life and circle of friends during his stay in Denmark, we have but little information. While in Sorø he rarely visited Copenhagen, and he does not appear to have come into frequent contact with members of the German circle; but with Klopstock, Cramer, J. H. Schlegel and G. B. Funk he was on friendly terms.[4] There is a record of a visit of Basedow

[1] Pastor Goeze, Lessing's antagonist, was among Basedow's opponents.

[2] *Luxdorphiana*, Copenhagen, 1791, p. 28, *Pro Memoria* from Count Danneskjold to the king dated October, 1767.

[3] C. L. Sander, *Bidrag til Pædagogik og dens Historie*, I, p. 121.

[4] *Minerva*, Copenhagen, February, 1801, p. 125.

to Copenhagen in 1768, after he had been dismissed from the Danish government service, for the purpose of consulting with Klopstock, Cramer, Oeder and Resewitz as to his future pedagogic plans.[1] With Gerstenberg, who regarded him as one of the greatest pedagogues of the century,[2] Basedow was probably more intimate than with any other member of the German circle. There was a certain similarity between the two men, in their quick enthusiasms and lack of balance. In his patron, von Quaalen, Basedow had a good friend, who was always ready to exert his influence on his behalf. Not only had Basedow friends and admirers among the more progressive of the Danes, such as Sneedorff and Rothe, but also among the most orthodox clergy and the most devoted pietists.[3] Bishop Harboe of Seeland, a prominent Danish divine, although severely orthodox himself, was a friend of Basedow and on several occasions protected him against accusations and persecutions. In Sorø, where he had married for the second time, Basedow had many friends. The treatment of Basedow by the Danish government is another instance of its generosity toward the German writers within its borders. When in 1771 he accepted, with the permission of the Danish government, a fairly lucrative post in Dessau,[4] where he was to superintend the schools and seminaries of the state, he still retained an annual pension from Denmark. Even after he left Sorø, Frederick V continued to contribute to the cost of publication of his educational works. Bernstorff, who thoroughly approved of Basedow's educational ideas, showed on all occasions the utmost generosity towards his protégé, and had it not been for his powerful protection, Basedow would have had to leave Sorø before he did.

It is difficult to point to any direct influence of Basedow on

[1] C. L. Sander, *op. cit.* p. 121.

[2] During his earlier years Gerstenberg took a keen interest in the education of his children and on one occasion wrote to ask Basedow his advice regarding the education of his son; see A. M. Wagner, *op. cit.* I, p. 81.

[3] Heinrich Rathmann, *op. cit.* pp. 16 ff.

[4] In Dessau Basedow was to receive a salary of 1100 thaler; see *Minerva*, Copenhagen, February, 1801, p. 129.

Danish literature or on Danish intellectual development. His educational reforms, continued afterwards by Campe, Salze and other German educationalists, had later an influence on Danish education[1]; but in Basedow's time Denmark had not progressed to a point where it could absorb his ideas. The stolid and conservative mass of the Danish people was unable to appreciate their boldness and originality, and it heartily disliked the violent and revolutionary language in which they were expressed. Orthodoxy was still strong in Denmark. Basedow's colleagues at Sorø, as Sneedorff also found, did not welcome contact with new ideas. Had Basedow met with a more favourable reception at Sorø, and had he found a more tolerant and more widely intelligent audience in Denmark, he might have made that country a focus for new and important educational ideas, and the Danish government would certainly have gained greater honour for its generous treatment of a man who some years later was acclaimed as a genius and benefactor by all Europe and as one who had suffered in the cause of religious and political freedom. It was only the higher educated classes, the court circles, to which such men as Bernstorff belonged, such patriotic and progressive writers as Sneedorff and Rothe, and a few of the more enlightened clergy, who admired the vigour and fearlessness with which Basedow expressed ideas which were often unpopular, but which were always interesting and stimulating. Many of these men realized that Basedow was fighting against stupid and outworn dogmas, for freedom and truth in religion and for the liberation of education from a harmful ecclesiastical influence.

[1] N. M. Petersen, *op. cit.* v, I, 28.

CHAPTER SIX

The MINOR MEMBERS of THE GERMAN CIRCLE

In addition to the more prominent members of the German circle in Copenhagen there were many German writers, who although not well known to the world outside Denmark, exercised an influence on the literary and intellectual development of the country of their adoption. The number of these writers was by no means inconsiderable. They had been for the most part attracted to Denmark by the lack of prospects in their own country and by the generous hospitality offered by Count Bernstorff and the Danish government. Not all of these writers left Denmark when Count Bernstorff was dismissed from office. Many of them found there an assured living and a permanent home.

Johann Heinrich Schlegel[1] came to Copenhagen in 1748 as tutor to the sons of Count Christian Rantzau. His brother Elias, whose success in Denmark had probably attracted him to that country, died in 1749. In 1758 J. H. Schlegel went to the Academy of Sorø in charge of the young Counts Rantzau. There he stayed for two years, occupying for a time the chair of History. In 1760 he returned to Copenhagen, where he lived until his death in 1780. In the Danish capital Schlegel seems to have been on friendly terms with most of the members of the German circle. J. A. Cramer he had already known in Leipzig. Count Bernstorff, who appears to have taken a lively interest in Schlegel's historical work,[2] extended to him, as to so many others of the circle, his generous patronage. To Count Moltke Schlegel dedicated his edition of his brother Elias' works.[3]

[1] 1726–80.

[2] Bernstorff read through the manuscript of Schlegel's *Geschichte der Könige von Dänemark*, adding to it his own remarks. See F. Rønning, *op. cit.* I, p. 74.

[3] Published 1761–70.

A. G. Carstens seems to have been one of the few intimate friends whom Schlegel made in Copenhagen.[1]

The number and variety of posts held by Schlegel bear testimony to the wide range of his interests.[2] In 1760 he was made secretary to the Danish Chancellery. In the same year he became professor of Philosophy in the University of Copenhagen, where he lectured on the Fine Arts and on Practical Philosophy. In 1763 he was made secretary to the "Selskab til de skjønne og nyttige Videnskabers Forfremmelse", a position which he held up to his death. In 1766 he became professor of Geometry at the Art Academy in Copenhagen, in 1770 Royal Historiographer, and in 1778 Royal Librarian. Through these various offices Schlegel had ample opportunity to contribute to Denmark's intellectual development. His interest in Danish language and literature seemed to justify his appointment as secretary to the Danish Society, and his university lectures on the fine arts appeared at first as if they might contribute to the movement started by Sneedorff towards the improvement of literary taste in Denmark. His idea for the founding of a typographical society for the publication of literary work in Denmark was an excellent one.[3] Before Mallet had declared the importance of northern mythology[4] Schlegel had studied Icelandic in the *Edda* of Resenius and had realized the significance of this new field. He proposed a special nordic department in the Royal Library and wished to make that library more accessible to the public than it had hitherto been.[5]

It cannot be said, however, that the influence which Schlegel exercised was always to the benefit of Danish interests. He was hardly fitted for the somewhat delicate position in which, as a foreigner, he found himself in Denmark. He possessed none of the tact of his brother, Elias, and he was possibly the

[1] J. H. Schlegel, *Betragtninger*, Copenhagen, 1779, p. 81.

[2] "Ved de Stillinger, han efterhaanden indtog, havde han tilstrækkelig Lejlighed til at vise, hvor vidt en Fremmeds literære Virksomhed lod sig forene med vor egen" (N. M. Petersen, *op. cit.* v, I, p. 15).

[3] L. Magon, *op. cit.* p. 273.

[4] *Histoire de Dannemarc*, Copenhagen, 1758–77.

[5] C. F. Bricka, *op. cit.* xv, p. 81.

most unpopular member of the German circle in Copenhagen. His undue idea of his own importance and his self-seeking nature made him many enemies among the Danes. Already in 1763, the year in which he took over the secretaryship to the Danish Society, the anti-German feeling was beginning to develop in Denmark. His lectures at the university were attended by very few students. He was regarded as an intruder, who was occupying positions which could have been much more suitably occupied by Danes. As a critic of Danish literature he was declared to have but few qualifications.[1] His declaration that the arts and sciences in Denmark were on a lower level than in other countries[2] did not serve to make him more popular. Furthermore, such literary powers as Schlegel did possess were mainly critical, and he contributed to the over-emphasis of criticism, which prevented the Danish Society from exercising a helpful influence on young Danish writers. The society only met once a year and Schlegel gradually acquired an undue influence in its decisions.[3] On the communications of the society only the name of the secretary appeared, and Schlegel's prominent connection with it caused it to be regarded by many Danes as a German, and not as a Danish society.

Schlegel's personal unpopularity and the anti-German temper of the Danes during the latter years of his life in Copenhagen have somewhat obscured the services, which he rendered to Denmark. Yet he was one of the first members of the German circle to interest himself in Danish language and history. His *Afhandling om det danske Sprogs Fordele og Mangler i Sammenligning med det tyske og franske Sprog*[4] bears witness to his linguistic interests. Schlegel's main intellectual interest, however, was in historical research, and in this field he rendered

[1] Schlegel's Danish critics declared that his Danish was very faulty. See C. H. Pram, *Minerva*, xv, p. 164.

[2] J. H. Schlegel, *Betragtninger*, Copenhagen, 1779, pp. 143–5.

[3] L. Magon, *op. cit.* p. 275.

[4] This work Schlegel wrote in Danish for a prize, which it did not obtain; it was, however, because of it that Schlegel was in 1763 appointed secretary to the Danish Society. Schlegel had shown the manuscript of this work to Sneedorff and the latter had advised against publication.

valuable services to the study of history in Denmark.[1] His *Geschichte der Könige von Dänemark aus dem Oldenburgischen Stamme*,[2] continuing as it did the study of Danish history begun by Hans Gram, Langebek and Holberg, is one of the most important works published in Denmark in the eighteenth century.[3]

Helferich Peter Sturz[4] came to Copenhagen in 1764. During the four preceding years he had been private secretary to Chancellor von Eyben in Glückstadt. Von Eyben, appreciating Sturz' ability and realizing that his opportunities would be much greater in Copenhagen, sent him there with many useful letters of introduction.[5] It was not long before Sturz obtained a footing in the Danish capital. In the year of his arrival, through the influence of Count Rantzau, he was appointed to a secretaryship in the Department of External Affairs and shortly afterwards he was made private secretary to Count Bernstorff. Living as he did in Bernstorff's house, Sturz quickly obtained introductions to the leading members of the German circle, to the Danish court and to Copenhagen society. The time he spent in Bernstorff's service[6] was the happiest time of his life, "heitrer Morgen einer trüberen Zukunft".[7] He was working constantly under the eyes of Denmark's greatest statesman and became himself "a statesman, man of the world, poet, writer and artist".[8] At Bernstorff's evening meetings with his family and intimate

[1] N. M. Petersen, *op. cit.* v, 1, p. 16.

[2] Published 1769–77 in two volumes.

[3] C. Paludan-Müller, "Dansk Historiografi i det 18. Aarhundrede" in *Hist. Tidsskrift*, Fifth Series, IV, pp. 1 ff. Schlegel's work was favourably reviewed by Gerstenberg in the *Hamburgische neue Zeitung*, ed. Fischer, p. 354.

[4] Born at Darmstadt 1736; 1753–7 studied at Jena, Göttingen and Gieszen; 1764 went to Copenhagen; 1772 banished; granted a pension by the Danish government; subsequently lived at Glückstadt and Altona; then in Bremen, where he died in 1779. Cp. M. Koch, *H. P. Sturz*, Munich, 1879.

[5] H. P. Sturz, *Schriften*, Zweite Sammlung, Leipzig, 1782, Vorrede.

[6] 1764–71.

[7] Letter from Sturz to Boie, dated November 9, 1777; see *Deutsches Museum*, 1777, pp. 459–65; Zimmermann, Schlegel's biographer and bosom friend, writes: "Dies waren seine goldenen Jahre; er lebte in Bernstorffs Hause mit Klopstock die seligsten Tage seines Lebens, von denen er so oft mit Entzücken und Wehmuth sprach und schrieb" (H. P. Sturz, *Erinnerungen aus dem Leben des Grafen Johann Hartwig Ernst von Bernstorff*, Leipzig, 1777, Introduction, p. 8).

[8] *Ibid.*

friends Sturz was always present, and in describing these evenings he pays a grateful tribute to Bernstorff's generous character and brilliant intellect:

> Wir hingen alsdann an Bernstorffs Mund, und labten uns mit Sokratischer Weisheit. Hier entfaltete sich sein Herz und sein Geist; der Schleier der Würde fiel nieder, und die erhabene Seele glänzte in ihrer eigentümlichen Schönheit: wir verlieszen ihn nie, ohne wärmer für die Tugend zu empfinden, ohne unterrichtet und gebessert zu seyn.[1]

It is from Sturz' accounts of Count Bernstorff and of Klopstock[2] that we gain some idea of the personal relations which existed among the members of the German circle. With Klopstock, who was for some time in Bernstorff's house, Sturz was on particularly intimate terms. Hardly a day passed without their meeting each other[3] and in Klopstock's skating and walking expeditions Sturz usually took part. Of the author of the *Messias* he writes in terms of warm friendship and admiration.[4] With Gerstenberg, too, Sturz was on intimate terms and was a regular attendant at the musical evenings at Gerstenberg's house at Lyngby. J. A. Cramer, J. B. Basedow, J. C. Oeder, and J. J. von Berger, all members of the German circle, were also among his friends.

Sturz was one of the ablest members of the German circle.[5] He had an unusual gift for languages. Of French, Italian and Spanish he had a fair command, and he possessed an uncommon knowledge of English literature. Within six months of his arrival in Copenhagen he was able to speak and write the Danish language correctly.[6] Although Sturz, like Schönborn, the brothers Stolberg and K. F. Cramer, began his literary education in the school of Klopstock and the German circle, yet, like these writers he, too, developed beyond these beginnings.

[1] *Erinnerungen aus dem Leben des Grafen Johann Hartwig Ernst von Bernstorff*, p. 141.

[2] *Deutsches Museum*, November, 1777, pp. 459 ff.

[3] M. Koch, *op. cit.* p. 40.

[4] See Chapter II, pp. 70 ff., *supra*.

[5] His biographer Zimmermann calls him "ein Genie der ersten Klasse"; see *Hannoversches Magazin*, 1776, XLI, p. 636.

[6] H. P. Sturz, *Schriften*, Zweite Sammlung, Leipzig, 1782, Vorrede.

For the *Messias* Sturz does not express an unqualified admiration.[1] The ideas which Lessing expressed in the *Hamburgische Dramaturgie* were not without their influence on him. He, too, believed that the German drama should take a path between the over-boldness of the English and the over-timidity of the French. Sturz' letter, addressed to the friends and patrons of the German Theatre in Hamburg and prefixed to his five act prose drama, *Julie* (1767), contains ideas strongly reminiscent of Johann Elias Schlegel's dramaturgic theories. To Lessing's critical work Sturz gives high praise.[2] Unlike Klopstock and Cramer, he realized that literary criticism might do much for the development of German literature. Yet with Klopstock as with Gerstenberg, the two outstanding figures of the German circle, Sturz reveals certain points of contact. He detested mere imitators[3]; he was interested in old German literature and he saw in the old nordic literatures a new field, where much original material might be gathered. Although Sturz made no direct contributions to Gerstenberg's *Schleswiger Litteraturbriefe*, yet it is probable that his ideas had a certain influence upon them. Like J. E. Schlegel and J. A. Cramer, Sturz edited a periodical in Copenhagen. At the beginning of 1767 Breding, a Dane, had founded in the Danish capital a journal entitled *Der nordische Sittenfreund*. It was of poor quality and the similarity of its title to that of *Der nordische Aufseher* seemed likely to lead to confusion with Cramer's periodical. In the same year Sturz began the publication of *Die Menechmen oder zwey Wochenschriften von gleicher Statur in vier Aufzügen*. In the first part Sturz declared that he had undertaken the work with the in-

[1] "Aus der Phantasie allein kann der bildende Künstler niemals ein Werk schaffen; er bedarf des sinnlich greifbaren Vorbildes" (*Deutsches Museum*, November, 1777, pp. 459 ff., in an article by H. P. Sturz on Klopstock).

[2] "Ich rede nicht von der Berliner Bibliothek; dieses Werk enthält Männerarbeit, wenn sich auch gleich ein seichtes Blättchen über Klopstock mit einschleicht" (*ibid.*).

[3] "Wie können wir ein eignes Theater erwarten, wenn wir ewig übersetzen und wenn unsere Schauspieler fremde Sitten mit deutschen Gebärden ausdrücken sollen? Wann wagen wir es endlich einmal zu seyn, was wir sind?" (H. P. Sturz, *Geschichte des deutschen Theaters*, 1766).

tention of convincing the world that in Denmark one cannot lightly offend against good taste in so vulgar a manner as *Der nordische Sittenfreund* had done. In his periodical, which had but a short life, Sturz followed Gottsched's lead and used parody as a literary weapon.

The high esteem which Bernstorff entertained for Sturz, resulted in due recognition by the Danish government of his merits. In 1768 he was made a Danish Legationsraad and in the same year he accompanied the Danish king, Christian VII, on a royal tour in England and France.[1] In both of these countries Sturz made a good impression. He made friends with such prominent people as Samuel Johnson, Garrick, Angelica Kauffmann and with Madame Geoffrin, Galiani, d'Alembert and Helvétius; with several of them he afterwards maintained a correspondence. In 1768, on his return to Copenhagen from this journey, he was made Director of the Post Office. The fall of Bernstorff in 1770 brought about a change for the worse in Sturz' fortunes. He did not leave Copenhagen with his patron. Bernstorff, thinking that it might help him to have some friends still at the Danish court, asked him to remain there under Struensee. Struensee had been Sturz' travelling companion on the royal journey, but the relations between the two men had never been cordial. In 1772, under the pressure of the anti-German agitation against Struensee, Sturz was dismissed from his secretaryship in the Department of Foreign Affairs. Count Rantzau, his former patron, offended by Sturz' close association with Count Bernstorff, made no effort to help him. Shortly afterwards, on the day before his marriage, he was arrested on no definite charge and kept in prison for four months without a trial. After his release he was banished from Copenhagen.[2] From this unjust treatment Sturz never recovered.

In spite of *Die Menechmen* and the part which Sturz, with

[1] H. P. Sturz, *Briefe eines Reisenden* (1777), contains an account of his journey.

[2] For an account of the latter years of Sturz' life see H. P. Sturz, *Schriften*, Zweite Sammlung, Leipzig, 1782, Vorrede by Zimmermann.

his *Gespräche zweier Müsziggänger*,[1] played in the fight for the liberty of the press in Denmark, he can hardly be said to have exercised any definite influence on the development of Danish literature.[2] During his stay in Denmark his literary activities were chiefly within the German circle and were concerned rather with German than Danish literature, and the great popularity which he enjoyed in Copenhagen and in Hamburg, was for the most part among German-speaking people.

Unlike most of the members of the German circle, A. G. Carstens did not come to Denmark from Germany. He was born in Copenhagen in 1713, of German parents. Of the literary men in Copenhagen about the middle of the eighteenth century Carstens was perhaps the best fitted to reconcile the German and Danish elements in Denmark's intellectual and literary life. His wide reading in, and deep knowledge of the classics, his familiarity with the languages and literatures of France and England, and the fact that he had as easy a command of the Danish language as he had of German, his mother tongue, were qualifications which were not common at that time; and he possessed and freely exercised the valuable gift of stimulating and inspiring young writers. Frederikke Brun, after having spoken of Carstens' learning and literary taste and of his powers of appreciation of ancient and modern literatures, says: "Denne ædle Mand var Værn og Støtte for hvert opblomstrende Talent, Ewalds og Baggesens faderlige Velgjører",[3] and this high praise is confirmed by all subsequent Danish critics. This helpful influence Carstens exercised at an important stage of Denmark's literary and intellectual development; and he did much for the study of Danish history,[4] language and literature. By all the

[1] Published at Copenhagen, 1771.

[2] "Der var ogsaa andre Mænd, som, uden at gribe mærkelig ind i den danske Literatur, i den tyske have vundet et hædret Navn, som H. P. Sturz" (N. M. Petersen, *op. cit.* v, 1, p. 32).

[3] Fr. Brun (Münter), *Ungdoms Erindringer*, ed. Louis Bobé, Copenhagen, 1917.

[4] To the new interest in nordic literature Carstens made a contribution in the advice which he gave to Mallet as to his *Histoire de Dannemarc*; see Mallet's preface to this work.

members of the German circle Carstens was liked and highly respected. Klopstock and Gerstenberg were his chief friends within the circle. With the former Carstens kept up a correspondence long after the poet had left Copenhagen, and in a letter to Carstens from Hamburg dated April 8, 1788, Klopstock assured him of his unfailing friendship.[1]

It was in his relations with Johannes Ewald that Carstens rendered the greatest service to Danish literature. He had met the young Danish poet in 1764, at a time when Ewald was in need of help and encouragement. Carstens extended both to him in generous measure. He possessed what the younger Ewald lacked, a sense of restraint and proportion, and to the Danish poet, who was then uncertain of his path, Carstens gave all that his own literary taste, disciplined by wide and careful reading in ancient and modern literatures, enabled him to give. Of all the members of the "Selskab til de skjønne og nyttige Videnskabers Forfremmelse",[2] there was none who took more trouble than Carstens in criticizing carefully the works submitted for publication or prizes,[3] and the help which he gave to Ewald when, in November, 1773, he submitted *Balders Død* to the society, is but one example of his generous interest in the Danish poet. In a letter, accompanying Ewald's work, which Carstens sent to Luxdorph, a member of the society, he says that he finds great merit in the piece, but that there are passages which should be altered; while Luxdorph's opinion expressed in his diary[4] was that *Balders Død* did not seem to him to have been written by a sane man, and in his letter to the society he spoke very disparagingly of Ewald's work. The other members of the society were more favourable and Carstens

[1] "So oft ich Jemanden spreche, der von Kopenhagen kömt, so rede ich auch von Ihnen" (J. M. Lappenberg, *op. cit.* p. 324).

[2] Founded 1759. Gerstenberg declared Carstens to have been the founder of this society; see letter from Gerstenberg to Rahbek quoted in *Archiv für das Studium der neueren Sprachen und Literatur*, CXXXVI, p. 25. A. M. Wagner supports Gerstenberg's view, *op. cit.* I, p. 90; but Magon opposes it; see L. Magon, *op. cit.* p. 523, note 482. It is probable that Carstens was one of the founders of the society.

[3] P. F. Suhm, *Werke, ed. cit.* XIV, p. 262.

[4] November 12, 1773.

especially defended the work warmly. At the March meeting of the society in 1774 *Balders Død* was awarded a prize on the understanding that it was to be published after certain changes had been made in consultation with Carstens. It was published in 1775.[1] That Ewald fully realized the debt under which he lay to Carstens is shown by his grateful allusion to his benefactor:

> Jeg skulde uden hans Hjælp have kunnet blive en Mand af Indfald og Lune, maaske selv min daglige Cirkels Beundring...Hvorledes skal jeg finde Ord, der værdig nok udtrykke min Taknemmelighed mod den Mand, der ved at tæmme og styre min alt for brusende Aand, ved at vise mig de Afgrunde, som jeg havde at frygte for...gjorde mig bekvæm til at naa det.[2]

It was a generous and well-deserved tribute; but Carstens was conscious of his own limitations. He knew that his strength did not lie on the creative, but rather on the critical side of literature. The list of his works is not a long one, although his treatise, *Om aabne Vocalers Medvirkning i det poetiske Udtryks Styrke og Livagtighed* (1766) with its supplement *Samtale om Vocalernes Sammenstød i danske Vers* (1767), was up to that time the only Danish work on poetic theory to be translated into German.[3]

It was in 1752 that A. F. Büsching (1724–93) came from Germany to Sorø as tutor to a son of Count Lynar. Sneedorff was at Sorø at that time and for this patriotic Danish writer, Büsching expressed a warm admiration.[4] After some months in Sorø Büsching resigned his tutorship and went to Copenhagen, where he was soon in touch with both Danish and German writers. Although a member of the German circle, Büsching did not confine his attention entirely to matters concerning German literature, and it was not long before he observed that Denmark suffered from the lack of a learned periodical, which might express the actual development of Danish literature. To remedy this defect Büsching, against the advice of many Danes,

[1] F. Rønning, *op. cit.* II, p. 235.

[2] J. Ewald, *Samlede Skrifter*, *ed. cit.* III, pp. 244 f.

[3] J. H. Schlegel's translation of this work was published in the *Neue Bibliothek der schönen Wissenschaften*, IV, p. 1, where Carstens was warmly praised.

[4] A. F. Büsching, *Beyträge*, VI (1789), p. 204.

but possibly under the influence of Count Bernstorff with whom he was on a friendly footing, determined to bring out such a periodical. In 1753 the *Nachrichten von dem Zustande der Wissenschaften und Künste in den königlichen Reichen und Ländern* issued its first number. It was dedicated to Bernstorff and J. L. Holstein and its avowed purpose was to correct the false impressions which existed abroad regarding Denmark, an object dear to Bernstorff's heart. It did not merely achieve this immediate object. Büsching's periodical is still a useful source of information regarding Danish literature between 1753 and 1768. From his enterprise Büsching gained much credit in Danish eyes; it procured for him "den Credit eines Patrioten, den ein Ausländer in Dänemark nicht leicht sich erwerben kann, weil man ihm aus Eifersucht nicht trauet".[1] In April, 1754 Büsching left Copenhagen to return to Germany. He himself tells us that at his farewell visit to Count Holstein, at that time governor of the University of Copenhagen, the latter asked him to remain and said that he would try to obtain for him a position at the University. Bernstorff, too, thought that Büsching should wait a little to see what he might obtain in Denmark.[2] In spite of these friendly dissuasions Büsching left Copenhagen and the first volume of the *Nachrichten*, published on July 12, 1754, is signed by him as professor of Philosophy in the University of Göttingen. After his departure the *Nachrichten* was continued by others until 1768, in which year it ceased to appear.

Although Matthias Claudius,[3] like Gerstenberg, was legally a Danish subject, he was, of course, really a German, and is to be regarded as a member of the German circle. In a letter to Gerstenberg from Reinfeld, dated October 2, 1763, Claudius enquires of his friend as to the possibilities of his finding employment in Copenhagen: "Stirbt in Copenhagen nicht ein Secretair oder braucht nicht ein junger Herr einen Hofmeister

[1] A. F. Büsching, *Beyträge*, VI (1789), p. 220. [2] *Ibid.* pp. 226 f.

[3] Born at Leinfeld in 1740; studied in Jena 1759–63; in Copenhagen 1764–65; from 1768 on in Hamburg; then edited *Der Wandsbecker Bothe*; in 1788 in Altona; died in Hamburg in 1815.

mit ihm auf die Universität zu gehen?".[1] Finally in 1764, through his uncle, Josias Lorck, Claudius obtained a position as secretary to Count J. L. Holstein.[2] His stay in the Danish capital was of short duration. Already in August, 1765, he had returned to Reinfeld.[3] There is but little material available on Claudius' Copenhagen period,[4] and it is difficult to trace any influence of this writer on Danish literature. He seems to have found his friends exclusively among members of the German circle. Gerstenberg he had known previously in Jena, but the Gerstenberg he meets now is the Gerstenberg of the *Gedicht eines Skalden* and of the *Briefe über Merkwürdigkeiten der Litteratur*. At the musical evenings in Gerstenberg's house in Lyngby Claudius was a regular attender. Klopstock found him as enthusiastic a skater as himself and rarely did he miss one of Klopstock's favourite excursions.[5] Of his friend, G. F. E. Schönborn, who was then in Copenhagen, Claudius probably saw a good deal, and it is more than likely that it was in Copenhagen that Claudius first met the two young Counts Stolberg with whom he was later connected. The German circle exercised a strong influence on Claudius and the impressions he received during his short stay in the Danish capital formed the foundation of his later literary activities.[6] It was there that his interest in Shakespeare and in German and nordic antiquity was aroused; but although in Claudius' letters of that period the bardic names of "Wotan" and "Hermann" occur, and although he took part in the turmoil occasioned by Gerstenberg's *Gedicht eines Skalden* and the *Briefe über Merk-*

[1] Carl Redlich, *Ungedruckte Jugendbriefe des Wandsbecker Boten*, Hamburg, 1881, p. 8.

[2] L. Magon, *op. cit.* p. 210.

[3] W. Stammler, *Matthias Claudius*, Halle, 1915, pp. 31 ff.

[4] See R. Petersen, *Matthias Claudius og hans Vennekreds*, Copenhagen, 1884, p. 45; see also W. Stammler, *op. cit.* p. 32.

[5] Among the members of the German circle Claudius enjoyed a reputation as a fast skater. Klopstock's ode *Der Eislauf* is said to have been dedicated to him; see W. Stammler, *op. cit.* p. 32.

[6] See W. Herbst, *Matthias Claudius*, 1857, p. 47; also R. Petersen, *op. cit.* p. 41: "Den poetiske Anskuelse, der siden fremtræder i hans Skrifter, men som fik en stærk Tilsætning af hans egen ejendommelige Natur, er for største Delen Frugten af denne Periode."

würdigkeiten der Litteratur yet he never altogether yielded to the bardic fever. Klopstock exercised a greater influence on Claudius than did Gerstenberg. It was he who introduced him to the world of poetry and revealed to him nature, the fatherland and God as sources of literary inspiration.[1] That Claudius had enjoyed his stay in Copenhagen and would have been willing to return there is indicated by the fact that in 1770 Klopstock asked Count Bernstorff to appoint Claudius professor at Altona Gymnasium,[2] while in 1775 Gerstenberg vainly tried to have Claudius appointed as organist in a Copenhagen church.[3]

It was through Matthias Claudius that in 1764 his friend, G. F. E. Schönborn,[4] was attracted to Copenhagen.[5] During the first few years of his residence there Schönborn lived with Pastor Josias Lorck at Christianshavn,[6] but in 1768 he was appointed as tutor to a cousin of the Danish minister, Count Bernstorff, in whose house he lived for the following two years. For Bernstorff Schönborn, in common with all the other members of the German circle, had a great respect. The important place occupied by Schönborn in the history of the German circle is hardly warranted by the number of his published works. The little that he did write was scattered for the most part in different periodicals.[7] From the Copenhagen period only one poem of his has survived.[8] Inspired by Klopstock, Schönborn attempted a translation of the Pindaric hymns and gave one of these translations to Gerstenberg for publication in the con-

[1] W. Herbst, *op. cit.* p. 43.

[2] *Bernstorffske Papirer, ed. cit.* II, p. 318, and I, p. 519.

[3] Adolf Langguth, *Christian Hieronymus Esmarch und der Göttinger Dichterbund*, Berlin, 1903, pp. 99 and 137; referred to by L. Magon, *op. cit.* p. 77.

[4] Born 1737 at Stolberg in the Harz; 1758 studied theology at Halle University; 1764–71 in Copenhagen; 1771 went to Hamburg; 1773 to Algiers; 1778–1802 in London; died in 1817.

[5] *Zeitschrift der Gesellschaft für Geschichte der Herzogtümer Schleswig-Holstein*, I, Kiel, 1870, p. 131.

[6] J. G. Rist, *Schönborn und seine Zeitgenossen*, Hamburg, 1836, p. 10.

[7] For example the *Freiheitsode* (1776) in the *Musenalmanach*, Göttingen, 1776, ed. by Boie; and *Der Rhein* in Matthisson's *Lyrische Anthologie*.

[8] *Die Freiheitsode*, dedicated to his brother-in-law, Pastor Müller. It reveals Klopstock's influence; see W. Herbst, *op. cit.* p. 61.

tinuation of the *Briefe über Merkwürdigkeiten der Litteratur*.[1] Perhaps the most extraordinary personality of the German circle,[2] Schönborn was less important for his works than for his talents, the recognition he won from a wide circle of important friends, and the respect which such men as Count Bernstorff, Klopstock and Gerstenberg accorded him. The two latter, as well as J. A. Cramer and Sturz, were his close friends; with the young Counts Stolberg, Christian and Friedrich Leopold, he appears also to have been on terms of friendship. The widespread popularity enjoyed by Schönborn is attested by a "Gesamtbrief" sent from Kiel in 1776 to him—he was then in Algiers—and signed by Klopstock, Ehlers, Büsch, F. L. Stolberg, J. A. Cramer, Frau Ehlers, Noodt, Frau Fabricius, Margarete Dimpfel, E. Schmidt, Vosz and Frau von Winthem. In 1771 Schönborn followed Bernstorff and Klopstock to Hamburg, but returned to Copenhagen in 1773 with a nephew of the former. In the same year he went to Algiers as secretary to the Danish consulate there, and in 1778 he was transferred to London where he served the Danish government for twenty-four years. In London he was an intimate friend of Reventlow, the Danish ambassador to England. In both these positions Schönborn served the Danish crown and people with the utmost zeal and loyalty.[3]

When Cramer was in Quedlinburg G. B. Funk,[4] then a student in theology at Leipzig, had consulted him with regard to his fitness for the church as a profession.[5] In 1756 Cramer invited him to come to Copenhagen as tutor to his son Karl Friedrich and promised to help him with his theological studies.[6]

[1] *Zeitschrift der Gesellschaft für Geschichte der Herzogtümer Schleswig-Holstein*, Kiel, 1870, I, p. 131.

[2] P. Döring in *Der nordische Dichterkreis und die Schleswiger Litteraturbriefe*, Sonderburg, 1880, speaks of "Schönborn...mit seinem Gesicht wie Eichenrinde und seinem Herzen wie Blumenduft".

[3] *Reventlowske Papirer*, *ed. cit.* IV, p. 284.

[4] Gottfried Benedik Funk, born 1734 at Hartenstein in Saxony; studied at Freiburg and Leipzig; 1756 came to Copenhagen; 1769 left Copenhagen for Magdeburg, where he died in 1814. For Funk's life see Jördens, VI, pp. 124 ff.

[5] *Allgemeine deutsche Biographie*, VIII, p. 201.

[6] G. B. Funk, *Schriften*, Berlin, 1921, II, p. 307.

Funk's first impressions of the Danish climate were not altogether favourable: "Billig sollten unter so einem Himmel nur Freygeister wohnen",[1] he writes in a letter to a friend; but he recognizes gratefully the generous treatment accorded by the Danish government to German writers: "Sollte ich mir das vollkommenste Glück in dieser Sterblichkeit wünschen, das ich mir denken kann, so wäre es diesz: die dänische Regierung nach Sachsen zu versetzen, und selbst dann in Sachsen zu seyn".[2] During the thirteen years which Funk spent in Cramer's house in the Petristræde, it was a favourite meeting-place for the members of the German circle. For Cramer and for Klopstock Funk possessed an unbounded admiration.[3] To both of them Funk's musical tastes and his literary interests rendered him sympathetic. Throughout his life Funk was a tremendous worker. The range of his reading in the classics was unusually wide.[4] During his stay in Copenhagen theology and the oriental languages were his chief interests. He found time, however, for occasional contributions to *Der nordische Aufseher*, and he was the only writer other than Gerstenberg to play any considerable rôle in the *Briefe über Merkwürdigkeiten der Litteratur*. Four of these letters were probably written by Funk[5]; the first on Abbt's *Vom Verdienste*, the seventh on Gottsched's idea of a German grammatical dictionary, and the twenty-fifth and twenty-sixth on *Kritische Sammlungen einer dänischen Privat-Gesellschaft*. In 1760–1 he issued a translation of Du Bos' *Réflexions critiques* under the title *Kritische Betrachtungen über die Poesie und Mahlerey*, and in 1764 of J. H. Schlegel's Danish treatise as *Abhandlung über die Vorteile und Mängel der dänischen Sprache*. In 1769 Funk left Copenhagen to assume the position of subrector of the Domschule at Magdeburg.

Another member of the German circle has been mentioned as a possible contributor to Gerstenberg's *Briefe über Merk-*

[1] G. B. Funk, *Schriften*, II, p. 310. [2] *Ibid.* [3] *Ibid.* p. 312.

[4] In Funk's diary for the year 1753 there is a list of the classical works read by him during the year; see P. Döring, *op. cit.* pp. 19 f.

[5] A. M. Wagner, *op. cit.* I, pp. 67 f. See also Chapter III, p. 101, note 3, *supra*.

würdigkeiten der Litteratur.[1] It was probably P. Kleen who contributed the sixth letter[2] to Gerstenberg's collection. Kleen was born in Glückstadt in 1732 and came to Copenhagen in 1756 to assume a position as clerk in the Royal Army Commissariat. The German prose translation of Tullin's prize poem *Om Skabningens Ypperlighed*, entitled *Die Schönheit der Schöpfung*,[3] is by Funk.

In addition to J. A. Cramer there were three other members of the German circle who were pastors to churches in or near Copenhagen, F. G. Resewitz,[4] Balthasar Münter and Josias Lorck. Klopstock, who had previously known Resewitz in Quedlinburg, succeeded in procuring his appointment in 1767 as second preacher to the German Petrikirche in Copenhagen. Two years before, when the pulpit of this same church had been rendered vacant by the death of Dr Eberhard Hauber, Resewitz' name had been proposed, but Balthasar Münter was appointed. Münter himself pressed for Resewitz' appointment as second preacher to the church in 1767.[5] Resewitz had already some reputation as a theologian and as a literary man, before he came to Copenhagen. In spite of his connection with the Berlin party and the *Litteraturbriefe*, he was received in friendly fashion by the members of the German circle and he was soon on a good footing with Klopstock, J. A. Cramer, J. H. Schlegel and G. B. Funk. His work at the Petrikirche allowed him plenty of leisure.

Eminent theologian as Resewitz was, it was with pedagogic reform and the organization of philanthropic work that his interests were most closely engaged. With Balthasar Münter he carried on the school and poor relief organization of the Petrikirche, and with such success that he was soon given a wider field in which to exercise these activities. The pamphlet, *Über*

[1] A. M. Wagner, *op. cit.* p. 67. [2] Omitted in the edition by Weilen.

[3] Copenhagen, 1765.

[4] Born in Berlin, 1729; 1747 at Halle, where he studied theology; 1767–75 in Copenhagen; 1775–95 Abbot of Klosterbergen; 1806 died at Magdeburg.

[5] *Geschichtsblätter für Magdeburg*, 1885, p. 160, article by M. Kawerau on Resewitz.

die Versorgung der Armen,[1] in which Resewitz emphasized the necessity of organization in poor relief work, won the favourable attention of Christian VII, and in 1771 Resewitz was entrusted with the poor relief organization for the whole of Copenhagen. Under Struensee's ministry Resewitz was able to continue this work, and in 1771 he published his *Nachrichten an das Publikum von der Verfassung der Armenpflege in Copenhagen und von der Realschule des bisherigen Waisenhauses*. The question of school reform was at that time very much to the fore in Denmark and Resewitz was well qualified to discuss it. In 1773 he published his pamphlet, *Die Erziehung des Bürgers zum Gebrauche des gesunden Menschenverstandes und zur gemeinnützigen Geschäftigkeit*, which gives the results of the attempts at pedagogic reforms. Resewitz points out that three types of schools were necessary: agricultural schools in the country, technical schools in provincial towns and for the working classes in the large towns, and Realschulen and Gymnasien for the middle and upper classes in the large towns. For the proposed Realschule in Copenhagen Resewitz submits a very detailed plan. The school was to educate boys for business careers. French, English and Italian were to be taught and possibly Dutch. Danish history and geography were to be on the curriculum, and the scholars were to be instructed only in what would be useful to them later in business. The object was to develop in the pupils "a healthy common sense". This work of Resewitz is important in the history of German pedagogy and is typical of the views and strivings of German rationalism in education. Resewitz gave for the first time clear and practical expression to the vague ideas of educational reform which were then in the air. He pointed out paths full of promise to modern educationalists. It was in Copenhagen that Resewitz produced this important work, and as a result he was entrusted with the organization of the Realschule in the Danish capital. The only two schools of this type then in existence were one in Berlin and the other the Waisenhaus in Potsdam, and neither corresponded to Resewitz'

[1] Copenhagen, 1769.

ideas. Berlin was attempting to turn out both scholars and business men, and Potsdam wished to educate both soldiers and citizens.[1] In addition to his poor relief and educational work Resewitz delivered lectures on theology at Copenhagen University. His time was so fully occupied that he frequently found it necessary to get a student to preach in his stead, a habit which aroused a certain amount of resentment among the congregation of the Petrikirche.[2] After Count Bernstorff left Copenhagen Resewitz stayed on, but his position there after Struensee's fall was by no means agreeable, and in 1775 he left Copenhagen for Klosterbergen.[3]

Balthasar Münter[4] came to Copenhagen from Lübeck in 1765. His reputation as a theologian and preacher had preceded him, and it was not long before he had made his mark in the Danish capital. The German congregation of the Petrikirche, to which Münter was appointed, included the best known and most influential members of the German colony in Copenhagen. It had existed as a congregation from the time of the Reformation and was attended by the court. In the Petristræde, where the church was situated, were the residences of J. A. Cramer and Münter, and in this quarter was for many years the natural meeting-place for the Germans in the Danish capital. To the memoirs of Münter's only daughter, Frederikke, we are indebted for some information as to the German circle and the milieu in which she and her father moved.[5] Klopstock, Cramer and Gerstenberg were Münter's first acquaintances in Denmark and for many years his most intimate friends. In Münter's house Klopstock read his latest odes aloud, Sturz let his wit and humour play and Schönborn developed his philosophical system. Von Berger, Carsten Niebuhr, Gerstenberg and Basedow were also visitors. Like Cramer, Münter had always the

[1] *Geschichtsblätter für Magdeburg*, 1885, p. 169. [2] *Ibid.* p. 161.

[3] *Nyeste Skilderi af Kjøbenhavn*, 1823, XXXIX, p. 650.

[4] Born in Lübeck 1735; 1754 studied theology at Jena; 1765 appointed to the Petrikirche in Copenhagen; 1793 died in Copenhagen.

[5] Frederikke Brun, *Wahrheit aus Morgenträumen*; see also L. Bobé, *Frederikke Brun og hendes Kreds hjemme og ude*, Copenhagen, 1910.

most friendly feelings for Denmark and regarded himself and his family as adopted Danes. When his son, Fritz, in a letter home expressed his pleasure at having set foot on German soil his father reproved him. "Du har ikke nogensomhelst Aarsag til at glæde sig saa hjertelig over at have forladt den danske Jord".[1] In his time Münter was regarded as the best preacher in Denmark. His sermons were translated into Danish and used by Danish preachers.[2] Münter wrote many hymns, and his first collection, published in 1772, was dedicated to Klopstock and Cramer. For the schools and poor of his parish Münter was an untiring worker. He was just as fearless a preacher as was Cramer, and against Struensee's arbitrary rule he spoke out in no uncertain manner.[3] Münter was in the secret of the conspiracy to bring about Struensee's fall and his daughter, Frederikke, relates how she, who suspected something regarding the conspiracy, was locked up that she might not betray it. In 1772 Münter was asked to prepare Struensee for death. His *Bekehrungsgeschichte des Grafen J. F. Struensee*,[4] written under the impression that he had converted Struensee from materialism, was translated into many languages and brought Münter a European reputation. Münter's excellent qualities were fully appreciated in Denmark by both Danes and Germans.[5] In 1767 he was made an honorary Doctor of Theology of the University of Copenhagen and in 1769 a member of the Royal Academy of Sciences. P. F. Suhm refers to Münter as "en Theolog, begavet med største Dømmekraft og Taalsomhed, fremragende ved ypperlig Veltalenhed en Støtte for de fattige, lykkelig i sit hele Liv".[6]

Josias Lorck, uncle of Matthias Claudius and pastor of the

[1] B. Münter, *Briefe vom Hause*, 1781–2, and quoted by L. Bobé. *op. cit.*

[2] *Preuszische Jahrbücher*, CXXXII, pp. 230–49, article by Rudolph Kayser, "Deutsches Leben in Dänemark".

[3] B. Münter, *Predigten*, 1772, p. 120. Münter's feelings against Struensee were perhaps intensified by the fact that the latter's accession to power had deprived him of part of his income.

[4] 1772–3.

[5] *Zeitschrift für vergleichende Literaturgeschichte*, Neue Folge, X, p. 249. See also C. F. Weisze, *Selbstbiographie*, p. 84.

[6] *Adr. Cont. Efterretninger* 1793, No. 242; quoted by L. Bobé, *op. cit.*

German church at Christianshavn, had helped Büsching with the *Nachrichten* when it was started in 1753; he took over the editorship in 1756 and continued the periodical until 1768, when it ceased to appear.

It was not only the German pastors and men of letters who exerted an influence in Denmark under Frederick V and Christian VII: there were also German scientists and artists, who made important contributions at a time when the Danish sciences and arts had not developed very far. In 1752 the botanist, J. C. Oeder,[1] came to Copenhagen and in 1762, at the request of some influential Danes and assisted by O. F. Müller, Wahl and other Danes, he started the *Flora Danica*, one of the most important scientific productions of the period. There had at first been opposition to Oeder's undertaking this work on the grounds that a foreigner, handicapped by his ignorance of the language, could not gather the necessary information as he travelled through the country; but when Oeder's work appeared it was hailed with unanimous approval.[2] Oeder's interests were not entirely confined to botany. Political economy and agrarian reform held for him a strong attraction, and during the years 1755 to 1760, when he was visiting Norway, primarily to gather botanical information, he was asked by Bernstorff and Moltke to enquire into the economic conditions in that country.[3] He was one of the first writers in Denmark to propose a definite scheme for giving the Danish peasants freedom from feudal obligations, and his work *Bedenken über die Frage: wie dem Bauernstande Freiheit und Eigenthum verschaffet werden könne*[4] foreshadowed changes which later came to pass in Denmark. Oeder's words "ownership and property" became the slogan of the liberal party.[5] After Bernstorff's fall Oeder remained in Denmark to help with the plans for agrarian reform.

[1] Born at Anspach in 1728; studied at Leipzig; 1752 came to Copenhagen; 1754 became professor of Botany at the University of Copenhagen; died in 1791.

[2] A more modern Danish literary critic, N. M. Petersen, terms it "en af vor Literaturs Prydelser"; *op. cit.* v, 1, p. 29.

[3] L. Magon, *op. cit.* p. 153.

[4] Published 1769.

[5] F. Rønning, *op. cit.* II, p. 390.

C. G. Kratzenstein came from St Petersburg to Copenhagen in 1753 as professor of Physics in the University of Copenhagen. The study of the natural sciences was beginning to develop in Denmark at that time, and by his experiments, lectures, and writings, Kratzenstein did much to lay the foundation for an investigation of the laws of nature.[1]

J. M. Preisler and J. C. Pezold were two members of the German circle in Copenhagen who contributed to the cultivation of the arts in Denmark. Preisler had been discovered in Paris by Count Bernstorff,[2] and it was through him that the German engraver came to Copenhagen in 1744. In 1750 he was appointed professor in the recently founded "Kongelige Maler- og Tegneakademi." Preisler was a member of the summer colony at Lyngby and was on friendly terms with Klopstock and Cramer. Klopstock wished him to make a series of engravings for the *Messias* and vignettes for a collection of his odes.[3] J. C. Pezold, the sculptor, came to Copenhagen in 1750. He executed many commissions for statues in the public squares and gardens of Copenhagen. J. J. Dusch did not contribute much to the development of Danish art, in spite of the great reputation which he enjoyed. In 1766[4] he was appointed professor of the Fine Arts in Altona Gymnasium. Dusch had been attacked by Lessing in his *Briefe die neueste Litteratur betreffend* and he was consequently well disposed towards the circle of Klopstock and Cramer, of which he later became a member. Through his *Nordische Beiträge zum Wachstum der Naturkunde und der Wissenschaften und Künste überhaupt*[5] and his *Briefe zur Bildung des Geschmacks*,[6] in both of which works he illustrated his remarks by references to northern works of art, he made

[1] Kratzenstein was not popular in Denmark, partly because he never showed any desire to learn the Danish language; see N. M. Petersen, *op. cit.* v, 1, pp. 31 ff.

[2] L. Magon, *op. cit.* p. 206.

[3] F. Muncker, *Klopstock*, p. 338.

[4] Koch gives 1762 as the date of Dusch's appointment; but 1766 is probably correct; see L. Magon, *op. cit.* p. 519, note 292.

[5] 1757–8.

[6] 6 vols, 1764–73.

himself popular in Denmark. Frederick V helped him to defray the cost of publication of his writings.[1] His *Moralische Briefe zur Bildung des Herzens* was translated into Danish.[2]

Johann Just von Berger, a physician, was called from Germany to Copenhagen by Count Bernstorff in 1752.[3] An intimate friend of Bernstorff, he later became court physician. At his hospitable home the members of the German circle met frequently for musical evenings. It was Carsten Niebuhr, a German, who led the famous Danish expedition to Arabia in 1761. Michaelis, the originator of the plan, urged that a Dane should be appointed as leader, but that honour went to Niebuhr.[4] In 1767 he returned to Copenhagen after having spent six years in Arabia, and he remained in the Danish capital until 1778. Karl Christian Clauswitz, the son of a professor of theology in Halle, was a tutor in the house of the Stolbergs. The theologian, Georg Ludwig Ahlemann, came to Copenhagen in 1750 as private secretary to Count Dehn, a member of the Danish Council.[5] For Count Bernstorff Ahlemann had a great admiration and he later wrote the first biography of the Danish minister.[6]

[1] L. Magon, *op. cit.* p. 214.

[2] Translated by Jens Bech and published 1773–4 under the title *Moralske Breve til Hjertets Dannelse.*

[3] *Preuszische Jahrbücher*, CXXXII, pp. 230 ff.

[4] L. Bobé, *Frederikke Brun*, Copenhagen, 1910, p. 328.

[5] Aage Friis, *Bernstorfferne og Danmark*, II, pp. 36 ff.

[6] G. L. Ahlemann, *Über das Leben und den Charakter des Grafen J. H. E. Bernstorff*, 1777.

CHAPTER SEVEN

J. A. SCHEIBE and MUSIC IN DENMARK. THE MUSICAL MEMBERS of THE GERMAN CIRCLE

BETWEEN 1740 and 1775 no native name in Danish music rivalled in importance that of the German composer and musical critic, Johann Adolf Scheibe.[1] His works and the musical activities of some of the members of the German circle in Copenhagen are deserving of some attention, not only from the point of view of German music, on which they had an influence, but also from the point of view of music in Denmark where, like the other arts at that time, music was at a low ebb. Between 1740 and 1750 important changes were taking place in musical conditions in Denmark. During the reign of the pietistic Christian VI[2] "Comedianter, Liniedansere eller Taskenspillere" were forbidden, and in these lower forms of entertainment the opera was included. With the accession of Frederick V to the Danish throne there came a return of gaiety to public life. Within a short time were established in Copenhagen a German theatre, a French theatre under the protection of the court and the new Royal Theatre of Holberg on Kongens Nytorv. Opera, too, was revived, but it was the Italian and not the German opera which was played under royal patronage at Christiansborg in 1748.

Before coming to Denmark Scheibe was Kapellmeister to Friedrich Ernst, Margrave of Brandenburg. The Margrave had

[1] Born in Leipzig in 1708; 1725 studied law there, and was a member of Gottsched's circle; he then turned to music and, after living in Prague, Gotha and Sondershausen, went to Hamburg, where he edited the *Critische Musikus* (1737–40); in 1740 to Kulmbach as musical director to the Margrave of Brandenburg; in the same year to Copenhagen; in 1749 to Sønderborg; died in 1776.

[2] 1730–46.

some connection with the Danish court and through his and Count Bernstorff's influence Scheibe was called to Denmark as Court Musical Director in 1740,[1] and lived there until his death in 1776. He thus forms a link between those Germans who, like Johann Elias Schlegel, were in Denmark before the middle of the century and the members of the German circle, who grouped themselves round Klopstock. Scheibe came to Copenhagen with a reputation already made. From 1737 to 1740 he had edited in Hamburg the well-known musical periodical, *Der critische Musikus*. He had championed German opera and had gained an unenviable notoriety by his attack on Sebastian Bach in 1737.[2] In a letter to Gottsched written from Altona on September 3, 1740, Scheibe writes:

E. M. von demjenigen Glück, welches mir anjetzo begegnet ist, am ersten Nachricht zu erteilen, habe meiner Schuldigkeit gemäsz zu seyn erachtet. Es haben mich nämlich S. Mayt. der König von Dännemarck zu Dero wirklichen Capelldirektor unter einer ansehnlichen Besoldung allergnädigst ernennet, und ich werde wenigstens d. 12. oder 13. Sept. von hier nach Copenhagen zu gehen [haben], um diese Bedienung anzutreten. Da anjetzo kein Capellmeister daselbst ist, so musz ich diese Stelle zugleich mit vertreten, und es ist die grosze Hoffnung da, dasz es mit der Zeit und vielleicht bald um die Music besser stehen werde als bisher,...so werde ich allen Fleisz anwenden, dasz sowohl die Music als die Poesie ein anderes Ansehen gewinne, als sie einige Zeit in diesen Ländern gehabt haben.[3]

In the same year Scheibe announced to Gottsched his safe arrival in Copenhagen. He had found the court orchestra very much disorganized and had a great deal of work in connection with the celebration of the king's birthday. He goes on to say: "Der Hof fängt auch an, einen Geschmack an der Music zu bekommen und wir haben sehr oft Tafelmusic. Die Capelle wird auch vermehrt werden; doch werde ich alles anwenden, dasz diese Vermehrung mit lauter Deutschen geschieht".[4]

[1] N. M. Petersen, *op. cit.* IV, p. 422. See also Carl Roos, *Breve til Johann Christoph Gottsched fra Personer i det danske Monarki*, Copenhagen, 1918.

[2] Scheibe considered Bach responsible for his having failed to obtain a position as organist.

[3] Carl Roos, *op. cit.* p. 84.

[4] Dated December 9, 1740, *ibid.* p. 86.

This determination of Scheibe to strengthen the German musical influence in Denmark was doomed to partial disappointment through the popularity of the Italians. Sarti, with his light, tinkling rhythms and his cloying melodies, represented an entirely different school from that of Scheibe. The latter was unable to conceal his dislike for both the Italians and their music, and quarrels took place between the two composers; in 1749 Scheibe was dismissed from his court conductorship with a pension of 400 daler, which he retained until his death.[1] He retired to Sønderborg, where he opened a school of music. At the beginning of the 'sixties the favour of the court turned again toward Scheibe and through the influence of J. A. Cramer he was able to return to Copenhagen.

Since the operatic field in Denmark was barred to Scheibe's reforming zeal during his most vigorous years, he devoted his attention chiefly to church and concert music. On March 27, 1742, he wrote to Gottsched from Copenhagen informing him that he had given passion music in the royal chapel and that this was the first time such music had been performed in Denmark. He declared that he had good hopes of improving the royal orchestra by the addition of singers and instrumentalists.[2] Of the "Musikalske Societet", founded in 1744, Scheibe, with Holberg, was a prominent member and took a leading part in its activities until 1748, when the society, owing to the greater popularity of the Italian music, ceased to exist. Church music, oratorios and passion music by such German composers as Reinhard, Kaiser, Telemann, Hasse and Graun, were studied and performed.[3] That Holberg had a high opinion of this society is indicated by his words in one of the epistles:

Det musikalske Societet bestaar af adskillige Liebhabere og af alle Slags Stands-Personer, henved 40 udi Tallet, naar de alle ere samlede. De samme have udi en kort Tid saaledes tiltaget udi Musiken, at mange af dem kand passere for Mestere. Og, saasom dette Societet tiener till Konstens Forfremmelse, og tillige med er en Zirath for

[1] Schroeder, *Lexikon*, VI, p. 491. [2] Carl Roos, *op. cit.* Letter No. 9.
[3] Angul Hammerich, "Gluck som Kapelmeister i København" in *Vor Fortid*, I, 1917, Nos. 19–20, pp. 457, 472.

Staden, ønske alle dets Vedligeholdelse, helst, saasom det kand skee ved en gandske maadelig Bekostning.[1]

In addition to concerts, instruction in music was given by a college of music, and the object of improving musical taste in Denmark was very seriously pursued. There were four professional members of the college, of whom Scheibe was appointed one in 1745. His colleagues were Iversen and Foltmar, who played in the court orchestra, and one Ortmann.[2] In 1750 a new musical society was formed with headquarters in the Raadhusstræde. Although no longer residing in the capital, Scheibe still followed musical events there with unabated interest; it was he who wrote both the text and the music for the opening performance of the new society, and from him we have an account of its formation.[3] The Raadhusstræde society had considerable success. It continued its existence until 1773, when it had to yield to the competition of a younger and more vigorous rival society. This latter society had been founded in 1767 and met in the Bryggernes Laugshus. Its musicians were chiefly amateurs and the audiences drawn for the most part from the middle classes. In the year of its foundation Scheibe was made an honorary member of the society in recognition of his services to Copenhagen concerts. Although this new society attempted such serious works as Händel's *Alexanderfest* and Graun's *Der Tod Jesu*, there were complaints that the social side of its activities was unduly emphasized. The current periodicals of the time complained of the "livlige Passiaren" at the concerts and express the wish that: "de unge Herrer, som kommer i Koncerten alleneste forat drive Spøg med hinanden, vilde vælge et andet Sted til deres Sammenkomst".[4]

Scheibe was one of the most prolific composers and musical critics of his time, and the most important of his works

[1] L. Holberg, *Epistler*, No. 179.

[2] V. C. Ravn and Angul Hammerich, in *Festskrift i Anledning af Musikforeningens Halvhundredsaarsdag*, Copenhagen, 1886, p. 39.

[3] J. A. Scheibe, *Abhandlung vom Ursprunge und Alter der Musik*, Altona and Flensburg, 1754, Vorrede, p. 63.

[4] W. Behrend, *Illustreret Musik Historie*, 1897, p. 924.

were published in Denmark; but not all of them possess interest from the Danish point of view. In 1745 he had published a new and more ample edition of his periodical, *Der critische Musikus*. In 1747 he composed passion music for the *Gudelige Tanker* of G. G. Treschow. In 1749 he produced his *Thusnelda*, a musical play in four acts. The *Abhandlung vom Ursprunge und Alter der Musik insonderheit der Vokalmusik*, one of his best critical works, was published in Altona in 1754 by order of the Danish king. His *Schreiben an die Herrn Verfasser der neuen verschiedenen Schriften* appeared in Copenhagen in 1765 and was an answer to certain criticisms of his cantata on the occasion of the confirmation of the Prince Royal of Denmark. Scheibe composed several pieces of music for special occasions, chiefly in Copenhagen. In 1746 he wrote a lament ("Sørgecantata") on the death of Christian VI. *Die Patrioten* was written on the occasion of the birthday of the Prince Royal; the words were by J. A. Cramer. In 1751 Scheibe celebrated in music the inauguration of a hall of music and in 1752 the entry of the reigning queen into Copenhagen; his passion music, *Thränen der Sünder*, was published in 1754.

Scheibe's publications were not limited altogether to music. He had acquired a fair, although not a perfect mastery of the Danish language, and he had a genuine interest in Danish literature, possibly strengthened by his friendly intercourse with Holberg. The number of Scheibe's translations from Danish into German was considerable.[1] Among them were Pontoppidan's *Naturhistorie von Norwegen* in two parts (1753–4),[2] the first part of the same author's *Dänischer Atlas* (1765), C. P. Rothe's *Tordenskjold* (1753), Charlotte Biehl's plays in two volumes (1767), Holberg's *Fabeln* (1751 and 1761) and the same author's *Peder Paars* (1750). Scheibe issued a second translation of this latter work in 1764, together with an account of the life and writings of Holberg. He declared

[1] For a full list of Scheibe's translations from the Danish see Nyerup and Kraft, *Litteraturlexikon*, Copenhagen, 1820, p. 528.

[2] A new edition of this translation was brought out in 1769.

himself well fitted for this latter task, since he had plenty of available material and could count on the help of some friends of Holberg; besides which he himself had for six years known the Danish dramatist in familiar intercourse.[1] In the preface to this translation Scheibe says that he has made some improvements by eliminating coarse passages and adding passages of his own, and by changing the characters to suit better a German audience. But the liberties which Scheibe took with Holberg's work resulted in the loss of much of the strength and wit of the original *Peder Paars*.[2] Holberg himself was not satisfied with Scheibe's first translation, but he admitted that it was a difficult matter to make an adequate translation of such a work.[3]

As one might expect from the many allusions to music in Holberg's works, his interest in musical art was neither superficial nor transitory.[4] It is related that the Danish dramatist, reputedly so hard a man, had to conceal his tears and emotion when he heard Scheibe's cantata for the death of Christian VI.[5] He regarded the theatre and music as two of the most important factors in the cultural development of his fellow-countrymen. The art of the theatre could hope for nothing under Christian VI, and Holberg welcomed the presence in Denmark of so able a composer and musical critic as J. A. Scheibe. With most of Scheibe's musical ideas Holberg was in agreement, and the bond of friendship between the two men was strengthened by their common dislike of Italian music.[6]

[1] J. A. Scheibe, *Holbergs Peder Paars übersetzt*, Copenhagen, 1764, Vorrede, pp. xxiv–xxv. Holberg's account of his own life in *Epistolae ad virum perillustrem* only goes up to 1744, but he continues it in letter 447 of his *Epistler* (Part v).

[2] N. M. Petersen, *op. cit.* IV, 1871, p. 422.

[3] Holberg, *Epistler*, No. 447.

[4] One of Holberg's speeches at Borck's College dealt with music. It was not printed and was probably lost in the fire of 1728. See Erik Abrahamsen, *Holberg og Musikken*, in *Musik*, September 1, 1922, No. 117.

[5] *Ibid.*

[6] J. A. Scheibe, *Holbergs Peder Paars übersetzt*, Copenhagen, 1764, Vorrede, p. cix. Holberg expresses his hostility to Italian music in *Epistler*, Nos. 286, 299 and 373.

They considered it hurtful to the interests of operatic and concert music and of the theatre; it was introducing into the Danish churches too much instrumental music and an element of extravagant sentimentality, which both Holberg and Scheibe heartily disliked. To Scheibe's attacks on Italian music Holberg gave vigorous support. He voices a keen regret at the abandonment of the suave harmonies of the French school for the irregular dissonances of the Italian:

> Thi de Slags Folk (de moderne Musici) væmmes nu omstunder ved alt hvad er sødt og harmonisk, og finder ikke Smag, uden i Dissonancer, og hvad som skurrer i Ørene. Denne fordervede Smag haver nu allevegne indsneget sig, og det i saadan Grad, at om een af de Gamle stod op igen, og anhørte een af de nu brugelige anseeligste Concerter, vilde han bilde sig ind, at Instrumenterne accorderede ikke med hinanden, eller at Strængene paa hvert Instrument ikke vare stemmede: den gamle Music var simpel, men derhos naturlig, behagelig og harmonieuse: den nye derimod er konstig, men tilligemed unaturlig og skurrende.[1]

In one of his epistles Holberg expresses anger at the interest shown by Copenhagen in Italian opera: everywhere, he says, one hears talk of the heroes and heroines of opera and the singing and reciting of Italian operatic passages. He declares that the Italian singers "skieldede, klamredes, snorke, grædede og sukkede efter Takten"[2] and goes on:

> De Compositioner, som nu gøres sigte meer til Konst end Angenemhed, meer for at give Musicantere og Sangere noget at exercere sig paa, end at fornøye Tilhørerne....Det gaar med Skrifter som med vor Tids Musique hvorudi Harmoni og naturlig Sødme har maattet give Plads til Konsten.

Holberg's interest in music was not merely an academic one. Scheibe relates that Holberg practised the 'cello; he himself tells us he played the violin and alludes to himself as being regarded as "en af de dygtigste Fløytespillere i Byen".[3] When without money on his first foreign trip he earned some by playing the flute.[4] At Oxford his fellow-students complimented

[1] Holberg, *Epistler*, No. 33.
[2] *Ibid.* No. 286.
[3] *Ibid.* No. 157.
[4] Sigurd Müller in *Samtiden*, VIII, 1897, p. 338.

Holberg on his mastery of this instrument and on his knowledge of the English language.[1]

Scheibe's strong aversion to the Italian school of music did not date from his sojourn in Denmark, but from the time when he was a member of Gottsched's circle in Leipzig. Of Gottsched's musical ideas Scheibe was, as he himself acknowledges, a fervent disciple.[2] Gottsched, too, waged war against the old style of opera and advocated music in harmony with the spirit and action of the drama. The attacks on Italian music which he delivered in *Die vernünftigen Tadlerinnen* were supported by Scheibe in *Der critische Musikus*.[3] In the preface to the second edition of this work (1745) Scheibe says that it was the fashion to laud all the Italian musical follies to the skies and to admire them with clasped hands and bent knees; his summons to avoid these unpatriotic extravagances is addressed to the Danes as well as to his fellow-countrymen: "Laszt uns also, verehrteste Landsleute, Hand an dieses grosze Werk legen! Laszt uns das von den Ausländern zu unserm und der Musik Verderben entlehnte Unnatürliche und Verächtliche fliehen!"[4] It was from Holberg that Scheibe derived his strong interest in the development of the national spirit in Denmark and, like Holberg, he saw in the popularity of Italian music the development of a school of music, which was utterly foreign to Danish as well as to German ideas. In his *Vom Ursprunge und Alter der Musik* Scheibe was not afraid to put forward what was then a new and somewhat startling idea, that the origin of harmony was to be found among the peoples of the north.[5] His admiration for the musical qualities of the northern languages appears to have been genuine. He considered that the Danish

[1] E. Abrahamsen, *op. cit.* p. 116. [2] *Critischer Musikus*, II, pp. 88–110.

[3] Lessing agrees with these ideas of Scheibe on musical reform, possibly not being aware of their Gottschedian origin. See Lessing, *Hamburgische Dramaturgie*, No. 26, July 28, 1767.

[4] *Critischer Musikus*, Copenhagen, 1745, p. 111.

[5] Although Scheibe was the first to express this idea, it did not gain much prominence until Jean Jacques Rousseau espoused it. Rousseau's French critics declared the idea untenable, but it is now generally accepted. See Fétis, *Biographie des Musiciens*, VIII, 1844, p. 78.

language was particularly well fitted to express such emotions as love or sorrow and that it was a superior musical medium to the French:

> Det egner sig særdeles godt for Musik, og lader sig uden Vanskelighed sætte paa Noder og synge. Det klinger ogsaa meget godt, især naar det er kjærlige (zärtliche) eller sørgelige Tanker, som synges. Det overgaar i musikalsk Henseende langt det franske. Og dette kan jeg bedst bevidne af Erfaring.[1]

Of the contemporary Danish writers Johannes Ewald was the first to realize the musical possibilities of the Danish language, and he gratefully acknowledges the debt which he owed to Scheibe and to his advocacy of the collaboration of poet and musical composer: "Han var mig en Fader og det er vist, at om der findes noget i mine poetiske Arbejder, som i Hensigt til det Musikalske kan fortjene Bifald, saa har jeg hans lærerige Omgang, hans kærlige Undervisning ene at takke derfor".[2] To the use of vowels in poetry and their musical effect Ewald paid particular attention. In *Der critische Musikus* Scheibe had already emphasized their importance. In *Balders Død* the observation of the unities of time and place and the development of the characters in agreement with the action reveal the influence of Scheibe, Gottsched's disciple.[3] To Ewald Scheibe was a true friend and counsellor; this friendship came at an impressionable time of the young poet's life and was among the formative influences of his early years. The meeting between the two men probably occurred at the time of the death of Frederick V. The royal Kapelmester, Sarti, was then abroad and Scheibe was commissioned by the court to procure a mourning cantata. Ewald submitted a poem which Scheibe accepted and for which he later wrote the music.[4]

[1] *Abhandlung vom Ursprung und Alter der Musik, ed. cit.* p. 66, note in Danish translation.

[2] Johannes Ewald, *Samlede Skrifter, ed. cit.* v, p. 233.

[3] Torben Krogh, *Zur Geschichte des dänischen Singspiels im achtzehnten Jahrhundert*, Copenhagen, 1924, p. 109.

[4] It was first performed in 1768 with considerable success; see *Dansk Museum*, 1782, p. 692. Ewald and Scheibe collaborated on several pieces of music among which was the *Sørgecantata ved Christi Grav*.

To his German compatriots in Copenhagen Scheibe appears to have been well-known. He had met Johann Elias Schlegel so early as 1743. In a letter to Gottsched, dated April 18 of that year, Scheibe thanks Gottsched for having enabled him through a letter of introduction to make the acquaintance of Schlegel[1]; and in December, of the same year, he writes that Schlegel had translated into German for him the quotations from Aristotle in the second part of the new edition of *Der critische Musikus* on which he was then working.[2] In 1765 Scheibe wrote the music for Schlegel's *Procris und Cephalus*. There was much in common between the two men to bring them together. Scheibe, like Schlegel, was interested in the theatre and he agrees with the latter's attitude to Holberg's comedies, as he had expressed it in his *Zur Errichtung eines neuen dänischen Theaters*.[3] Both men were pioneers, both were stronger in criticism than in creative work and betrayed in their writings a lack of that warmth and imagination, which might have impressed their ideas more deeply on their generation. Like Schlegel, Scheibe had a keen interest in Danish language and literature and was friendly with many of the more enlightened Danes.

At a later date Scheibe came into contact with the members of the German circle, rather through his musical than through his literary interests. For some time he and Gerstenberg lived together in Copenhagen,[4] and that they were on friendly terms is indicated by Gerstenberg's intervention with Scheibe on Ewald's behalf, when the award for the mourning cantata was to be made on the occasion of the death of Frederick V.[5] In 1765 Scheibe wrote the music for Gerstenberg's *Ariadne auf Naxos*.[6] He had intended to compose the music for another cantata of Gerstenberg, *Klarissa im Sarge*, but the music for

[1] Carl Roos, *op. cit.* pp. 95 and 97.

[2] *Ibid.*, letter to Gottsched, p. 96.

[3] J. A. Scheibe, *Übersetzung von Peder Paars*, Copenhagen, 1764, Vorrede, p. cix.

[4] Cp. a letter from J. C. Book to Gerstenberg (1765), quoted by A. M. Wagner, *op. cit.* I, p. 195, note 40.

[5] See Chapter III, pp. 111 f., *supra*.

[6] It appeared in 1767.

this never appeared. The composer, Christopher Gluck, spent the winter of 1748–9 in Copenhagen as conductor at the Italian Opera House. In the history of music Scheibe is regarded as the forerunner of Gluck, and some record of the meeting of the two men and of the relations between them would have been interesting. In such of Scheibe's letters as exist there is, however, no such record. Gluck was not then the great reformer of music, which he later became, and little is known of this period of his life. Musical critics, however, date the change in Gluck's style of composition from his stay in Copenhagen, and it is generally assumed that Scheibe had an influence on Gluck, who, while in the Danish capital, was an interested spectator of Scheibe's championship of classical music and of his attack on Italian opera.[1] While in Copenhagen Gluck produced only one composition of his own, a cantata on the occasion of the birth of the young prince, later Christian VII. The first work composed by him after his Copenhagen season was the *Telemacco*,[2] and musical critics see in this work a breaking away from the purely Italian type of opera.[3]

Scheibe had not the genius which enabled Gluck to carry through his reforms. His musical talent was not equal to his reforming zeal; but he possessed a great store of musical learning; he was quick and accomplished in musical matters,[4] and his theoretical works, by reason of the novelty of their ideas and the clarity of their expression, take a high place in the musical literature of the eighteenth century. The bulk of these works was written in Denmark; but, although Scheibe had many friends in the country of his adoption, in his lifetime he met with recognition from a relatively small group of "cognoscenti" among whom, however, were Holberg and Johannes Ewald. Ewald speaks of him as "denne højst fortjente og, som jeg

[1] Angul Hammerich, *op. cit.* Scheibe in the introduction to his *Thusnelda, ein Singspiel in vier Aufzügen*, 1749, entitled *Von der Möglichkeit und Beschaffenheit guter Singspiele*, expresses ideas which Gluck later adopted in his opera *Alceste*. See Torben Krogh, *op. cit.* p. 109.

[2] 1749–50.

[3] Angul Hammerich, *op. cit.* p. 472.

[4] V. C. Ravn and Angul Hammerich, *op. cit.* p. 67.

frygter, for lidet paaskjønnede Mand", and many later Danish critics considered that Scheibe hardly received the recognition which was due to him. As with Basedow, the numerous quarrels and disputes in which Scheibe was engaged in maintaining the validity of his views prevented him from becoming popular with the peace-loving Danes.[1] A new time and new musical ideals caused Scheibe's music to be forgotten. Imagination and feeling came into their own and deposed his rationalistic, Wolffian art; but it should not be forgotten that Scheibe's cantatas and oratorios were the first attempt to exploit the qualities of the Danish language in the field of music.[2] That there were some Danes who realized the importance of his ideas and of the contribution which he made to Denmark's music is indicated by a generous tribute written four years after his death:

> Naar han satte Musik, saa troede han at maatte følge Digterens Tanker, at maatte lade Tonerne stræbe at opvække lige saadanne Forestillinger i Tilhørernes Sjæl som Digteren ved Ordene, og da var det naturligt, at de fleste nægtede ham Bifaldet, thi de fleste skjøtte ikke at erindres om, at de have en Sjæl....Kun faa erindre sig den høje Vellyst som de nød ved at høre en Ewalds Poesie ledsaget af en Scheibes Musik. Men hos disse faa er Scheibe udødelig som Ewald.[3]

Music was not the least of the bonds which attracted the members of the German circle to one another and held them together. Gerstenberg, Klopstock, J. A. Cramer, Claudius and Funk, all took an active interest in music. In *Der nordische Aufseher* there was much more space devoted to the musical art than was usual at that time in a moral periodical. Four of Funk's essays in *Der nordische Aufseher* treat of musical subjects[4]: Article 80 deals with *Die Musik als ein Teil einer guten Erziehung* and article 179 is entitled *Einige Anmerkungen über die Musik beym Gottesdienste.* In article 11*b* of the same periodical Cramer makes an appeal for a "majestic and touching" church

[1] E. L. Gerber, *Lexikon der Tonkünstler*, II, Leipzig, 1792, p. 315.
[2] C. F. Bricka, *op. cit.* XV, 1901, p. 101.
[3] *Almindelig dansk lit. Journal*, 1780, p. 386.
[4] Articles 80, 152, 153, 179.

song. Sturz has given an account of the musical evenings of the German circle at Gerstenberg's house at Lyngby.[1] Of one such evening, on the occasion of receiving a visitor from Hamburg, Gerstenberg writes to Klopstock:

> Von Bach war seine ganze Rede voll. So was Mannichfaltiges! So was Neues und Reifes und Vollendetes hatte er nie gehört. Den Abend sang er; wir hatten in aller Eile Violinen, Flöten, Oboen, Hörner, Bässe zusammengebracht, machten da in der Geschwindigkeit ein kleines Concert, das sich hören liesz.[2]

And in a letter of Klopstock to Cäcilie Ambrosius the author of the *Messias* says:

> Gerstenberg und seine Frau singen sehr gut und sehr nach meinem Geschmacke. Wir haben eine deliciöse kleine Sammlung von Musik. Wir lesen Melodien aus, die uns vorzüglich gefallen. Wir machen Texte dazu, wenn sie noch keine haben, wir ändern andere Texte oder wir nehmen auch irgend einer Melodie, die uns nicht gefällt, einen Text, der uns gefällt, und bringen ihn unter eine andere Melodie. Wir singen aber auch viele scherzhafte Sachen, z. E. die Gerstenberg muss mir sogar griechisch singen.[3]

Both Gerstenberg and his wife played the piano well, to which fact J. H. Vosz, in a letter to his fiancée, Ernestine Boie, bears witness: "Die Gerstenberg singt und spielt ganz vortrefflich, weit natürlicher und empfindungsvoller als die Windhem und Gerstenberg ist ebensosehr Meister in Beiden".[4] Frederikke Brun tells of Gerstenberg and his wife singing Klopstock's *Selmar und Selma* to the melody of the composer, Neefe.[5]

Gerstenberg's interest in music did not originate in Copenhagen. It had been awakened by his intercourse with the composer, Rosenbaum, while he was still attending Altona Gymnasium,[6] and it continued through his life. During the years which Gerstenberg spent in Copenhagen, he was working

[1] See Chapter III, p. 93, *supra*.

[2] J. M. Lappenberg, *Briefe von und an Klopstock*, Braunschweig, 1867, p. 273.

[3] *Ibid.* p. 192, No. 98.

[4] *Briefe von J. H. Vosz*, I, p. 286, dated December 5, 1775.

[5] F. Brun, *Wahrheit aus Morgenträumen und Idas ästhetische Entwicklung*, Aarau, 1824, p. 64.

[6] A. M. Wagner, *op. cit.* I, p. 15.

at cantatas and an opera, writing against Italian music, advocating a closer union between poet and musical composer, and through his correspondence with Claudius, Emanuel Bach and others he was keeping in close touch with musical developments elsewhere. His *Ariadne auf Naxos*, generally accounted one of the best cantatas in eighteenth-century music, and the only cantata which Gerstenberg completed, was published in 1767. *Clarissa im Sarge* was not completed. Only the beginning of his opera, *Peleus*, has survived.[1] In 1770 Gerstenberg published a short essay on the shortcomings of Italian songs, entitled *Über Recitativ und Arie in der italienischen Singkomposition*. In maintaining, as he did in this work, that the Italian recitative ran counter to the spirit of the German language, Gerstenberg, like Scheibe, was fighting a battle for Danish as well as for German music.

It had already been pointed out by Du Bos, whose *Réflexions critiques* Gerstenberg knew, that classical poetry had had a much more intimate relation to music than modern poetry,[2] and Gerstenberg had the vision, which was realized later, of a German drama, which could be combined with music. He attempted the translation into German of two famous monologues, that of Socrates before drinking poison, set to music by Emanuel Bach, and Hamlet's monologue "To be or not to be". In this desire of Gerstenberg for a closer union between music and poetry there may be discernible, too, the influence of Scheibe's *Der critische Musikus*. Already in the *Sorøske Samlinger* there is a reference to this work. Scheibe had evidently complained of some unfairness in the criticism in Gerstenberg's periodical of one of his productions, and Gerstenberg assures him that there was no unfriendly intention in the criticism, but that the critic was a personal friend of Scheibe and an admirer of his music.

To such eager music-lovers as Claudius and Gerstenberg and,

[1] In a letter from Gerstenberg to Klopstock; see J. M. Lappenberg, *op. cit.* p. 274.

[2] Du Bos, *Réflexions critiques*, III.

indeed, to all the musical members of the German circle, Philipp Emanuel Bach, who went to Hamburg as musical director shortly before Claudius, was an interesting personality. It was partly through Claudius and partly through direct correspondence with Bach, that Gerstenberg was enabled to keep up his connection with the Hamburg composer. In his letters to Gerstenberg Claudius gave a detailed account of the personality and musical activities of Bach; and it was Claudius who promised to send Gerstenberg occasional numbers of Bach's weekly musical periodical, *Musikalisches Vielerlei*, which had begun to appear on January 5, 1770, and which contained music by good composers for all instruments.[1] Bach was interested in the musical possibilities of Gerstenberg's poems. He promised to set *Clarissa im Sarge* to music[2] and asked Gerstenberg to send him some contributions to his periodical.[3] Through his correspondence with Emanuel Bach, J. C. F. Bach, Claudius, Gluck and Nicolai,[4] Gerstenberg did much to keep the Danes in touch with musical developments outside their own country, and in these letters he shows a real understanding of, and love for music, such as no other member of the German circle, with the exception of Scheibe, possessed.

Klopstock had a naturally true and delicate feeling for music; his verse is usually characterized by perfect rhythm; but he was greatly inferior to Gerstenberg both in his practical and theoretical knowledge of music. He played no instrument and only in later years sang in chorus.[5] In a letter written in 1767 to Cäcilie Ambrosius, Klopstock says: "Ich bin ein sehr verliebter Liebhaber der Musik, und ob ich gleich selbst weder spiele noch singe, so habe ich doch ein Flügel-Clavier auf meiner Stube. Ich singe wohl bisweilen ein wenig mit, wenn es leicht ist, was

[1] Letter from Claudius to Gerstenberg from Hamburg, 1770; see Carl Redlich, *Ungedruckte Jugendbriefe des Wandsbecker Boten*, Hamburg, 1881, p. 19.

[2] *Ibid.* See also La Mara, *Musikerbriefe*, I, pp. 207 ff.

[3] *Ibid.* p. 20.

[4] R. M. Werner, "Gerstenbergs Briefe an Nikolai" in *Zeitschrift für deutsche Philologie*, XXIII, p. 59.

[5] F. Muncker, *op. cit.* p. 361.

gesungen wird".[1] Although, through his relations with Gerstenberg, Emanuel Bach and Gluck, Klopstock was able to develop his musical knowledge considerably, he always retained certain narrowing prejudices. He considered music only from the standpoint of poetry and he thought more of vocal than of instrumental music. Of the latter he knew but little. He held that music had no moral influence and was therefore inferior to poetry, but he regarded it as higher than the plastic arts since it touches the heart more. Klopstock acknowledges quite frankly his lack of knowledge of the theory of music: "Ich bin, wie verliebt ich auch in die eigentliche, wahre, simple Musik bin, doch ein Laye in allem, was musikalische Theorie heiszen kann und ich habe nur seit ehegestern die Lehre vom Tacte ein wenig studirt".[2] Of the changes in musical conditions in Copenhagen during his sojourn there Klopstock does not speak. He makes no mention of Scalabrini, Sarti or even Scheibe, although the latter was called to Copenhagen by Bernstorff, Klopstock's patron and friend.

It is significant that it was in 1764, the year of Gerstenberg's arrival in Copenhagen, that Klopstock's interest in music awakened. Between the two men their common love of music was a strong bond. From the musical side of his intercourse with Gerstenberg Klopstock derived a great deal of pleasure and profit. He persuaded him to set some of his odes and extracts from the *Messias* to music,[3] and in 1767 they collaborated on a new German text for the *Stabat Mater*. It was Gerstenberg who introduced Klopstock to Händel's musical works.[4] Assisted by Gerstenberg and Funk, Klopstock wrote new poems and altered old ones to suit certain melodies.[5] In the history of song-writing in the eighteenth century Klopstock's odes

[1] J. M. Lappenberg, *op. cit.* p. 192.
[2] *Ibid.* p. 158; letter to Denis, dated November 22, 1766.
[3] *Vierteljahrsschrift für Musikwissenschaft*, VII, p. 189.
[4] F. Muncker, *op. cit.* p. 363.
[5] Funk relates that Klopstock used frequently to go to the former's house early in the morning to awaken him in order to try over new songs; see G. B. Funk, *Schriften*, II, p. 314.

occupy an important place, and foremost in Klopstock's musical interests was the desire to see the musical qualities of his own poetry evoked; he tried repeatedly to find a composer who could set his poems to music. His negotiations to this end with C. G. Krause of Berlin, whose music to Ramler's *Ptolemäus und Berenice* had delighted him, and with J. A. Hasse, the famous Viennese conductor, proved fruitless; but in 1759 Klopstock came into touch with Christopher Gluck, at that time in Vienna,[1] where Klopstock was known through his *Hermannsschlacht*, which he had dedicated to the Emperor Joseph II. In a letter to Ebert, dated July 14, 1770, Klopstock says: "In allem Ernste wird der Hermann in Wien im künftigen Jahre aufgeführt werden. Gluck arbeitet schon an der Composition"[2]; but the *Hermannsschlacht* music was never finished. Gluck did, however, write several accompaniments to Klopstock's odes and published seven of them as songs. Like Klopstock, Gluck believed in a closer union between poetry and music.[3] In the melodies of the bardic poetry Klopstock felt a keen interest. In a letter to Ebert he speaks of Macpherson having promised to send him some old melodies of Ossian from which he could study the rhythm of the old bardic music.[4] With Angelica Kauffmann Klopstock maintained a frequent correspondence on the subject of nordic melodies.

The debt which Danish music owed to Scheibe and the musical members of the German circle was no small one. Danish writers in general, and Johannes Ewald in particular, were roused by the desire of these writers to realize a close connection between poetry and music. Klopstock and Gerstenberg tried to link up the old northern melodies with the literary productions of the bardic school. Scheibe continued on the musical side the tradition which J. E. Schlegel had begun, that of pointing out the qualities and possibilities of the modern Danish

[1] Klopstock and Gluck did not meet until 1775; F. Muncker, *op. cit.* p. 362.
[2] J. M. Lappenberg, *op. cit.* p. 229.
[3] Gluck declared that music should clothe the text as their silken veils did the Grecian dancers; see H. P. Sturz, *Schriften*, *ed. cit.* I, p. 184.
[4] J. M. Lappenberg, *op. cit.* p. 218, letter dated May 5, 1769.

language and the interest of the older bardic literature. The patriotic ideas, which he had absorbed from Gottsched in his Leipzig days, he put at the service of the Danish people. Scheibe enjoyed a musical reputation such as no Dane then possessed and his vigorous opposition to the Italian school of music, his bold declaration that the origin of harmony had been among the northern peoples, and his assertion of the claims of the Danish language as a musical medium were all blows at the artistic prestige of the Latin countries and indications of independent lines of development, which meant much at that time to Danish music.

The aloof attitude of many of the members of the German circle towards the Danes reflected that of the rest of the Germans in Denmark to the Danish population.[1] Had there been closer intercourse with those Danes who were interested in literature, the contribution which the German circle made to Danish literary development, might have been still greater.[2] Yet there were a large number of German writers in Copenhagen who did take an interest in Danish literature and exercised a very considerable influence on its development; and although the German circle was and remained German, yet in forming a just picture of Danish literature during the years between 1750 and 1770, one must begin with and constantly refer to the influence and works of the members of this circle.[3] It was in Danish literature a period of preparation. A new poetry was introduced, a new aesthetic and moral attitude to the Bible, a ruthlessly free-thinking philosophy; foundations were laid for a theory of education; attention was drawn to the latest discoveries in the natural sciences; the liberation of the Danish peasants was

[1] The Danish government appears to have protected the Germans in Denmark from contact with the Danish language and people. German priests were introduced into German communities in Copenhagen and other parts of Denmark. See H. L. Møller, *Kong Christian den Sjette*, pp. 112 ff.

[2] Although Holberg lived for three years (1751–4) after Klopstock's arrival in Denmark, these two writers never met, so far as is known.

[3] Just Bing, *Klopstock og den Klopstockske Kreds i Danmark.* (*For Kirke og Kultur*, v, p. 608.)

advocated; a new literary criticism and a new method in the treatment of the history of literature were introduced; and in all of these significant developments the German writers in Denmark played an important part.[1] They continued the work which Holberg had begun, that of bringing the Danes into touch with ideas which were then moving in Western Europe, and, during a period which was poor in native talent, they prevented Danish literature from becoming narrow and parochial.

Yet Holberg, Falster and Tullin had good reason to complain of the favour shown to Klopstock and Cramer by Danish statesmen. For over thirty years, while positions and pensions were freely offered to German men of letters and while money was being squandered on foreign adventurers, Danish literature received but little help from the government.[2] For this attitude to native literature the Danish prime minister was largely responsible. Like Holberg, Bernstorff wished to give Denmark a share in the general culture of the time; but, differently from him, he had no idea of developing Danish nationality or of encouraging the use of the Danish language in literature. It is difficult to decide now whether Bernstorff could have found at home men who could equally well have attacked the problems for the solution of which he employed so many Germans; but the result of his attitude towards Danish literature was that Danish men of letters lost courage when they saw that only foreigners were allowed to sun themselves in the presence of the Danish ministers.[3] It is a shameful fact that Michaelis had to remind the prime minister that the expedition to Arabia should be led by a born Dane or Scandinavian and that the nation, which was to bear the cost of the expedition, should harvest the honour.[4]

[1] N. M. Petersen, *op. cit.* v, 1, p. 32.

[2] The Danish writer, P. F. Suhm, complains that only 700 daler were spent annually on the Royal Library, at that time a private library, while he himself spent from 4000 to 5000 daler a year on his own library. In 1775 Suhm's library was made a public one. See P. F. Suhm, *Samlede Skrifter*, xv, Introduction, pp. 95–6.

[3] J. C. Fabricius, *Efterladte Reventlowske Papirer*, 1895–7, vi, p. 580.

[4] J. D. Michaelis, *Literarischer Briefwechsel*, 1, p. 318.

The foregoing chapters treat only of the period up to the fall of Bernstorff. Some of the members of the German circle still remained in Copenhagen after that unhappy event. But in Bernstorff the circle had lost its protector and in Klopstock its intellectual leader. There was none to replace these two men, and, although the German writers continued to meet in the houses of J. J. von Berger, J. M. Preisler and Balthasar Münter and in the Bernstorff Palais, where, after 1772, Andreas Peter Bernstorff, nephew of the creator and patron of the circle, lived, yet the spirit that informed the German circle in Copenhagen had departed. From now on the German muse found its home in the fatherland and the light of Copenhagen grew dim before the approaching glory of Weimar.

APPENDIX

HANS PONTOPPIDAN'S TRANSLATION of KLOPSTOCK'S *MESSIAS*

According to a note at the beginning of his manuscript, Hans Pontoppidan gave his translation of Klopstock's *Messias* (see *supra*, p. 79) to the publisher to the Court and University Library, Schultze, in 1786, with a view to its publication. Schultze, however, was unable to secure a sufficient number of subscribers; and the translation was consequently never printed. An unnamed person made a copy in which the author inserted corrections. The work is dedicated to the Queen of Denmark: "Deres Majestæt Min Allernaadigste Dronning, Juliana Maria, allerunderdanigst tilegnet af Oversætteren, Hans Pontoppidan, Sogne Præst i Rönne og St Knuds K. paa Bornholm." Both original and copy are in the Royal Library in Copenhagen. The following verses from the beginning of the epic will give some idea of its quality:

FÖRSTE SANG

Syng udödelig Siel! de syndige Menneskers Frelsning,
Hvilken Jehova Messias, i Manddommen haver fuldendet;
Og ved hvilken paa nye han Adams forlorede Slægte
Guddommens Kierlighed, ved Pagtens Blod haver skienket.

Saaledes skeede den Eviges Villie. Forgieves oprörte
Satan sig mod den guddommelig Sön. Forgieves Judæa
Mod ham opstod. Han giorde, fuldbragte den store Forsoning.
Men O Værk, som ikkun Gud alværende kiender!
Tör sig vel Digter Konsten af sit Mörke dig nærme?

Hellige hende, Aand Skaber! for hvem jeg stille tilbeder!
Föer hende mig, som din Efterlignerske hellig henrykket,
Fuld af udödelig Kraft, i forklaret Skiönhed i möde,
Rust hende ud, med hiin dybsindig eensomme Viisdom,
Hvormed du forskende Aand! Guddommens Dyb gjennemskuer.

Saaledes skal jeg Lyes og Aabenbaringer kjende,
Og den store Messias Forlösning værdig besynge.
Kiende I Dödelige! eders Slægtes fornyede Ære?
Da eders Skaber, som Forlöser paa Jorden nedstiger.
O saa hörer min Sang! og I saa Ædle for alle!

Dyreste Venner af Jesu vor elskværdige Midler!
Siele, som med den tilkommende Dom fortroelig omgaaes!
Hörer og synger den evige Sön, ved gudeligt Levnet!
Nær hiin hellige Stad, der sig vanhelliget ilde,
Og sin höje Udvælelses Krone, uvidend bortkasted,

Fordum Guds synlige Herligheds Stad, de hellige Fædres
Pleiemoder, nu et Blods Altar af Mordre udgydet;
Her er det Messias sig nu fra Folket lösriver,
Hvilket dyrket ham vel, men ikke med saadanne Hierter
Som for den Alseendes Øyne ulastelig blive.

BIBLIOGRAPHY

I. ORIGINAL SOURCES.

A. Works and letters of members of the German circle and of those in contact with them.

Bernstorffske Papirer. Ed. Aage Friis. Copenhagen, 1904–13. I, II.
Cramer, J. A. Letters in:
  Briefe deutschschreibender Gelehrten, II, pp. 133–48.
  Archiv für Litteraturgeschichte, XIII, pp. 455 ff. and V, pp. 581 ff.
  Seufferts Vierteljahrsschrift, IV, pp. 59–61.
Funk, G. B. Schriften. Berlin, 1821.
Gram, Hans. Breve fra. Ed. Herman Gram. Copenhagen, 1907.
Holberg, L. Epistler. Copenhagen, 1865–75.
Klopstock, F. G. Briefe von und an. Ed. J. M. Lappenberg. Braunschweig, 1867.
Michaelis, J. D. Literarischer Briefwechsel. Leipzig, 1794. I.
Rabener, G. W. Briefe. Ed. C. F. Weisze. Leipzig, 1772.
Reventlowske Papirer. Ed. L. Bobé. Copenhagen, 1895 ff. IV, V and VI.
Schlegel, J. E. Briefe an Bodmer. Ed. G. F. Stäudlin. Stuttgart, 1794.
—— Briefe an F. von Hagedorn. Hagedorns Poetische Werke. Ed. Eschenburg. Hamburg, 1800. V.
Sturz, H. P. Leben und Charakter des Grafen Bernstorff. Leipzig, 1777.
—— Article in Deutsches Museum, June, 1776.
Suhm, P. F. Samlede Skrifter. Copenhagen, 1798. IX, X, XIV and XV.

B. Danish and German literature relating to the German circle and published during the years 1750 to 1800.

(1) General Works.

DANISH:

Biehl, C. D. Mit ubetydelige Levnetsløb. Ed. L. Bobé. Copenhagen, 1909.
—— Breve om Kong Christian VII. Ed. L. Bobé. Copenhagen, 1901.
—— Interiører fra Kong Frederik den Femtes Hof. Ed. L. Bobé. Copenhagen, 1909.
Brun, Frederikke. Ungdomserindringer. Ed. L. Bobé. Copenhagen, 1917.
Ewald, J. Samlede Skrifter. Copenhagen, 1914–24. I, V and VIII.
Langebek, J. Det kongelige danske Selskabs Begyndelse. Copenhagen, 1768.

Langebekiana. Copenhagen, 1794.
Luxdorphiana. Copenhagen, 1791.
Sneedorff, J. S. Skrifter. Copenhagen, 1775–7. VII and VIII.
Tullin, C. B. Samlede Skrifter. Copenhagen, 1770–3. II.
—— Den patriotiske Tilskuer. Sorø, 1761.

GERMAN:

Cramer, K. F. Klopstock, er und über ihn. Hamburg, 1780.
Herder, J. G. Werke. Ed. Suphan. Berlin, 1877–1913.
Lessing, G. E., see (3) German critical periodicals, below.

(2) Literary and critical periodicals published in Denmark, 1750–1800.

Büsching, A. F. Nachrichten von dem Zustande der Wissenschaften und Künste in den kgl. dänischen Reichen und Ländern. Copenhagen and Leipzig, 1754–7. II.
—— Beyträge zu den Lebensgeschichten denkwürdiger Personen. Hamburg, 1783–9. III and VI.
Dansk Maanedsskrift. 1865. I.
Dansk Minerva. 1816. III.
Dansk Magazin. Copenhagen, 1745–52.
Dänische Bibliothec. Copenhagen and Leipzig, 1738–46.
Dänisches Journal. 1767. I.
Dansk Anti-Spectator. Copenhagen, 1744–5.
Dansk Spectator. Copenhagen, 1744–5.
Deutsches Museum. November, 1777.
Fortgesetzte Nachrichten von dem Zustande der Wissenschaften und Künste. Copenhagen, 1762. II.
Mercure Danois. Copenhagen, 1753.
Nye Tidender om lærde Sager, 1745.
Om de kjøbenhavnske Lærde Tidender fra 1720 til vor Tid. In Dansk Litteraturtidsskrift, 1834, Nos. 1–9, pp. 38–43, and pp. 321–33.

(3) German critical periodicals.

Bibliothek der schönen Wissenschaften und der freyen Künste. Leipzig, 1757–65.
Hamburgische Dramaturgie. Lessings Werke. Ed. Lachmann-Muncker. IX and X. Leipzig, 1893–4.
Briefe, die neueste Litteratur betreffend. *Ibid.* VIII. 1892.

(4) Records and publications of Copenhagen learned Societies, 1750–70. In addition:

Malling, O. Om Sorø Akademie in For Historie og Statistik, 1822. I, pp. 1–36.
Molbech, C. Det kgl. danske Videnskabernes Selskabs Historie 1742–1842. Copenhagen, 1843. XVI.
—— Om Sorø Academie. Copenhagen, 1847.

Rahbek, K. L. Om Selskabet til de skjønne og nyttige Videnskabers Fremme, dets Stiftelse (1759) og Stiftere. In Dansk Minerva, 1816. III, pp. 228–55.

Tauber, E. G. Træk af Sorø Academies ældre Historie 1623–1771. In Blandinger fra Sorø. Copenhagen, 1831. I, pp. 159–67.

(5) Impressions of foreign travellers in Denmark in the eighteenth century.

Molesworth, R. Account of Denmark in the year 1692. London, 1694.

De La Vrigny. Relation en forme de Journal fait en Dannemark. Rotterdam, 1706.

II. OTHER SOURCES.

C. Danish and German literature from 1800 to the present time.

(1) Relating more particularly to the German circle.

Bobé, L. F. Brun og hendes Kreds, hjemme og ude. Copenhagen, 1910.

Döring, P. Der nordische Dichterkreis und die Schleswiger Literaturbriefe. Sonderburg, 1880.

Kayser, R. Deutsches Leben in Dänemark. In Preuszische Jahrbücher, 1908. CXXXII, pp. 230–49.

Koch, M. H. P. Sturz und Abhandlung über die Schleswigischen Litteraturbriefe. Munich, 1879.

Löwenfeld, R. Eine deutsche Tafelrunde in Kopenhagen. In Nord und Süd, 1897. LXXXIII, pp. 165 ff.

Magon, L. Ein Jahrhundert geistiger und literarischer Beziehungen zwischen Deutschland und Skandinavien 1750–1850. I. Dortmund, 1926.

Møller, H. L. Kong Christian den Sjette. Copenhagen, 1889.

Schmidt, K. Klopstock und seine Freunde. Halberstadt, 1810. I.

(2) Of more general interest.

SCANDINAVIAN:

Blanck, A. Den nordiske Renässansen i sjuttonhundretalets litteratur. Stockholm, 1911.

Kjøbenhavns Skilderi. Copenhagen, 1813.

Møller, J. Om Danmarks skjønne Litteratur under Kong Christian VI, og om Kongens Ulyst til Skuespil. In Det skandin. Litt. Selskabs Skrifter, 1832. XXIII, pp. 197–256.

Nielsen, O. Kjøbenhavn paa Holbergs Tid. Copenhagen, 1884.

Paludan, J. Danmarks Litteratur i Holbergstiden. Copenhagen, 1913.
—— Deutsche Wandertruppen in Dänemark. In Zeitschrift für deutsche Philologie. xxv, 3, pp. 313 ff.
—— Fremmed Indflydelse paa den danske Nationalliteratur i 17. og 18. Aarh. Copenhagen, 1913.
—— Holbergs Forhold til det ældre tyske Drama. In Historisk Tidsskrift. vi, 2.
Rønning, F. Rationalismens Tidsalder. Copenhagen, 1886. i, ii.

GERMAN:

Danzel, T. W. Gottsched und seine Zeit. Leipzig, 1848.
—— Lessings Leben und Werke. Berlin, 1880.
Haym, R. Herder. Berlin, 1877–85. i.
Koch, M. Gottsched und die Reform der deutschen Literatur. Berlin, 1866.
Köster, A. Die deutsche Literatur der Aufklärungszeit. Heidelberg, 1925.
Prutz, R. E. Ludwig Holberg. Stuttgart, 1857.
Wagner, A. M. H. W. von Gerstenberg und der Sturm und Drang. 2 vols. Heidelberg, 1920–4.
Waniek, G. Gottsched und die deutsche Literatur seiner Zeit. Leipzig, 1897.
Weddigen, F. H. O. Die Einwirkung der deutschen Literatur auf die dänische. In Germania, 1899. iv.
—— Geschichte der Einwirkung der deutschen Literatur auf die europäischen Kulturvölker der Neuzeit. Leipzig, 1882.

FRENCH:

Van Tieghem, P. La Mythologie et l'ancienne Poésie scandinaves dans la littérature européenne au dix-huitième siècle. In Edda, 1919, 1920. Reprinted in Le Préromantisme, Paris, 1924.

D. (1) Danish and German histories of literature published since 1800.

DANISH:

Hansen, P. Illustreret dansk Litteraturhistorie. Copenhagen, 1883–6.
Horn, F. W. Den danske Litteraturs Historie. Copenhagen, 1881. (Also in German and English translation.)
Petersen, N. M. Bidrag til den danske Litteraturs Historie. Copenhagen, 1867–71. iii–v.
Rahbek, K. L. and Nyerup, R. Den danske Digtekunsts Historie. Copenhagen, 1800.
—— Den danske Digtekunst under Christian VII. Copenhagen, 1828.
—— Den danske Digtekunst under Frederik V. Copenhagen, 1819.

GERMAN:

Goedeke, K. Grundrisz zur Geschichte der deutschen Dichtung. 2te (3te) Aufl. Dresden, 1910.

Hettner, H. Literaturgeschichte des 18. Jahrhunderts. Braunschweig, 6te Aufl. 1913. III.

Schweitzer, P. Geschichte der skandinavischen Literatur bis auf die skandinavische Renaissance im 18. Jahrhundert. Leipzig, 1886.

(2) Biographical Dictionaries.

Allgemeine deutsche Biographie, 1875 ff.

Bricka, C. F. Dansk biografisk Lexikon. Copenhagen, 1887 ff.

Ehrencron-Müller. Forfatterlexikon. Copenhagen, 1924.

Genealogisk og biografisk Archiv. Copenhagen, 1840 ff.

Kirkehistoriske Samlinger. Copenhagen, 1874 ff.

Personalhistorisk Tidsskrift. Copenhagen, III, V.

(3)

Friis, A. Bernstorfferne og Danmark. 2 vols. Copenhagen, 1913–19.

Hansen, O. Filosofien i Danmark i det 18. og 19. Aarhundrede. Copenhagen, 1897.

Holm, E. Danmark-Norges Historie 1720–1814. Copenhagen. 1898. II, III.

SPECIAL SOURCES FOR CHAPTER I.

ORIGINAL SOURCES:

Holberg, L. Den danske Skueplads. Copenhagen, 1750. Fortale.

Schlegel, J. E. Werke. Ed. J. H. Schlegel. Copenhagen, 1761–70.

—— Ästhetische Schriften. Ed. A. von Antoniewicz. Stuttgart, 1887.

—— Briefe an Bodmer. Stuttgart, 1794.

Schlegel, J. H. Introduction to J. E. Schlegel, Werke. Copenhagen, 1770. V.

SOURCES, 1750–1800:

Bielefeld, J. F. Progrès des Allemands. Breslau, 1752.

Herder, J. G. Criticisms of J. E. Schlegel. In Allgemeine deutsche Bibliothek. Berlin, 1767–74.

Koch, F. J. Kompendium der deutschen Literaturgeschichte, 1795–8.

SOURCES, 1800 TO PRESENT TIME:

(1) For J. E. Schlegel.

Antoniewicz, A. von. Introduction to J. E. Schlegels Ästhetische und Dramaturgische Schriften. Stuttgart, 1887.

Mayer, F. Ein Vorläufer Lessings. Oberhollabrunn, 1869.

Rentsch, J. J. E. Schlegel als Trauerspieldichter. (Dissertation.) Erlangen, 1890.

Schmid, C. H. Nekrolog vom Leben der Dichter. Berlin, 1785. I, pp. 231–66.

Seeliger, K. J. E. Schlegel. In Mitteilungen des Vereins für Geschichte der Stadt Meiszen. 1888. II, pp. 145–88.

Söderhjelm, W. Om J. E. Schlegel särskildt som Lustspeldiktare. Helsingfors, 1884.

Walzel, O. J. E. Schlegel als Trauerspieldichter. Leipzig, 1890.

—— Beiträge zur Kenntnis J. E. Schlegels. Vierteljahrsschrift für Literaturgeschichte, I, 1888.

Wolff, E. J. E. Schlegel. Berlin, 1889.

—— Gottscheds Stellung im deutschen Bildungsleben. Kiel and Leipzig, 1895–7. II.

(2) For Holberg and the Danish Theatre.

Aumont, A. and Collin, E. Det danske Nationalteater. Copenhagen, 1896–9.

Flögel, C. F. Geschichte der komischen Litteratur. Liegnitz and Leipzig, 1784–7. IV, pp. 322 ff.

Hansen, P. Den danske Skueplads. Copenhagen, 1902.

Kahle, B. Holberg. In Neue Heidelberger Jahrbücher. XIII, pp. 144–72.

Knudsen, C. Holbergs Tid og Oplysningstiden. Svendborg, 1913.

Löwen, J. F. Geschichte des deutschen Theaters. Hamburg, 1766.

Martensen, J. Om Holberg og den efter Frederik Vs Tronbestigelse gjenoprettede danske Skueplads. In Museum, 1894, I, pp. 23–56.

Müller, S. Holberg og hans Samtid. Copenhagen, 1897.

Nielsen, H. Holberg i Nytidsbelysning. Copenhagen, 1923.

Nyström, E. Den danske Komedies Oprindelse. Copenhagen, 1918.

Overskou, T. Den danske Skueplads. Copenhagen, 1860. II.

Paludan, J. Om Holbergs Niels Klims. Copenhagen, 1878. Pp. 321 ff.

Schlenther, P. and Hoffory, J. Dänische Schaubühne. 2 vols. Berlin, 1885.

Schwarz, F. Historisk Efterretning om den danske Skueplads. In Lommebog for Skuespilyndere. 1785. Pp. 205–70.

Skavlan, O. Holberg som Komedieforfatter. Kristiania, 1872.

Smaae Bidrag til det danske Theaters Historie. In Nyt Aftenblad, 1825, pp. 177–9, 190–1.

Trier, H. Holberg og den danske Skueplads. In Danske Studier, 1907, pp. 140 ff.

(3) General.

Belouin, G. De Gottsched à Lessing. Paris, 1909.

Poensgen, M. Theorie der Tragödie von Gottsched bis Lessing. (Dissertation.) Leipzig, 1899.

Prutz, R. E. Vorlesungen über die Geschichte des deutschen Theaters. Berlin, 1847.
Schmid, C. H. Theorie der Poesie nach den neuesten Grundsätzen. Leipzig, 1767. Pp. 379 ff., 486 ff., 490 ff.
—— Chronologie des deutschen Theaters. Leipzig, 1775.
—— Anweisung zur Kenntniss der besten Bücher. Leipzig, 1784.
Stolpe, P. Dagspressen i Danmark. Copenhagen, 1878–82. v.

SPECIAL SOURCES FOR CHAPTER II.

ORIGINAL SOURCES:

Klopstock, F. G. Contributions to Der Nordische Aufseher. Copenhagen and Leipzig, 1758–61.
—— Briefe von und an Klopstock. Ed. J. M. Lappenberg. Braunschweig, 1867.
—— Odes of the Copenhagen period. In Klopstocks Oden, Stuttgart, 1889.

SOURCES, 1750–1800:

Baggesen, J. Labyrinthen. Ed. L. Bobé. Copenhagen, 1909.
Journal Étranger, August and September, 1760; October and November, 1761.
Rahbek, K. L. Über Klopstocks Verdienste um die dänische Litteratur. In Kieler Blätter, 1819, II, pp. 235–42.
Stenersen, P. K. Critiske Tanker over de rimfrie Vers. Copenhagen, 1752.
Sturz, H. P. Klopstock. In Deutsches Museum, November, 1777.
Thiesz, J. O. F. G. Klopstock. Altona, 1805.

SOURCES, 1800 TO PRESENT TIME:

(1) For Klopstock.

Adler, F. H. Herder und Klopstock. (Thesis.) Cleveland, Ohio, 1914.
Bailly, E. Étude sur la vie et les œuvres de Klopstock. Paris, 1888.
Berg, T. Neue Mitteilungen über Klopstocks Aufenthalt in Dänemark. In Euphorion, XXIV, pp. 331–42, 562–70.
Bing, J. Klopstock og den Klopstockske Kreds i Danmark. In For Kirke og Kultur, V, pp. 587–608.
Diez, C. Essai sur Klopstock. 1859.
Doering, J. M. H. Klopstocks Leben. Jena, 1853.
Gruber, J. G. Klopstocks Leben. Leipzig, 1832.
Langer, L. Klopstock und der Sport. In Über Land und Meer, 1903, XLV, No. 23.
Muncker, F. Friedrich Gottlieb Klopstock. 2te Aufl. Berlin, 1900.
Scheel, W. Klopstocks Kenntnis des germanischen Altertums. In Seufferts Vierteljahrsschrift, 1893, VI, pp. 186–212.

(2) For Klopstock and Ewald.

Bobé, L. J. Ewalds Levnet og Meninger. Copenhagen, 1911.
Brix, H. Johannes Ewald. Copenhagen and Christiania, 1913.
Hammerich, M. Ewalds Levnet. Copenhagen, 1882.
Jørgensen, A. D. Ewalds Levnet. Copenhagen, 1888.
Molbech, C. Ewalds Levnet. Copenhagen, 1831.
Moller, H. Beiträge zur Charakteristik der Dichtungen J. Ewalds. 1906.

(3) General.

Braitmaier, F. Geschichte der poetischen Theorie. 2 vols. Frauenfeld, 1888–9.
Euphorion, III, Ergänzungsheft, pp. 38–54, and VI, pp. 67–83.
Jæger, H. En Kristiania Poet fra forrige Aarhundrede. In Litteraturhistoriske Pennetegninger, 1878.

SPECIAL SOURCES FOR CHAPTER III.

ORIGINAL SOURCES:

Gerstenberg, H. W. von. Samling af adskillige Skrifter til de skjønne Videnskabers og det danske Sprogs Opkomst og Fremtarv. Sorø, 1765.
—— Briefe über Merkwürdigkeiten der Litteratur. Ed. A. von Weilen. Stuttgart, 1890.
—— Rezensionen in der Hamburgischen neuen Zeitung, 1767–71. Ed. O. Fischer. Berlin, 1904.
—— Gedicht eines Skalden. Copenhagen, 1766.
—— Ugolino. Hamburg, 1768.
—— Korrespondenz mit Nikolai. In Zeitschrift für deutsche Philologie, XXIII, pp. 43–67; and Euphorion, X, pp. 56 ff. and XVIII, pp. 162 ff.
—— Ungedruckte Briefe aus dem Nachlasz H. W. von Gerstenbergs. In Archiv für das Studium der neueren Sprachen, CXLI, pp. 3 ff.
—— Contributions to Bibliothek der schönen Wissenschaften. Leipzig, 1757–65.

SOURCES, 1750–1800 (ca.):

Baggesen, J. Labyrinthen. Ed. by L. Bobé. Copenhagen, 1909.
Den danske Tilskuer. 1818, pp. 743–56.
Ewald, J. Levnet og Meninger. Ed. L. Bobé. Copenhagen, 1911.
Morgenblatt, 1810, CLXXXVI.
Rahbek, K. L. H. W. von Gerstenberg. In Kieler Blätter, 1819, II.
Schmidt, G. P. Gerstenbergs Biographie. In Iris og Hebe, 1809, I, pp. 1–26.

SOURCES, 1800 TO PRESENT TIME:

(1) For Gerstenberg and Danish Literature.

Fischer, O. Gerstenberg als Rezensent der Hamburgischen neuen Zeitung. In Euphorion, 1903, x, pp. 56–76; 1911, xviii, pp. 162–4.

Hamel, R. Grundsätze und Grundzüge moderner Dramatik bei H. W. von Gerstenberg. In Kritische Studien und Essays, 1900, pp. 278–94.

Jacobs, M. Gerstenbergs Ugolino. In Beiträge zur germanischen und romantischen Philologie, Germanische Abteilung, xiv. 1898.

Strausz, L. von. Nordische Literatur und deutsches Geistesleben. In Schleswig-Holsteinische Zeitschrift für Literatur, i, pp. 371–80, 408–14.

(2) Northern Mythology.

Batka, R. Altnordische Stoffe und Studien in Deutschland. In Euphorion, vi, pp. 67 ff.

Ehrmann, E. Die bardische Lyrik im 18. Jahrhundert. Halle, 1892.

Freytag, L. Nordische Dichtungen in deutscher Übersetzung. In Magazin für die Litteratur des In- und Auslandes, 1880, pp. 636 ff.

Golther, W. Die Edda in deutscher Nachbildung. In Zeitschrift für vergleichende Litteraturgeschichte, 1893, vi.

Grohmann, W. Herders nordische Studien. Leipzig, 1899.

Pfau, W. Das Altnordische bei Gerstenberg. In Vierteljahrsschrift für Literaturgeschichte, 1889, ii, pp. 161 ff.

Weber-Lutkow, H. Nordische Dichtung in deutscher Sprache. In Internationale Literaturberichte, 1900, p. 193.

SPECIAL SOURCES FOR CHAPTER IV.

ORIGINAL SOURCES:

Cramer, J. A. Contributions to Der Nordische Aufseher. Copenhagen and Leipzig, 1758–61.

Sneedorff, J. S. Den patriotiske Tilskuer. Sorø, 1761.

Taber, J. H. Diary quoted in Dansk Maanedsskrift, 1865, i, p. 104.

—— Autobiographie. In Block. Den svenske Geistligheds Historie, ii, p. 437.

Tullin, C. B. En Maidag. Samlede Skrifter. Copenhagen, 1770–3.

SOURCES, 1750–1800 (ca.):

Baden, J. Article in Universitets Journal, ii, 2, pp. 49–61.

Birch, H. J. Haandbog for Præster, 1795, ii, pp. 153–82.

Ebeling, F. W. J. A. Cramer. In Hannoversche Magazin, 1768, xxxiv, pp. 533 ff.

Feddersen, J. F. Nachrichten von dem Leben und Ende gutgesinnter Menschen, 1790. vi, pp. 276–313.

Høst, J. K. J. A. Cramer. In Chronos, 1822, II, pp. 95–100, and Clio, 1813, I, pp. 71–82.
Meusel, W. Das gelehrte Teutschland. Lemgo, 1783.
Møller, J. Canzler J. A. Cramer. In Nyt. theol. Bibl. 1823, III, pp. 3–37.

SOURCES, 1800 TO PRESENT TIME:

Archiv für Litteraturgeschichte, VI, pp. 329 ff.
Blümcke, A. Cramers Leben. Greefswald, 1910.
Dansk Maanedsskrift, 1865, I, pp. 96 ff.
Kirkehistoriske Samlinger. Copenhagen, 1874 ff. IV, p. 329.
Krähe, L. C. F. Cramer. Leipzig, 1907.
Luehrs, P. M. Der nordische Aufseher. (Dissertation.) Heidelberg, 1909.
Molbech, C. Ewalds Levnet. Copenhagen, 1831.
Veeck, O. J. A. Cramer. In Religion in Geschichte und Gegenwart, 1909, I.

SPECIAL SOURCES FOR CHAPTER V.

ORIGINAL SOURCES:

Basedow, J. B. Reden über die glückselige Regierung Friedriks V. Sorø, 1761.

SOURCES, 1750–1800 (ca.):

Høst, J. K. J. B. Basedow. In Chronos, 1822, II, pp. 104 ff.
Meier, J. B. J. B. Basedows Leben, Charakter und Schriften. Hamburg, 1791–2.
Rathmann, B. H. Lebensgeschichte J. B. Basedows. Magdeburg, 1791.
Sander, C. L. J. B. Basedow. In Minerva, 1801, I, pp. 113–43.
Suhm, P. F. J. B. Basedow. In Deutsche Monatsschrift, December, 1790, pp. 281–316.

SOURCES, 1800 TO PRESENT TIME:

Bidstrup, J. Holberg og Sorø Akademi. In Museum, 1893, II, pp. 32–50.
Bruun, C. Lidt om Sorø Akademis Historieskrivere i det 18. Aarhundrede. In Soransk Tidsskrift, 1870, I, 2, pp. 121–44.
Diestelmann, R. J. B. Basedow. Leipzig, 1897.
Kirkehistoriske Samlinger. IV, I, pp. 28–32, and IV, pp. 328 ff.
Koch, L. Nogle Bemærkninger om L. Holberg og Sorø. In Historisk Tidsskrift, VI, 1887, I, pp. 195–207.
Swet, C. Beiträge zur Lebensgeschichte und Pädagogik J. B. Basedows. (Dissertation.) Leipzig, 1898.

SPECIAL SOURCES FOR CHAPTER VI.

(1) For Matthias Claudius.

Deinhardt, J. H. Leben und Charakter des Wandsbecker Boten. Gotha, 1864.
Herbst, W. Matthias Claudius. Gotha, 1857.
Mönckeberg, C. Matthias Claudius. Hamburg, 1869.
Petersen, R. Matthias Claudius og hans Vennekreds. Copenhagen, 1884.
Stammler, W. M. Claudius der Wandsbecker Bote. Halle, 1915.
Ungedruckte Jugendbriefe des Wandsbecker Boten. Ed. C. Redlich, Hamburg, 1881.

(2) For F. G. Resewitz.

Kawerau, W. F. G. Resewitz. In Geschichtsblätter für Magdeburg, 1885, pp. 149–95.
Nyeste Skilderi af Kjøbenhavn, 1823. XXXIX, pp. 648 ff.

(3) For Schönborn.

Rist, J. G. Schönborn und seine Zeitgenossen. Hamburg, 1836.
Zeitschrift der Gesellschaft für die Geschichte der Herzogtümer Schleswig-Holstein. Kiel, 1870. I, pp. 29 ff.

(4) For H. P. Sturz.

Bobé, L. H. P. Sturz. In Vierteljahrsschrift für Literaturgeschichte, 1891, IV, pp. 450–65.
Koch, M. H. P. Sturz. Munich, 1879.
Merzdorff, T. H. P. Sturz. In Archiv für Litteraturgeschichte, 1878, VII, pp. 73–92.
Sturz, H. P. Geschichte des deutschen Theaters. Schriften. Leipzig, 1786.
Zimmermann, J. G. H. P. Sturz. In Hannoversches Magazin, 1776, XLI, pp. 636 ff.
—— Preface to H. P. Sturz. Schriften. Zweite Sammlung. Leipzig, 1782.

(5) For J. H. Schlegel.

Paludan-Müller, C. Dansk Historiographie i det 18. Aarh. In Historisk Tidsskrift, V, IV, pp. 1 ff.
Schlegel, J. H. Betragtninger. Copenhagen, 1779.

(6) For B. Münter.

Münter, B. Briefe vom Hause, 1781–2.
Weisze, C. F. Selbstbiographie. Leipzig, 1806.

SOURCES FOR CHAPTER VII.

(1) For J. A. Scheibe.

ORIGINAL SOURCES:

Scheibe, J. A. Critischer Musikus. Copenhagen, 1745. II.
—— Abhandlung vom Ursprung und Alter der Musik. Altona and Flensburg, 1754. Vorrede, p. 63.
—— Holbergs Peder Paars übersetzt. Copenhagen, 1764.
—— Letters in Breve til J. C. Gottsched fra Personer i det danske Monarki. Ed. by C. Roos. Copenhagen, 1918.

SOURCES, 1750–1800 (ca.):

Almindelig Dansk Lit. Journal, 1780, pp. 386 ff.
Gerber, E. L. J. A. Scheibe. In Hist. Biogr. Lexikon der Tonkünstler, 1792, II, pp. 412 ff.

SOURCES, 1800 TO PRESENT TIME:

Behrend, W. J. A. Scheibe. In Illustreret Musikhistorie, 1897, p. 924.
Eitner, R. J. A. Scheibe. In Quellenlexikon der Musiker, 1900–4.
Fétis, F. J. J. A. Scheibe. In Biographie des Musiciens, VII, pp. 444 ff.
Hammerich, A. Gluck som Kapelmester i København. In Vor Fortid, 1917, I, Nos. 19–20.
Internationale Musikgesellschaft, Sammelbände, II, 1910, pp. 654 ff.
Jørgensen, A. D. Johannes Ewald. Copenhagen, 1888.
Krogh, T. Zur Geschichte des dänischen Singspiels im 18. Jahrhundert. Copenhagen, 1924.
Minor, J. C. F. Weisze. Innsbruck, 1880.
Musikforeningens Festskrift, 1884, I.
Nyerup, C. Litteraturlexikon. Copenhagen, 1826.
Ravn, V. C. J. A. Scheibe. In Nationaltidende, January 18, 1883.
Schroeder, H. Lexikon der Hamburgischen Schriftsteller. VI, p. 491.
Worm, J. Lexicon. II, pp. 330 ff.

(2) For other subjects of the chapter.

Abrahamsen, E. Holberg og Musikken. In Musik, September, 1922, No. 117.
Claudius, M. Letters in Ungedruckte Jugendbriefe des Wandsbecker Boten. Hamburg, 1881. Pp. 19 ff.
Funk, G. B. Contributions to Der nordische Aufseher. Copenhagen, 1758–61.
Gerstenberg, H. W. Briefe an Nikolai. In Zeitschrift für deutsche Philologie, XXIII, pp. 59 ff.
Koller, O. Klopstock als Musikalischer Ästhetiker. In Jahresberichte der Landesoberrealschule zu Kremsier, 1884.
Müller, S. Holberg. In Samtiden, 1897, VIII, pp. 338 ff.

INDEX

For EU product safety concerns, contact us at Calle de José Abascal, 56–1°, 28003 Madrid, Spain or eugpsr@cambridge.org.

www.ingramcontent.com/pod-product-compliance
Ingram Content Group UK Ltd.
Pitfield, Milton Keynes, MK11 3LW, UK
UKHW012347130625
459647UK00009B/608

* 9 7 8 1 1 0 7 4 8 7 5 0 5 *